PHILOSOPHY AN

Philosophy, Aesthetics and Cultural Theory

Series Editor: Hugh J. Silverman, Stony Brook University, USA

The *Philosophy, Aesthetics and Cultural Theory* series examines the encounter between contemporary Continental philosophy and aesthetic and cultural theory. Each book in the series explores an exciting new direction in philosophical aesthetics or cultural theory, identifying the most important and pressing issues in Continental philosophy today.

Derrida, Literature and War, Sean Gaston

Foucault's Philosophy of Art, Joseph J. Tanke

The Literary Agamben, William Watkin

PHILOSOPHY AND THE BOOK
EARLY MODERN FIGURES OF MATERIAL INSCRIPTION

DANIEL SELCER

continuum

Continuum International Publishing Group
The Tower Building   80 Maiden Lane
11 York Road   Suite 704, New York
London SE1 7NX   NY 10038

www.continuumbooks.com

© Daniel Selcer, 2010

All rights reserved. No part of this publication may be reproduced or transmitted in any form or by any means, electronic or mechanical, including photocopying, recording, or any information storage or retrieval system, without prior permission in writing from the publishers.

British Library Cataloguing-in-Publication Data
A catalogue record for this book is available from the British Library.

ISBN: HB: 978-1-4411-1321-4
      PB: 978-1-4411-5009-7

Library of Congress Cataloging-in-Publication Data
Selcer, Daniel.
Philosophy and the book: early modern figures of material inscription / Daniel Selcer.
  p. cm.
Includes bibliographical references (p.).
ISBN 978-1-4411-1321-4 – ISBN 978-1-4411-5009-7 1. Materialism–Europe–History–17th century. 2. Philosophical literature–Europe–History and criticism. 3. Figures of speech in literature.
  4. Books in literature. I. Title.

B825.S399 2010
190.9'032–dc22   2009044689

Typeset by Newgen Imaging Systems Pvt Ltd, Chennai, India
Printed and bound in Great Britain by CPI Antony Rowe Ltd, Chippenham, Wiltshire

For T

Laws die, books never.

　　　　　– from a fortune-cookie received in Chicago, 1998

CONTENTS

List of Illustrations	viii
Acknowledgments	ix
List of Abbreviations	xi
Introduction	1
Chapter 1 Infinite Mechanism and the Allegorical Library	22
Chapter 2 Encyclopedic Method and the Uninterrupted Ocean	58
Chapter 3 The Materialist Encyclopedia	89
Chapter 4 Reading and Repetition	122
Chapter 5 The Body and the Book	163
Conclusion: The End of the Book	194
Notes	203
Bibliography	234
Index	251

LIST OF ILLUSTRATIONS

1. Miniature by Jean Colombe in Boethius, *De consolatione philosophiae* (Bourges: 1476), Harley 4335, f.1. © The British Library Board.   51

2. The first page of the "Rorarius" article, Pierre Bayle, *Dictionnaire historique et critique*, 2nd edn. (Rotterdam: Leers, 1702), 2599. © John J. Burns Library, Boston College, Chestnut Hill, MA.   74

3. Detail of Figure 2.   75

4. Detail of a page from the "Ovid" article, Pierre Bayle, *Dictionnaire historique et critique*, 2nd edn. (Rotterdam: Leers, 1702), 2273. © John J. Burns Library, Boston College, Chestnut Hill, MA.   108

ACKNOWLEDGMENTS

Several major ideas in this book were first formulated under the guidance of Angelica Nuzzo and Niklaus Largier, both of whom have long been models for the historical and conceptual rigor and creativity in thinking to which I aspire. Many central elements of this project developed during long and frequent conversations with Michael Witmore, who helped to sharpen my vague obsessions into concepts and who was responsible for making Pittsburgh an exciting place to work on early modern thought. Our seminar, "Late Epicureanism: Varieties of Materialism in Early Modernity," co-taught during the spring semester of 2007, was crucial for the development of this book. I would like to thank the Philosophy, English, and Cultural Studies graduate students from Duquesne University and Carnegie Mellon University who participated, as well as the Duquesne students who have stuck with me through years of Descartes, Spinoza, and Leibniz seminars. Déborah Blocker is responsible for convincing me (perhaps despite herself) that many scholars working on the history of the book are secretly philosophers. Katherine Rudolph-Larrea may recognize here the fruits of her labor when many years ago she accidentally turned me into an early modernist. Christopher Braider's panels at several ACLA conferences provided the opportunity for me to present several parts of this work publicly for the first time. His comments, encouragement, and model of interdisciplinary scholarship have played a crucial role in its formulation. My colleagues at Duquesne University have provided a vibrant intellectual environment in which my work could develop and I owe all the members of the Philosophy faculty a true debt of gratitude. I would like to especially thank Jim Swindal for his unflagging support as Chair of the department as well as Fred Evans and Lanei Rodemeyer for their longstanding encouragement and camaraderie. This book and all the passions behind it owe more than I can possibly express to Theresa Smith, who taught me most of what

ACKNOWLEDGMENTS

I know about books and everything I know about paper and ink. Without her, this book would surely not exist.

A Fulbright fellowship supported research in Hanover and Berlin for parts of Chapters 1 and 2. A Presidential Scholarship Award from Duquesne University supported research for part of Chapter 3 and completion of the manuscript.

An earlier version of a section of Chapter 1 appeared as "The Labyrinth and the Library," *Graduate Faculty Philosophy Journal* 22, no. 2 (2001), 101–13. The bulk of Chapter 2 appeared as "The Uninterrupted Ocean: Leibniz and the Encyclopedic Imagination," *Representations* 98 (2007), 25–50. I am grateful to the editors of these journals for allowing me to give this material a new home.

LIST OF ABBREVIATIONS

A   G.W. Leibniz, *Sämtliche Schriften und Briefe*, ed. Berlin-Brandenburgerischen [form. Preussische] Akademie der Wissenschaften and Akademie der Wissenschaften in Göttingen, 48 vols. in 8 series (Berlin: Akademie Verlag, 1923–present). Cited by series, volume, and page.

AG   G.W. Leibniz, *Philosophical Essays*, ed. and trans. Roger Ariew and Daniel Garber (Indianapolis, IN: Hackett, 1989).

AP   Giorgio Agamben, *Potentialities: Collected Essays in Philosophy,* ed. and trans. Daniel Heller-Roazen (Stanford, CA: Stanford University Press, 1999).

AT   René Descartes, *Oeuvres de Descartes*, ed. Charles Adam and Paul Tannery, rev. edn., 11 vols. (Paris: Vrin, 1996).

ATP   Gilles Deleuze and Félix Guattari, *A Thousand Plateaus: Capitalism and Schizophrenia*, trans. Brian Massumi (Minneapolis, MN: University of Minnesota Press, 1987).

Cons.   Anicius Manlius Severinus Boethius, *The Theological Tractates and The Consolation of Philosophy*, ed. and trans. H.F. Stewart, E.K. Rand, and S.J. Tester, Loeb Classical Library 74 (Cambridge, MA: Harvard University Press, 1973). Cited by book, prose (pr.) or meter (m.) number, and line.

CR   René Descartes, *Regulae ad directionem ingenii, Texte critique établi . . . avec la version hollandaise du XVIIème siècle*, ed., trans., and commentary Giovanni Crapulli (The Hague: Martinus Nijhoff, 1966).

CSM   René Descartes, *The Philosophical Writings of Descartes*, ed. and trans. John Cottingham, Robert Stoothoff, and Dugald Murdoch, 3 vols. (Cambridge: Cambridge University Press, 1984–1991).

LIST OF ABBREVIATIONS

DF	Lorenzo Valla, *Dialogue on Free Will*, trans. Charles Trinkhaus, in *The Renaissance Philosophy of Man*, ed. Ernst Cassirer, Paul Oskar Kristeller, and John Herman Randall, Jr. (Chicago, IL: University of Chicago Press, 1948), 155–82.
Dict.	Pierre Bayle, *The Dictionary Historical and Critical of Mr. Peter Bayle* (1697, 1702), trans. Pierre Desmaizeaux (London: Knapton et al., 1734–1738). Translations frequently modified, via *Dictionnaire historique et critique*, 5th edn., 4 vols. (Amsterdam: Brunel et al., 1740). Cited by article (art.), remark (rem.), marginal citation (cit.), preface (pref.), or explanation (exp.).
DRN	Titus Carus Lucretius, *De rerum natura*, trans. W.H.D. Rouse and Martin Ferguson Smith, rev. edn., Loeb Classical Library 181 (Cambridge, MA: Harvard University Press, 1975). Cited by book and line.
FS	Christiane Frémont, *Singularités: individus et relations dans le système de Leibniz* (Paris: Vrin, 2003).
GA	Galileo Galilei, *The Assayer* in *The Controversy of the Comets of 1618: Galileo, Grassi, Guiducci, Kepler*, ed. and trans. Stillman Drake and C.D. O'Malley (Philadelphia, PA: Pennsylvania University Press, 1960).
GP	G.W. Leibniz, *Die Philosophischen Schriften*, ed. Carl I. Gerhardt, 7 vols. (1875–1890; reprint Hildesheim: Olms, 1996).
GW	Pierre Gassendi, *The Selected Works of Pierre Gassendi*, ed. and trans. Craig B. Brush (New York: Johnson Reprint Corporation, 1972).
H	G.W. Leibniz, *De l'horizon de la doctrine humaine (1693); Apocatastase panton (La Restitution universelle, 1715)*, ed. and trans. Michel Fichant (Paris: Vrin, 1991).
HB	Thomas Holden, "Bayle and the Case for Actual Parts," *Journal of the History of Philosophy* 42, no. 2 (2004), 145–64.
LB	Seth Lerer, *Boethius and Dialogue: Literary Method in the Consolation of Philosophy* (Princeton, NJ: Princeton University Press, 1985).
Lev.	Thomas Hobbes, *Leviathan, with selected variants from the Latin edition of 1668*, ed. Edwin Curley (Indianapolis, IN: Hackett, 1994).

LIST OF ABBREVIATIONS

MB Warren Montag, *Bodies, Masses, Power: Spinoza and His Contemporaries* (London: Verso, 1999).

Met. Publius Naso Ovid, *Metamorphoses*, trans. Frank Justis Miller and G.P. Goold, Loeb Classical Library 42 and 43, rev. edn. (Cambridge, MA: Harvard University Press, 1977). Cited by book and line.

OG Jacques Derrida, *Of Grammatology*, trans. Gayatri Chakravorty Spivak (Baltimore, MD: The Johns Hopkins University Press, 1974).

OT Michel Foucault, *The Order of Things: An Archaeology of the Human Sciences*, trans. Alan Sheridan (New York: Vintage, 1970).

RB Thomas M. Lennon, *Reading Bayle* (Toronto: University of Toronto Press, 1999).

RE Jonathan Israel, *Radical Enlightenment: Philosophy and the Making of Modernity, 1650–1750* (Oxford: Oxford University Press, 2001).

SP Etienne Balibar, *Spinoza and Politics*, trans. Peter Snowdon (London: Verso, 1998).

SW Baruch Spinoza, *Complete Works*, ed. Michael L. Morgan, trans. Samuel Shirley (Indianapolis, IN: Hackett, 2002). Spinoza's *Ethics (E)* and *Principles of Cartesian Philosophy* (*PPC*) will be cited by part, preface (Pref), definition (Def), axiom (Ax), proposition (P), lemma (L), postulate (Post), and enumerated definition of affect (AD). *Treatise on the Emendation of the Intellect (TdIE)* will be cited by section. The *Theological-Political Treatise (TTP)* will be cited by chapter. The *Political Treatise (TP)* will be cited by chapter and section. Spinoza's correspondence will be cited by letter number (Ep).

Theo. G.W. Leibniz, *Theodicy: Essays on the Goodness of God, the Freedom of Man, and the Origin of Evil*, ed. Austin Marsden Farrer, trans. E.M. Huggard (La Salle, IL: Open Court, 1985).

INTRODUCTION

> *All through these very lines of mine you see many elements common to many words, although you must confess that lines and words differ from one another both in meaning and in the sound of their soundings. So much can elements do, when nothing is changed but order; but the elements that are the beginnings of things* [primordia rerum] *can bring with them more kinds of variety, from which all the various things can be produced.*
>
> Lucretius, De rerum natura

In Lucretius' atomist poem *De rerum natura*, the fabric of the world is presented as an aggregational tissue of material micro-entities arranged in particular patterns with respect to one another and to the empty spaces between them. While explicating his Christianized version of this Epicurean atomism, Pierre Gassendi invoked what he designated "the similitude of the letters," a figure repeatedly used by Lucretius to exemplify the Epicurean claim that all the apparent diversity of the sensible world can be produced through the permutation of several fundamental classes of material *primordia*.[1] Just as the finite set of letters in a given alphabet can be combined and rearranged to produce an endlessly varied pattern of words and sentences, so may the complex arrangement of primordial atoms—differentiated only by shape, speed, weight, and location—produce trees, fields, animals, and all that appears to the senses. When Lucretius mobilizes this figure it nearly always takes this reflexive form, drawing the reader's attention to the text in which it is inscribed. Just as a finite series of letters may be arranged to produce a long and complex poetico-philosophical text proving an explanation of the nature of things (such as *De rerum natura*), so may the physical *primordia* of the world (i.e., material atoms) be ordered in such a way as to constitute a system of sensible objects.

When Gassendi takes up the similitude of the letters, he links it not only to the multiplication of sensible things but also directly to the explosion of books in the seventeenth century. "For as letters are the elements of writing," he remarks, "and from them are produced first syllables, then words, sentences, orations, and printed books, so atoms are the first elements of things from which the tiniest concretions, or molecules, are formed, and then larger and larger ones, and miniscule bodies, bigger ones, and finally very large and complex ones" (GW, 427). If, for Gassendi, a complex body is an aggregational thing formed by a multiplicity of primordial elements arranged in a particular way, then conversely, a written work or printed text is a mobile arrangement of sets of finite signs that can signify absolutely anything. Indeed, Gassendi extends the similitude of the letters even further than Lucretius. He makes the permutated letters form not merely the sensible objects surrounding his readers or the text they hold in their hands, but every book that has been or will be written. Where Lucretius claims that the letters making up the words on the page of his text were like atoms capable of accreting into the multiplicity of the world, Gassendi holds that the atomic bodies they analogize may produce worlds far stranger than any we will ever encounter. He writes,

> Just as letters with no more shapes than the ones we find in the alphabet can produce an innumerable diversity of words by the mere variation of their arrangement [*dispositio*], so great a diversity indeed that they suffice not only for all the books heretofore written, but also for all those yet to be composed, so it is logical that atoms with their innumerable shapes in various compounds may produce a diversity of qualities or appearances, far more innumerable beyond any proportion, I might even say infinitely more. (*GW*, 427–28)

When *De rerum natura* was rediscovered in the fifteenth century, it fumed and smoked like a slow-burning fuse. First printed in 1473, this extended poetic discussion of the principles of atomic materialism did not begin to achieve its real impact until the Lambin edition printed in 1564. Then it exploded in a philosophical and literary landscape just beginning to reshape itself through a new theoretical and aesthetic relation to bodies and embodiment—falling, projectile, colliding, dissected, staged, printed, and otherwise.[2] New forms of philosophical materialism emerged (Gassendi's being only the most prominent example), often retrospectively reconstructing a history for themselves stretching back to the antiquity of the Platonic Academy and rewriting the intellectual history of the still-unfolding European Renaissance along an Epicurean rather than neo-Platonic line.[3] In postmodern or post-postmodern reconstructions of these genealogies of modernity, we sometimes frame the early modern period as one that gives rise to consummate forms of idealism and dematerialization, or at least to a dialectic between the so-called rationalisms and empiricisms that seek to conquer the corporeal realm in the name of epistemological or economic-political empire. The contemporary philosophical imperative to do away with dualisms of every sort has resisted this dematerialization in the name of the lived, situated body and the corporeality of language. We sometimes forget that early modern thought—whether philosophical, scientific, poetic, or aesthetic—was in many ways defined by its obsession with corporeality. This obsession belonged, moreover, not only to those thinkers and writers who would come to be associated with the practices of experimentalism, corpuscularism, and the construction of empirical natural histories, but also to those who are now, rightly or wrongly, considered the forerunners of the dematerialization of the body, the disincorporation of language, the idealization of space, and the construction of hegemonic forms of rational subjectivity. While it is possible to argue (as this book will do) that some of these figures have been misread, even avowed enemies of the newly formulated legacy of atomism or the non-Epicurean mechanisms emerging in the wake of Galilean science found themselves immersed in a complex set of discursive fields that were in many ways bounded and defined by the seventeenth-century passion for matter. Thus, even those who resisted the "materialization" of early modern thought found themselves framed, at least to some extent, by the episteme of the body. This discursive framework held whether the matter in question was conceived in terms of its direct bearing on the now-valorized realm of the sensible, with respect to its theoretical power to provide an ontological framework of mathematical abstractions or fields of force-relations, through the theorization of insensible microstructures meant to knit together a world in corporeal dispersion, or even via contact with the sensuality of language in the encounter between reader and text, language and the letter.

Throughout the seventeenth century, one important rhetorical and conceptual framework in which this passion and the resistance to it were articulated will be treated here under the rubric of "figures of material inscription," organized by the image of the book. By figures of material inscription, I mean the field of philosophical metaphors associated with the printed volume, the manuscript page, ink and paper, and the minimum unit of literate culture, the letter. I call these metaphors "material" not only because they are frequently mobilized in the service of confrontations with the natural world understood as an irreducible site of corporeality, movement, and force, but also because the meanings they metaphorically transfer into the language of the concept are keyed to their very physicality. The uses of the figures that interest me here do not allegorize a set of abstract and incorporeal ideas (the idea of the book, the idea of paper) but refer specifically to the material objects of literate culture that confronted the bodies of those who wrote and thought in terms of them. The material figure of the book, in other words, does not refer to the capacity of a codex to evoke, through a series of conventional signs, a meaning that transcends the marks on its pages and thereby transports its readers to imaginary realms (mythological, natural, hypothetical, mathematical, etc.). Instead, the material figure of the book refers to the codex in its very corporeality: a physical object with a heft of its own, composed of folded and sewn leaves of paper or parchment, covered in ink arranged in particular typographical or scribal patterns, bound in boards, subject to the ravages of history, fire, commerce, loss, and the ink stained fingers of its readers.

These figures (not just the book, but its pages, their letters, and the ink with which they are written or printed) rely on a transference or displacement of meaning not so much from the realm of idealized form as from the quotidian encounters of readers and writers with the things that structure their reading and writing activities. These things are furthermore objects that channel those who encounter them into particular bodily postures and motions, whether those necessary for a scholar to read at a desk in a library, for a bookseller to hide clandestine materials under the counter when the bookshop is visited by the censor, or for the compositor to lock up a type forme to avoid misalignment during a print run. Think, for example, of the moment that Cicero is transformed for Petrarch, in the *Letters on*

INTRODUCTION

Familiar Matters, from "our prince of eloquence" into the heavy, bound object that has repeatedly fallen from the doorpost at the entrance to his library and seriously injured his leg.[4]

The book, letter, paper, and ink thus give rise to a second series of material figures of inscription, namely those constituted by the activities of writing and reading themselves. In this case, reading, writing, cataloging, printing, binding, and so forth are mobilized in philosophical texts as figures for the materialization of the body and the mind. As a result of the increasing penetration of literate culture into everyday early modern life and the associated proliferation of bodies taking up the postures and practices of reading and writing, objects associated with textual practice begin to accumulate at alarming rates and thereby to provoke new cultural anxieties. These anxieties eventually give rise to entirely new types of corporeal-intellectual activity: cataloging books in libraries, now too extensive for any single librarian to retain even in a well-constituted memory palace; creating and setting new typographical layouts that organize sentences on the printed page in hitherto unimagined ways; or even, as in Descartes' case, denouncing written material as an illegitimate source of knowledge, and exiting the library to enter the great book of the world, that is, the ranks of a mercenary army. Thus, we arrive at the third and final series of figures of material inscription (with which this book will actually begin), the institutions, systems, and artifacts that serve as touchstones for the early modern organization of knowledge and intellectual practice: the library, the encyclopedia, the textbook, and the historical-philosophical dictionary.

The particular virtue of philosophical interpretation structured by an engagement with figures of material inscription is that it operates simultaneously in the corporeal and conceptual registers, precisely as these metaphors do. The typical problems of addressing the status of figurative language in the philosophical text—explored extensively, for example, by Jacques Derrida, Paul de Man, Michèle Le Doeuff, and many others—are avoided, since figures of material inscription function most obviously and powerfully at precisely those junctures where the materiality of figuration is the conceptual question addressed by the philosophical text.[5] Spinoza, for example, will directly structure his arguments with reference to the figures of ink and paper when the question on the table is the capacity of meaning to exceed the history of its material embodiment. Were he simply to ask if meaning could be separated from paper and ink, nothing of real note would have taken place. Instead, paper and ink themselves become the figures for staging a confrontation between material history and immaterial sense. They are simultaneously metaphors for philosophical concepts and specific material objects with regard to which conceptual arguments are being staged. Leibniz, to give another example, turns to the figure of the infinite and total library at the specific moment when it is best suited to frame his solution to the problem of the infinite divisibility of the material continuum and to demarcate the line separating the real from the ideal. At this moment, the philosophical status of the figural image of the library is thrown into question. Is it merely an allegorical figure that makes Leibniz's ontological solution to the labyrinth of the continuity of the continuum easier to decipher (i.e., do language and thought function exclusively on a plane of pure ideality)? Or does the allegorical journey of the philosopher through its endless stacks and reading rooms correspond precisely to the transition in Leibniz's thought from a mathematical extensionalism to a "metaphysical atomism," that is, from a realm of merely ideal representation populated by figural numbers to one where bodiless, substantial points without parts are reconceived as the irreducible units of the real? The material figures of inscription to be pursued in this book are not exogenous metaphors, those that express ideas that precede their figural instantiation and thereby merely ornament the surfaces of concepts. Rather, the book, print, reading, writing, etc. are precisely the material bodies in which several types of early modern philosophical discourse circulate instead of mere rhetorical importations that structure textual presentation externally.

DECONSTRUCTION AND DEMATERIALIZATION

One precursor to a project investigating figures of the book in the history of philosophy (and metaphor in the philosophical text in general) is necessarily Jacques Derrida. The theoretical basis of this project, however, is more directly the analysis of the transition from the Renaissance episteme of signature and resemblance to the baroque framework of arbitrary systems of signification as elaborated by Michel Foucault.[6] Nevertheless, given the seeming proximity to Derrida's project, his work deserves to be addressed directly. This project is differentiated from Derrida's in several ways; most importantly, it is framed in materialist rather than textualist terms.

With respect to the figure of the book, this generates radically different results. In his early magnum opus, *Of Grammatology*, the figure of the book is ineluctably identified with a thoroughly onto-theological, philosophical phono- and logocentrism. The history of philosophy, Derrida argues, is fully congruent with the formation of the "book of the world" image. Philosophical discourse, argues Derrida, transforms the very language in which it is articulated into a prosaic bearer of a truth-value that fundamentally transcends it, thereby forgetting or violently erasing its own origin *in* and *as* language. The movement of philosophical language is always onto-logically retrospective and reconstitutive, standing as an "effacement of the signifier" and a restoration of being as the presence of the signified.[7] Philosophical discourse thereby transforms the ostensible object of its ontology—the world itself—into a surface inscribed by systems and structures already understood to be given or ordered by an extramundane authorial principle prior to the philosopher's sensible or intellectual encounter with things and concepts. The onto-theological history of philosophy, then, is the "becoming-prose of the world" (*OG*, 287).

Derrida's first chapter, "The end of the book and the beginning of writing," is a manifesto for a philosophical and literary revolution *against* the figure of the book and what Derrida sees as its ontological commitment to sacralization through the transformation of the world into the Word. In contrast to the book, Derrida's arche-writing operates in a post-metaphysical space, which primarily means that it is incommensurable with the logic and metaphorics of the book. For Derrida, the book is a totalized signifier and therefore necessarily involves the production of God or being conceived on the onto-theological model of presence: an infinite and perfect signified that necessarily precedes, creates, orders, authors, judges, and maintains the book in its existence. Thus, as a mechanism for the complete capture of the heterogeneous distribution of difference, the book is an apparatus for methodologically binding (and thereby producing) the absolute and the infinite within the boards of the world. When Derrida calls for a history of the metaphor of the book—begun by Ernst Robert Curtius, on whom Derrida relies for the bulk of his account of the book as metaphor, and perhaps completed by Hans Blumenberg, who effectively ignored Derrida's work—he overdetermines it by insisting that such a history must be one that "systematically contrasts divine or natural writing and the human and laborious, finite and artificial inscription" and that "follow[s] the theme of God's book (nature or law, indeed, natural law) through all its modifications" (*OG*, 15–16).[8]

Not only is the figure of the book a pernicious legacy of the history of metaphysics, Derrida argues, it has also lost its efficaciousness when confronted with the thought of difference. "What is thought today," he asserts, "cannot be written according to the line and the book, except by imitating the operation implicit in teaching modern mathematics with an abacus" (*OG*, 87). Despite a long and entrenched history of Derrida-reception that has framed him as a partisan of the book, despite the erudition with respect to the history of writing that permeates his oeuvre, despite his constant affinity for metaphors of inscription together with the inscription of metaphor, and despite the constant and unavoidable presence in his work of the charming whiff of nostalgia for a mechanism of communication and an object of study—the book—that he clearly thought was on the verge of technological supersession, in *Of Grammatology* Derrida is quite clear where he stands with regard to this figure.

> The idea of the book, which always refers to a natural totality, is profoundly alien to the sense of writing. It is the encyclopedic protection of theology and of logocentrism against the disruption of writing, against its aphoristic energy, and, as I shall specify later, against difference in general. If I distinguish the text from the book, I shall say that the destruction of the book, as it is now underway in all domains, denudes the surface of the text. (*OG*, 18)

The page fares no better in *Of Grammatology*: writing is what gives rise to homogeneous and objective spatiality that submits to geometrical measure or mathematical abstraction (i.e., the fields of Cartesian extension or Newtonian absolute space). Prior to this scriptive construction of a secondary, ideal field of spatiality is the heterogeneity of bodily relation, that is, the thoroughly differential field exuded or inhabited by the lived body of phenomenological experience. This lived body is only later dismembered via a scriptive order of intellection. Within the geometrically homogeneous space thereby produced, Derrida insists that traces of heterogeneity still remain such that this space is distributed according to a variety of corporeal systems and orders. For the Derrida of 1967 (he explicitly renounced this view in his late texts), the page is the model

INTRODUCTION

par excellence for the distribution of homogeneous, intellectualized, geometrical space.[9] "The surface of the page, the expanse of parchment or any other receptive surface," he writes, "distributes itself differently according to whether it is a model of writing or readings" (*OG*, 288). In the broad epoch of the onto-theological book, the page thus constitutes a surface to be organized by an action that stands fundamentally exterior to it. The gesture of writing distributes marks across the face of the page and at the same time determines the page to be a framework of localities, or a container that submits to the logic of geometrical abstraction. In this sense, the page—as the spatial field produced by writing and the material support for its scriptive marks—becomes sensible in the Kantian meaning of the term (an oriented and directional form for any and all experience), but it is at the same time stripped of all materiality (*OG*, 289). The page is produced by a more originary writing (an arche-writing) and corporeality or materiality are reserved for the "gestures" of "the body 'proper'" in its scriptive activity. In other words, outside of or prior to the act of inscription, the page is precisely nothing (*OG*, 56). Lacking all being, it "is" only as a set of retrospectively constituted, quasi-Kantian formal conditions for the possibility of inscription, which is to say that it comes to be only as a post hoc supplement to writing. Thus, the page is not only fully dematerialized but also metaphysically obliterated. For Derrida, in other words, the page comes to be through the imposition of writing, but is merely an ideal field of the distribution of localities wherein the real characters, whose formal condition it constitutes, will be inscribed. It is never paper or parchment or even a projected field of electrons, but only ever that "material support" that formally structures any and all appearance of the letter or the word.

In at least one sense, writing actually fares no better than the page in Derrida. The "arche-writing whose necessity and new concept I wish to indicate and outline here," Derrida writes, "I continue to call writing only because it essentially communicates with the vulgar concept of writing" (*OG*, 63). That is, arche-writing structurally mirrors but at the same time absolutely forsakes as the residue of metaphor the "vulgar" writing in which actual letters are inscribed in real ink on a physical, paper page. Unfortunately, were arche-writing somehow to be materially imprinted instead of remaining "the being-imprinted of the imprint" it would have allowed itself to be reduced to a form of presence, and for Derrida, this it cannot do (*OG*, 57).

At the same time, the often-repeated charge that the early Derridean program for the deconstruction of the priority of orality over writing and the voice over the hand amounted in the end to a purely textual idealism is in several respects exaggerated. Derrida did constantly insist on the materiality of the differential trace and on the corporeality of writing. Nevertheless, from the perspective of an ontology of the page, it looks obvious that the space in which Derrida's arche-writing takes place and the surface on which it is inscribed—the page—is thoroughly dematerialized. Its gathering in quires and binding in boards—the book—becomes, for Derrida, simply the retrospective totalization, intellectualization, and idealization of the body.[10] Here, the book is a thoroughly metaphysical "envelope" in which writing as such is sealed and from which a properly deconstructive theorization of arche-writing may one day free its readers. In short, when *Of Grammatology* announces that the book must be brought to an end in the name of writing, the book is purged of its function as an apparatus for the production of material effects and is thereby utterly idealized. At its limit, the book is virtually embedded as the formal character of the trace in a matter from which it is fundamentally alienated.

I will counter this dematerialization of the book and the page with an analysis structured by the material figures of inscription. Still, even a cursory look at the history of the figure of the book in philosophical writing certainly confirms Derrida's thesis that "book of the world" metaphors often or even usually function to sacralize a natural world seemingly on the verge of alienation from divinity. The "book of the world" figure may render nature intelligible by modeling natural philosophical investigation on scriptural exegesis. It may also serve to spiritualize a seemingly secular natural philosophical practice by framing it as the revelation of a still-hidden divine handwriting, thereby producing a textualization of nature that is, in fact, its metonymic investment with theological principle. Several times in recent memory, intellectual historians and philosophers of written culture have told this story of the sacralized figure of the book and without question it is ubiquitous within the pages of philosophical and theological early modern texts.[11] Bacon, for example, famously insisted that the study of the book of nature was the key to unlocking the mysteries of scripture and thereby to revealing the will of God.[12] Robert Boyle likewise insisted that the practices of experimental science allowed the philosopher "to read the stenography of God's omniscient hand."[13] Under these figures—and in a legacy stretching at least as far back in the philosophical tradition as Hugh of St. Victor and Nicholas Cusanus—the natural world is endowed with a measure of legibility that primarily serves to announce and increase the glory of its creator.

The price for allowing the investigation of things to serve as the ground for the expansion of human understanding of the natural universe, in other words, is that every iota of the knowledge so gleaned serves as a cosmological proof for the existence and perfection of the divine. The book of the world provides a supplement to scripture, or, in other cases, constitutes a second and unmediated instantiation of the divine word accessible directly to the natural philosopher. The familiar patterns of reading (scrutiny, perusal, etc.) and of rhetoric or dialectics (invention and judgment) thereby become direct modes of access to the traces left by God in the material world. Certainly, several of the figures of material inscription explored here are fully tied up in philosophical discourses connected by quasi-theological questions, such as the existence of God, the problem of theodicy, the confrontation between skepticism and belief, and even the proper exegetical method. Nevertheless, it would be an error to take these discourses to be fully structured by their contact with the theological, just as it would be absurd to propose a reading of Bacon wherein all that is powerful and interesting in his natural histories is the extent to which they unlock the meaning of scripture. That same caution needs to be exercised in the face of the profound arrogance expressed by some contemporary philosophers with regard to the history of philosophy ("just more of the same old onto-theology"). The ostensible object of a philosophical argument or the staging of a material figure of inscription may be connected to a theological question, but that does not mean that those theological stakes are the most central aspect of the concept or figure, or even that they are philosophically significant.

Consider, further, one of the most famous early modern figures of the book of nature, that presented by Galileo in *The Assayer*:

> Philosophy is written in this grand book—I mean the universe—which stands continually open to our gaze, but it cannot be understood unless one first learns to comprehend the language and interpret the characters in which it is written. It is written in the language of mathematics, and its characters are triangles,

circles, and other geometrical figures, without which it is humanly impossible to understand a single word of it; without these, one is wandering about in a dark labyrinth.[14]

In late 2008, at events marking the then upcoming International Year of Astronomy, several major Vatican officials seemed to announce the rehabilitation of Galileo as a man of the Church. Most prominently, Cardinal Tarcisio Bertone pointed to this passage and claimed that Galileo "was a man of faith who saw nature as a book authored by God."[15] Whatever the status of Galileo's religious commitments or lack thereof, Bertone's assumption that any invocation of the book of nature ultimately involves praising its transcendent author is unsurprising, given the long history of the figure's mobilization in the service of the theological attempt to recolonize the provinces of natural science. What is interesting, however, is that the attribution of this view to Galileo rests on a complete misreading of his text. Galileo's philosophical book of the universe is not the mathematical double of a scriptural truth whose glory it confirms, but an alternative to what he sees as the conceptual murkiness of fiction. Responding polemically in the same text to the Scholastic Oratio Grassi (with whom he had traded barbs over the Tychonian vs. Copernican cosmological models), Galileo's argument is that philosophy is not "a book of fantasy by some writer, like the *Iliad* or *Orlando Furioso*, productions in which the least important thing is whether what is written is true," but is instead written in the language of mathematics and legible to reason (*GA*, 183, trans. mod.). The book of nature, therefore, is thoroughly secularized by Galileo at the very moment when he launches the mathematical and corpuscular transformation of natural philosophy that would irrevocably shape the face of seventeenth-century philosophical thought. A secular material history of the book is therefore still possible, even when the terms of many of the early modern texts that it engages are structured by theological or onto-theological concerns.

MATERIAL HISTORIES OF THE BOOK

One of the major theoretical formations that organizes this project of reading figures of material inscription in early modern philosophical texts is the turn toward a materialist historiography of the book, the culture of print, scientific experiment and exchange, and the circulation of texts as they have been developed in recent decades. While this discourse has had minimal impact on the practice of the history of philosophy in the English-speaking world, the same cannot be said for the structure of humanistic inquiry in general, as the assumptions of many related disciplines have been thoroughly transformed by its results. While the engagement with figures of philosophical inscription presented here does not pretend to be a contribution to the material history of the book, print, or practices of reading, it has been strongly influenced by them. Thus, it is appropriate to offer an account of the impact of this approach on the project of articulating the philosophical stakes of figures of material inscription.

In 1979, Elizabeth Eisenstein published her monumental *The Printing Press as an Agent of Change* and thereby provoked a fundamental shift in the way that many intellectual, cultural, and literary historians considered the status of the objects of their theoretical and critical investigation.[16] Her thesis was broad, but it involved at least two major theoretical and historiographical claims that have more recently been contested. First, the material conditions for the production and circulation of texts—and specifically those that developed in the wake of the printing press—delimit the possibility of the development of intellectual culture and provide an ontological ground, of sorts, for literary, scientific, and philosophical practices. These "extrinsic" factors thus exert a measure of causal influence over significant elements of the "intrinsic" intellectual content of their objects, though Eisenstein was careful to deny that she was arguing for a full technological determinism. With Eisenstein, intellectual culture in the age of printing thus became "print culture," a form of cognitive life and corporeal practice oriented around and by the mechanisms of the press and the circulation of its products (especially, but not exclusively, books). Second, Eisenstein argued that early modernity in particular should be understood as the period of the stabilization and fixity of print artifacts, such that earlier epistemological problems concerning the identification and delimitation of texts (a legacy of scribal culture) disappear. Once the mechanisms of print culture became entrenched in intellectual life, she argued, texts were no longer defined by the particularity of their material form. Rather, their ubiquity, their (in principle) infinite reproducibility, and the stabilization of the conventions governing their format and appearance allowed for what we might call their *dematerialization*, whereby particular books and other printed matter became mere exemplars of a now inviolate authorial content that reappeared as an identical page each time another object with the same title and printing-house genealogy was examined or a new print run undertaken.[17]

While it has had a profound effect on critical practice even among those not particularly sympathetic to the details of her argument, in the three decades since its appearance Eisenstein's thesis has also been severely criticized. From one direction—call it evolutionary bibliographical pragmatics—bibliographers, intellectual historians, and historians of science from extremely diverse milieus (such as David McKitterick, Anthony Grafton, and Stillman Drake) have insisted that *The Printing Press as an Agent of Change* radically overestimates the disjunction between so-called scribal culture and print culture, and fails to acknowledge the profound sense in which the practices Eisenstein associates with the former continued to exert a significantly determinative influence on those she associates with the latter.[18] What is called for, they argue in very different ways, is a more nuanced account of the evolution of practices of reading, writing, and circulation as well as typographical and bibliographical presentation throughout the early modern period, rather than the epistemic and practical revolution Eisenstein's work presents. Scribal norms for the production and circulation of texts as well as the behavior of those associated with their production and reception survive well into early modernity and beyond, these critics argue, albeit under new labels and in significantly mutated forms.

From a very different direction—call it immanent bibliographical materialism—book historians and historians of science such as Roger Chartier and Adrian Johns have challenged Eisenstein's assertions about the nature of early modern textual stability and fixity. They accomplish this through careful analyses of the production of scientific and philosophical works, pointing to the complex collaborations required between authors, editors, printers (both legitimate and "piractical"), and booksellers, as well as censors and other state agents for the production of intellectual work.[19] Their approach is strongly influenced by the claim (advanced most forcefully by the avatars of the sociology of scientific knowledge Steven Shapin and Simon Schaffer, as well as by Bruno Latour) that printed artifacts are not merely mute bearers of knowledge but sites with respect to which "credit" must be established on extratextual, extra-argumentative, and even extra-discursive grounds.[20] Focusing (at the suggestion of Douglas McKenzie) on the nuances of printing-house practices and their correlates in the realm of the history of reading, Chartier and Johns affirm the singularity of material textual artifacts (as opposed to the repeatability and standardization endorsed by Eisenstein) and develop theoretical frameworks and methodological models for using this singularity as the interpretive touchstone for the production of histories of intellectual culture.[21] These positions can be described as "radical" in that they go so far as to affirm the theses that "authors do not write books: they write texts that become written objects" and that "new readers of course make new texts," that is, that the construction of textual objects involves an immanent dynamic interplay between readers, the objects they engage, and the histories of both.[22]

Also in the immanent bibliographical materialist camp, Johns elaborates arguments denying that anything corresponding to Eisenstein's "print culture"—understood as a more or less monolithic causal framework that imbues its objects with particular qualities such as typographical fixity—actually exists or ever existed.[23] Against Eisenstein's specific claim that the ubiquity of printing results in the stabilization of texts and their infinite reproducibility as identical instantiations of the same transcendental textual object (book object = x), Johns argues persuasively that the quantitative explosion of written culture, the development of a new series of forms for organizing or controlling its circulation (e.g., licensing regimes, printers' guilds, correspondence networks, learned societies, scholarly journals, etc.), and loci of resistance to that control (primarily in the form of "piratical" printing and cultural mechanisms by which "credit" may be awarded or withheld from print objects) in many cases *destabilized* texts. They do this by opening a myriad of new avenues through which readers may approach texts and by rendering more complex the chain of sovereign authorial production that connects authors to their texts and texts to their readers. Thus, rather than standing as an ahistorical hinge on which cultural and intellectual history turns, writing, printing, and reading become a series of practices enmeshed in particular milieus, practices, conflicts, and representations. Against Eisenstein, "print" is (as Johns insists) a result rather than a cause of culture, where culture itself is understood as a concatenation of material behaviors, dispositions, and objects rather than as an intellectual or aesthetic field that defines the formal conditions for the possibility of the appearance of any particular thing.

FIGURES OF MATERIAL INSCRIPTION

How might considerations of the thoroughly extrinsic material and cultural context surrounding a philosophical work's existence as a print object influence its interpretation, especially if the conceptual content of that work is not directly bound up with the vagaries of experimental protocol and the presentation or organization of empirical evidence to which a historian of science like Johns tends to key his analysis? Following the line pursued by Shapin, Schaffer, Johns, Chartier, and others as far as it leads in the realm of nonempiricist regimes for the production of philosophical truth might mean primarily directing interpretive attention to the specific milieu in which a work would have been encountered and read when it first appeared. It might also insist on an exploration of the conditions surrounding the constitution of the work as work, or the text as text. This is rarely an issue under the established pragmatic and technological norms for the production of academic or scientific work today, but the corresponding early modern norms were very much in flux during the explosion of seventeenth-century printed textual production. In this context, the concerns of the sociologists of scientific knowledge regarding the establishment of personal and textual "credit" may meet Eisenstein's fascination with the intensification of early modern textual stabilization under the banner of typographical fixity.

My project, however, does not proceed under the rubric of cultural history but of philosophy, and this book is certainly not a broad attempt to provide a history of the production, circulation, and social constitution of the meaning of seventeenth-century philosophical texts, although considerations related to these will play a role in the analyses that follow. Instead, this work is motivated by a conviction that the material, technological, and historical situation in which early modern texts were produced both shaped their rhetorical contours and constituted a reservoir of imaginative or metaphorical forms. Whether or not it was their intention, the work of historians of print culture, the book, reading, and the cultural-technological production and organization of knowledge has demonstrated that the figure of the book in its many modalities constitutes one of the dominant images that organize early modern philosophical and natural philosophical writing. Because it has focused almost exclusively on literary and cultural history even when directly concerned with the textual artifacts of scientific practice, this array of interdisciplinary scholarship has not directly addressed the effects of such changes in the early modern philosophical imagination. Conversely, attempts to elaborate the relationship in early modern philosophical texts between their rhetorical tropes or metaphorical figures and their argumentative content or metaphysical commitments have tended to advance an ultimately idealist position. This position is idealist in that it effectively reduces the concrete instantiation of such metaphors in the text of philosophy to the "material support" for the free play of imaginative language. Thus, an emphasis on the specific materiality of early modern philosophical text-objects leads to a bracketing of their conceptual content, or a preoccupation with the autonomy of their rhetoric blocks engagement with their materialization.

This book addresses that dilemma by investigating the mobilization of print, inscription, reading, and knowledge organization as metaphors in the work of a handful of major figures from the so-called continental rationalist side of early modern European philosophy. To explore these figures in relation to the concepts of materiality they explicate, I investigate images of the bound physical volume, the printed and inscribed page, ink and paper, libraries and their catalogs, encyclopedias, their synoptic tables, and their theoretical organization of the totality of human knowledge, as well as complex typographical, citational, and organizational systems of reference. Throughout this work I argue that these imaginative and rhetorical figures of the book are ineluctably linked to early modern attempts to grapple with theoretical problems surrounding the concept of matter. Figures of inscription play a privileged role in this endeavor in part because an engagement with the abstract problem of the nature of materiality forces any philosophical thinker to confront the material situation within which it takes place—one that is inescapably corporeal. With the ubiquity of paper and books, the institutions that organize and house them, epistolary networks, learned journals, paper instruments, etc. that shaped the contours of early modern philosophical reading, writing, communicating, and thinking, this engagement with the corporeal site for philosophical activity necessarily includes a confrontation with the materiality of texts, readers, and writers.

Of course, it is certainly not the case that the philosophers treated here were avowed materialists. In fact, neither Descartes, Leibniz, Spinoza, nor Bayle would accept that designation, especially under its dominant early modern form, atomism, or more generally, Epicureanism. The project does touch more tangentially on several figures who would accept the designation, Hobbes and Guillaume Lamy, for example. Nevertheless, all were denounced as materialists in the seventeenth century (or in Leibniz's case, repeatedly suspected of being one), and the question of why this was true will be a concern in what follows. I focus on the way their mobilizations of figures of inscription and of the book structure their engagements with the problematics of matter and materialization. This is worth investigating even when those engagements ultimately result in an apparent disavowal or reduction of the material to a metaphysically subordinate position (as in Descartes, though I will argue that this is retrieved when he turns from epistemology to natural philosophy). These connections are important even when they involve a denunciation of the dead letter of scriptive discourse in favor of its meaning-bearing signification (as in Spinoza, though I will argue that this is merely prefatory to his reformulation of materiality itself in terms of dynamic and productive power). Their strategies are significant even when they rest on a deliberate rhetorical and philosophical translation of materialist discourse into a spiritualized idealism (as in Leibniz, though I will argue that this is belied by his attention to historical allegorization and a reconceptualization of actuality as existential force). Finally, consideration of the way that figures of material inscription bear on philosophical concepts of matter is productive even when those figures are activated in the service of a direct critique of the mythological and metaphysical foundations of atomism (as in Bayle, though I will argue that his critical mode relies on an even more profound typographical materialism).

Chapter 1 develops an ontology of the page in connection with the metaphysics of ontological repetition that Leibniz elaborates under the figure of the infinite library. This library containing all possible books and therefore all possible histories of the world is connected to Leibniz's engagement with the labyrinth of the continuity of the continuum. Leibniz's solution to the question of how discrete, minimal, material elements can constitute an uninterrupted and continuous reality involves an idealization (not dematerialization) of matter itself, and the concomitant transformation of atomism into a theory of irreducible, immaterial, and yet metaphysically real substances. The translation of atomistic metaphors continues in Leibniz's tropological approach to another labyrinth, namely, human freedom. On both philosophical and rhetorical levels he develops an extremely complex intertextual and allegorical dialogue directly engaging Boethius' *Consolation of Philosophy* and Lorenzo Valla's "Dialogue on Free Will." This allegory is part of an attempt to reconcile the necessity seemingly implied by providentialism with the contingency apparently required for the real exercise of freedom and is simultaneously a Leibnizian entry into the debate over the inseparability of philosophy from its rhetorical form.

Chapter 2 continues to focus on Leibniz, with attention to his elaborate reflections on the proper method for the construction of a metaphysical encyclopedia. The methodological problem that Leibniz articulates through the encyclopedia is that of establishing a static taxonomy of human knowledge in the face of its fluidity and mutability. This constitutes an epistemological transformation of the continuum problem dealt with in Chapter 1, now overlaid with the issue of categorical organization. Since (in Leibniz's view) encyclopedic classificatory schemas are always inadequate to ever-shifting epistemological totalities, he proposes a radical system of infinite encyclopedic referentiality whereby each encyclopedic "entry" is constituted through an infinite system of perspectival reference to every other member of the same encyclopedic "world" of knowledge. Leibniz's unrealizable image of an infinitely indexical encyclopedia is a metaphysical radicalization of the elaborate *mise en page* and multilayered schema of notations structuring Pierre Bayle's *Historical and Critical Dictionary* (in which Leibniz makes an appearance).

Chapter 3 turns to Bayle's *Dictionary* and delves deeper into its critical project by elaborating the structures of referentiality mobilized by its typographical form. This allows the elaboration of Bayle's late seventeenth-century engagement with the major early modern theories of matter (especially neo-Epicureanism, Cartesian mechanism, corpuscularism), forms of resistance to them, and their links to the metaphysical problems of necessity and contingency elaborated in the earlier chapters on Leibniz. Bayle's commentaries on these topics are found in remarks to articles on philosophical figures, but issues surrounding materiality are also vigorously engaged in articles on more literary writers such as Lucretius and Ovid. Indeed, in these latter discussions, Bayle transforms a series of physical-theoretical debates (whether motion is an accident of matter or an inseparable primary mode, whether matter is intrinsically self-organizing or requires external teleological intervention, whether natural laws governing dynamic systems of matter in motion exclude or express "chaos") into occasions to advance a generalized poetics of early modern materiality. Transforming poets into philosophers and philosophers into poets, Bayle's texts confront problems bound up with the philosophical and rhetorical reactivation and transformation of Lucretian materiality. Bringing together Bayle's general strategy for the production and organization of this complex text-object, philosophical critiques of material poetic and rhetorical structures, and aesthetic engagements with natural philosophical and dialectical positions on materialism, this chapter traces Bayle's philosophical evaluation of the ontology of the page.

Chapter 4 brings these concerns with the physical principles of scriptive matter into contact with several episodes in the history of Cartesian reading and the specific ways in which they invoke the materiality of the book. I begin with a focus on the manner in which Descartes' texts mobilize figures of the apparatus of writing itself, exploring the ways in which paper, pen, and ink constitute a constant stream of example and metaphor in the Cartesian project for the elaboration of methodologically grounded certitude and natural philosophical knowledge. Of particular interest here is the constant performative reflexivity these figures invoke, as Descartes draws attention to the very pen with which he writes, the pages on which his letters appear, and the ink with which they are written. The chapter then turns to an account of Descartes' practices of philosophical reading, his critique of textual authority, and the machinations by which his texts determine the manner in which they will be read. Finally, the chapter takes up a strange episode in the history of philosophical reading, namely, Descartes' reflexive development of a form of methodological repetition. Providing an extremely close reading of key sections of *Rules for the Direction of Mind* and of the sometimes-bizarre intellectual gymnastics its commentators perform to deal with a series of textual and argumentative anomalies, the problematics of Cartesian methodological reading are shown to make significant philosophical contact with those of figuration, exemplarity, and repetition.

Chapter 5 turns to Spinoza who, as a young expositor of Cartesian philosophy, produced a philosophical commentary on Descartes'

INTRODUCTION

Principles of Philosophy that recast it in the geometrical form. Reading Spinoza's reading of Descartes and engaging with the broad set of anxieties regarding textual multiplication and repetition framed in earlier chapters, the first section focuses on a figure in Spinoza's text that poses the problem of distinguishing between two books written in an identical hand. An allegorization of the Cartesian distinction between formal and objective reality, this figure is also one site where Spinoza begins to articulate—via figures of material inscription—his radical break from the Cartesian project. In order to elaborate more fully the stakes of Spinoza's textual materialism, the next section turns briefly away from the figure of the book proper in order to explicate Spinoza's transformation of the notion of materiality and the concomitant implications this has for early modern political thought. Demonstrating that a properly Spinozan materialism involves a focus on the very problem of dynamic "disposition" and "arrangement" introduced by Lucretius' *De rerum natura*, the final section turns to Spinoza's formulation of a radically materialist exegetical method. Connecting the two-books figure of the first section with the theory of dynamic textual materialism in the second, this section argues that Spinoza elaborates a dynamic, materialist theory of meaning directly through an engagement with the materiality of writing.

CHAPTER 1

INFINITE MECHANISM AND THE ALLEGORICAL LIBRARY

> *Libraries are the enchanted domain of two major difficulties. They have been resolved, we know, by mathematicians and tyrants (but perhaps not altogether). There is a dilemma: either all these books are already contained within the Word and they must be burned, or they are contradictory and, again, they must be burned. Rhetoric is a means of momentarily postponing the burning of libraries (but it holds out this promise for the near future, that is, for the end of time). And thus the paradox: if we make a book which tells of all the others, would it or would it not be a book itself? Must it tell its own story as if it were a book among others? And if it does not tell its story, what could it possibly be since its objective was to be a book? Why should it omit its own story, since it is required to speak of every book? Literature begins when this paradox is substituted for the dilemma; when the book is no longer the space where speech adopts a form (forms of style, forms of rhetoric, forms of language), but the site where books are all recaptured and consumed: a site that is nowhere, since it gathers all the books of the past in this impossible "volume" whose murmuring will be shelved among so many others— after all the others, before all the others.*
>
> Michel Foucault, "Language to Infinity"

While Leibniz is in no sense a materialist, his philosophical work nevertheless grapples directly with many of the major conundrums facing early modern attempts to understand the nature and status of the material world. As I will show, even while Leibniz restricts the sphere of materiality to a derivative phenomenal level that operates in synchrony with a metaphysically real realm of immaterial substances and active forces, he rigorously adapts the vocabulary of Epicureanism in order to produce a "spiritualized atomism." Accomplishing this task involves a series of particularly rich engagements with philosophical textuality and rhetoric, organized tropologically under the figure of the infinite library.

In the *Theodicy* Leibniz describes the whole of his philosophical work as an attempt to follow a thread of Ariadne through "the two famous labyrinths in which our reason goes astray," both of which this chapter will bring into focus through an examination of Leibniz's use of the figure of the infinite library.[1] The first of these—the labyrinth of freedom—concerns the relation between contingency, necessity, determination, and freedom. The second is what Leibniz calls the labyrinth of the composition of the continuum. The problem itself is relatively simple. How can indivisible and distinct elements constitute a continuum? How, that is, can singularity possibly be thought, if the real is everywhere continuous, without interruption or break? As is well known, Leibniz affirms both extremes of these questions: what really exist are simple, irreducible unities or wholes, yet the totality of these unities constitutes a single, organically complete world. While one might attempt to understand this notion by turning immediately to Leibniz's elaboration of monadic expression and intrinsic predication, instead I will examine its effects on the specifically Leibnizian conceptions of the real and the ideal, and the sense in which these lead Leibniz to develop an ontology framed by figures of the labyrinthine infinite library and impossible total book that Foucault would later recognize. First, focusing on *A New System of the Nature and Communication of Substances and of the Union of the Soul and the Body* (1695), I explore Leibniz's account of the difference between organic and aggregational substances and argue that it cannot be too quickly identified with a distinction between the holistic and the mechanical. By locating a difference between the finite and the infinite within the realm of the mechanical, Leibniz lays the ground for an ontological distinction between the mathematical and metaphysical fields while articulating a unique mode of idealism under the rubric of a spiritualized atomism. Second, I demonstrate that the continuum problem ultimately entails a transition from the metaphor of the labyrinth to the figure of the infinite library (something I will consider in Leibniz's *Theodicy* and "Apokatastasis" fragments). In order to account for

Leibniz's transformation of the iconography of the library into a philosophical principle, I also examine the complex hermeneutic situation of Leibniz's use of allegory and dialogue. This structure involves texts by Boethius and Lorenzo Valla that frame Leibniz's own allegorical interpretation of rationality. The sometimes dizzying intertextual complexities of Leibniz's articulation of the relationship between philosophy, allegorical discourse, and a history of philosophical reading bring us back to Leibniz's solution to the labyrinth of freedom as developed in the *Theodicy*.

FINITE AND INFINITE MACHINES

In the geometrical and labyrinthine gardens of the Herrenhausen palace of the Electress Sophia (and of her daughter and Leibniz's pupil, Sophie Charlotte, Queen of Prussia) Leibniz formulated his best-known illustration of the principle of the identity of indiscernibles, challenging a critic to find two indistinguishable leaves that maintained distinct identities.[2] The labyrinth (along with its golden thread) is the most classical of metaphors, and its philosophical significance certainly does not begin with Leibniz or the seventeenth century.[3] The most frequently cited and direct source of the Leibnizian figure is a 1631 book by Libert Froidmont, interlocutor of Descartes and professor of philosophy at Louvain: *The Labyrinth, or On the Composition of the Continuum*.[4] Equally significant for Leibniz, however, is the figure's appearance a few years earlier in Descartes' *Rules for the Direction of Mind*. While this unfinished manuscript—to which I shall return in Chapter 4—remained unpublished until 1701, Leibniz had obtained a copy by at least 1675.[5] When Descartes circumscribes methodological thinking as "consist[ing] entirely in the ordering and arranging of objects on which we must concentrate our mind's eye if we are to discover some truth," he adds, "Anyone who sets out in quest of knowledge of things must follow this rule as closely as he would the thread of Theseus if he were to enter the Labyrinth."[6] The Cartesian search for truth by means of natural light was thus initially framed as a foray into the obscure maze of complex propositions. Discerning the simple elements of which they are formed is the methodological thread that saves the philosopher from the vicious Minotaur of ignorance and uncertainty presumably lurking at the center of this labyrinth. Descartes, in turn, had already found this image in the preface to Bacon's *Great Instauration*.

For Bacon, only method can lead us through the universe, which "to the eye of human understanding is framed like a labyrinth; presenting as it does on every side so many ambiguities of way, such deceitful resemblances of objects and signs, natures so irregular in their lines, and so knotted and entangled."[7] The image is also found in Comenius, Galileo, Harvey, and others, and was one of many obsessions of Athanasius Kircher, whose books impressed the young Leibniz.[8]

Leibniz shifts away from Cartesian method proper to affirm the analyticity of truth and decisively rejects the metaphorics of reduction and ascent. Nevertheless, he tackles Froidmont's labyrinth of the composition of the continuum precisely in the context of "simples" and their natures (and by extension, the problem of the infinite and its relation to body).[9] Leibniz quickly identified the infinite as the origin of both labyrinths, and described its problem as the skein of the ideal and the actual. As he would write in his 1695 notes on Simon Foucher's objections to the *New System*, "But, in actual substantial things, the whole is a result or assemblage of simple substances, or rather of a multitude of real unities. It is a confusion of the ideal with the actual which has muddled everything and caused the labyrinth of the composition of the continuum" (*AG*, 146, trans. mod.). In what sense do the ideal and the actual come to bear on the problem of this labyrinth, and what is the meaning of these terms for Leibniz?

In the *New System,* Leibniz criticizes his contemporaries for allowing their mechanism to conflate the natural with the artificial, as they see only a difference of degree between the organic and the mechanical (*AG*, 141–42). Here Leibniz can easily be taken to be reintroducing the classical distinction between that form of unity in which the parts are subordinate to the whole and that in which the whole is merely the sum of its parts. This view is certainly correct. However, Leibniz insists that while these terms mark a difference in kind, *both* aggregates and organic wholes are machines. The distinction is not between machines that are more or less complex on the one hand, and machines or nonmachines on the other, but between two really distinct forms of mechanism: the artificial machine, with its finite aggregation of parts (here he offers an army, a flock of sheep, a pond of fish, and a watch made of springs), and the natural or (as he will later call it in the *Monadology*) "divine" machine, with an actually infinite number of organs, a machine that is composed of machines all the way down, a machine in each of its parts, *ad infinitum* (*AG*, 142).[10] The organic, then, is an infinite or divine machine, composed of an infinity of organized parts, each itself an infinitely organized machine.

To return to our labyrinth: how can such an infinite machine remain singular? In what sense can this continuous whole be said to be composed of an infinity of organic parts? If its infinite parts are each ultimately real and distinct, then how can they compose a continuum? What is the nature of these "parts" such that they can achieve a truly substantial unity? And what, for that matter, could such a true unity be? Leibniz's answer to the final question is as unsurprising as it is dissatisfying: the unity of the organism is its form, as he writes, "corresponding to what is called 'I' in us" (*AG*, 142, trans. mod.). Nevertheless, the distinctions that Leibniz draws in explaining this answer offer substantial illumination for the problem of the actual and the ideal. Leibniz rejects a material atomism because it would require "links" or "relations" among substances, and these links must themselves be linked to that which they link, and so on in a vicious and infinite regress (*AG*, 142).[11] However, neither the implied circularity nor the regression of material atomism is ultimately important here. As elsewhere in his arsenal of arguments aimed at corpuscular philosophy, or what he calls "refined Epicureanism," Leibniz's objection really revolves around the notion that acceptance of a material atomism ultimately violates both the principle of the identity of indiscernibles and the principle of sufficient reason.[12]

In an unfinished dialogue written between 1679 and 1681, for example, Leibniz considers the possible Epicurean objection— probably one offered by Guillaume Lamy and confronted by Bayle (to be treated at greater length in Chapter 3)—that despite the obviously "well-made" nature of the world, a fortuitous concourse of material atoms necessarily produces "an infinite number of worlds in all varieties" (*A*, 6.4-c:2267). If this is the case, then the orderly nature of the world cannot constitute a proof for an extra-mundane authorial creative principle. Leibniz's response here is specifically framed in terms of bibliographical complexity. "It is very hard to believe," he writes, "that an entire library could have been formed one day by a fortuitous concourse of atoms" (*A*, 6.4-c:2267). His argument, however, turns simply on the vanishingly small "likelihood" of chance conjunctions of material bodies producing the precise artifactual objects that would populate the library's shelves, and he finds himself forced to admit its possibility.

If I should find myself transported into a new region of the universe, where I would see clocks, furniture, books, and fortresses, I would boldly wager all that I have that this would be the work of some kind of rational creature, although absolutely speaking it would be possible that it was not, and we could feign that there be, perhaps, a land in the extended infinity of things where books write themselves. This would nevertheless be one of the greatest coincidences of the world, and one would have to have lost his mind in order to believe that this land where I find myself is exactly the possible land where books are written by chance. One would prefer blindness rather than follow a supposition so strange, though it is possible that it is practical in the ordinary course of nature. (*A*, 6.4-c:2267–68)

As we shall see shortly, the phantasmagoria of the automatic and total library will return to haunt Leibniz's thought. In the context of the *New System*, however, where Leibniz is still focused on defining the precise difference between finite and infinite machines in order to solve the continuity problem, he replaces material atomism with what he calls a "substantial atomism," "that is," he writes, "real unities absolutely destitute of parts, which are the sources of actions, the first absolute principles of the composition of things, and, as it were, the final elements in the analysis of substantial things" (*AG*, 142). *Physical* points are merely contracted corporeal substances. These substantial atoms, on the other hand, are metaphysical points, points that alone "are exact and real." The real or the actual is the realm of these metaphysical points, of true unity without aggregation. In a fascinating twist, mathematical points are then defined as the points of view of these metaphysical points, the location in the nexus of the ideal from which the latter express the totality of the universe. The "ideal" is thus the realm of exactly what it says: the ideational, the viewpoint, and the perspective. This ideality is also the realm of the possible. Leibniz further describes these points of view or mathematical points as the modalities of the real, that is, the possible permutations of an actual single, simple unity constitute its ideal perception of the totality of which it forms a part. The possible or the ideal is the modality of the actual. Ultimately, this is an unsurprising position for Leibniz to take, as it is almost an Aristotelian tautology: matter (*hyle*) is understood as unformed potentiality (or that which is capable of taking an infinity of forms) and form (*morphe*) is taken to be nothing more than the actualizing of that matter in a particular.

Yet, there seems to be a paradox here. Metaphysical points—utterly devoid of parts—together can constitute an organic whole: a divine and infinite machine, actually divided into an infinity of real metaphysical points. How can a position like this allow Leibniz to defend the singularity of a given substance? Are we not thrown back into the labyrinth where the actuality of the whole is incommensurable with that of its parts? Responding to Leibniz in a 1695 letter to the *Journal des Savants*, Simon Foucher elaborated this objection when he suggested that the real metaphysical points that constitute the parts of the divine, organic, and infinite machine might be considered "unities which underlie the structure and reality of extension."[13] Foucher went on to take Leibniz to task for not going further, arguing that "the essential foundations of extension could never really exist," because points without parts—or alternately, wholes composed of an infinity of parts, each infinitely divisible into a further infinity of parts—could not really exist. This objection allows us to return to the question at hand. In his notes to Foucher's objection, Leibniz insists on his familiar claim that "Extension or space and the surfaces, lines, and points one can conceive in it are only relations of order or orders of coexistence, both for the actually existing thing and for the possible things one can put in its place" (*AG*, 146).[14] Thus, Leibniz's conception of space and spatiality (the centerpiece of his battle with Newton, and by extension, of Kant's with Leibniz) can be understood as the ontologization of Descartes' early methodological stricture: the order of reasons has become the order of existence. Extension, that is, has precisely no essential or actual foundation: it can be found only in the order of the ideal. Lines, planes, and figures are ideal things composed of merely ideal mathematical points—points of view or modalities of the real—and the mathematical continuum (a continuum of possibilities, modalities, and extremities of extension) cannot be composed of actual parts, but can be divided in any way we please. Correlatively, actual metaphysical points (true unities, real substances, the ultimate parts of organic and infinite machines) cannot compose a continuum (or can compose only an ideal continuum), because they are precisely actually infinite. The continuum in the order of the ideal has only indefinite parts. The continuum in the order of the real is not a continuum at all.

Instead of following the thread of analysis out of the labyrinth of the composition of the continuum, Leibniz has brought its very walls crashing down. Real unity is not to be found at the level of the unity of the organic machine. Rather, the very realm of the organic turns out to be an ideal aggregation, a modality or point of view, and no continuum at all. This real unity is found only in the infinity of metaphysical points that "compose" the organic. The artificial machine, by contrast, has neither a real unity nor real parts. Because the elements of its composition are finite and (in Leibniz's sense) mathematical, its unity or continuum is only ideal and modal.

What has happened to singularity? What constitutes the unity of the singular substance? Actual metaphysical points do not "compose" a continuum. Instead, they *are each* a continuum. The real continuum, that is, has precisely *no* parts. Singularity has not disappeared. It has been hypostasized, as each single, simple, partless metaphysical point explodes into a continuum that repeats an entire world. The infinite mathematical divisibility of the ideal has given way to the absolute: the actual infinite of the real. As Leibniz writes in *New Essays on Human Understanding*, "In all rigor, the true infinite, is only in the *absolute*, which is anterior to all composition, and is not formed by the addition of parts . . . And the true infinite is not a *modification*, it is the absolute; and indeed, it is insofar as one modifies it that one limits oneself and forms the finite" (*A*, 6.6:157–58).[15] Matter is not possibly or ideally divisible. It is actually divided, possessing only an ideal unity and composed of an infinity of metaphysical, partless points, each of which is in turn infinite. They are infinite no longer in division, but in their expression or unfolding of an entire world.

ALLEGORICAL REASON AND THE INFINITE LIBRARY

We have now seen part of Leibniz's solution to the problem of the composition of the continuum. What Leibniz does not explicitly discuss is the ultimate fate of the labyrinth. In dissolving the problem of the composition of the continuum by insisting on the incommensurability of the actual and the ideal, Leibniz ensconces us in a new maze—the monad and its freedom—a labyrinth no longer located in the possible, but in the actual infinity of the real. Leibniz's entry into this new labyrinth has exacted a double price. First, he has to allow an actual simple metaphysical unity that is itself an ideal continuum expressing an infinite totality of other such points. Second, in so doing he has relied on a suspect conception of the infinite—infinite divisibility together with progress *ad infinitum*—one under interrogation at least since Galileo and ultimately destroyed with Cantor. However, this shortcoming of the solution of the *New System* was something of which Leibniz was fully aware. During his tenure as the ducal librarian of Wolfenbüttel, Leibniz would often consider this new maze in the figure of a labyrinthine infinite library.[16] What would it mean to speak of an infinite library, and what would constitute the principle of its organization? Is not a library merely a heap of books, an aggregate in the most classical of Leibnizian senses? Is it not an arbitrarily ordered collection of determinate texts, a series of finite machines, each literally stitched together and bound by wood, paper, and leather? In what sense might this library provide a solution to the problems of this suspect infinite while still conserving the metaphysical unity of the singular? In his attempts to answer these questions, Leibniz presents two particularly powerful images of the library—the infinite library of possible worlds and the library of the eternal return conceived under the classical framework of *apokatastasis*.

In the closing pages of the *Theodicy*, Leibniz constructs a philosophical dialogue that turns on the appropriation, transformation, and allegorization not only of his principle of the optimum—the necessary existence of the best of all possible worlds—but also of his textual relationship to a history of philosophical iconography and to the possibility of a sustained conversation among himself, the fifteenth-century rhetorician, philologist, and dialectician Lorenzo Valla, and the sixth-century philosopher Boethius (*Theo.*, 366–76). As Leibniz engages Valla's 1439 *Dialogue on Free Will*, he connects his own mythical architecture of possibility with a narrative of philosophical allegory leading back to Boethius' *Consolation of Philosophy* from 524.[17] Furthermore, he understands that connection to be defined by the allegorization of philosophy and philosophical language. Not a mere translation of a philosophical position into allegorical language, but a refiguring of the relationship among philosophical conceptuality, allegorical language, dialogical form, and the site of philosophical reading, Leibniz's text weaves a web of multiple figures of reading, vengeful gods, enormous pyramids tunneled through by infinite libraries, dialogues within dialogues within dialogues, and the burning, penetrating eyes of Philosophy incarnate.

When Leibniz brings his own text into contact with those of Valla and Boethius, he does not simply present a series of interpretive critiques. In order to see what is ultimately at stake in Leibniz's transfiguration of Valla's allegorical dialogue, it will be useful to examine Valla's text first. This, in turn, will require an engagement with Boethius' text and the philosophical allegory to which Valla's dialogue responds. Rather than replying directly to Valla's arguments regarding the possibility of human freedom in the face of divine providential determination, Leibniz answers the dialogical and allegorical form of Valla's text with a dialogue and allegory of his own. This response involves Leibniz's literal insertion of Valla's dialogue into the pages of the *Theodicy*. Along with his explicitly philosophical response (aimed simultaneously at the positions of Cicero, Bayle, and Valla), this manipulation of textual figures provides Leibniz with the opportunity to present a rhetorical answer to Valla's use of allegory and to Valla's response to Boethius' *Consolation* (the explicit object of Valla's attack). That Leibniz is *reading* Valla—and that Valla is *reading* Boethius—necessarily become integral elements of Leibniz's textual strategy. I say "necessarily" because this staging and figuration of the scene of philosophical reading along with an allegorical reframing of philosophical discourse is already at issue in Valla's own response to Boethius as well as in Boethius' text itself.

What is important to explain here is the transformation that dialectical philosophical argumentation may undergo when it makes contact with the allegorical mode, and specifically when that mode is dominated by figures of inscription, print, and bibliographical organization. Some philosophers assert that the insertion of allegory into philosophical texts must take an instrumental form, reducing its figures to the trivial ornamentation of theoretical content and framing the philosophical concepts in play as its secret, interior, and determinate referents. These referents, then, merely symbolize a sequence of specific conceptual meanings and exhaust themselves in a finite gesture of interpretation. But if, as Paul de Man has suggested, allegory consists in the repetition of an unreachable anteriority with which it can never coincide, then insisting on this instrumentality would impoverish a philosophical discourse (like Leibniz's) concerned with problems of repetition and would refuse to engage productive and central elements of many philosophical texts that make use of allegory.[18] The first question is whether allegory may have a serious place within Leibnizian philosophical discourse, and the answer, as should by now be obvious, is yes. But if that is the case, further issues arise. Specifically, how can allegory function philosophically for Leibniz and how can the language of philosophy be allegorically transformed without rendering it nonphilosophical? The answers to these questions, as will be demonstrated, revolve around Leibniz's mobilization of the figure of the library.

What I describe as Leibniz's strategy of doubled allegory (the formulation of an allegory in response to an allegory, which simultaneously involves the allegorization of philosophical discourse as such) is already at issue in Valla's response to Boethius. Valla's text is figured by a series of rhetorical refusals to engage in both allegorical discourse and philosophical dialogue, even while it attacks philosophy both allegorically and dialogically.[19] Turning to Boethius' *Consolation*, the terrain of the allegorical, dialogical, and philosophical strategies to which Valla is responding will be considered. Boethius presents a relationship between allegorical and philosophical discourse that involves an interpretation of temporality, conceptually defining the moment at which philosophical dialectic must transform itself into allegory. At the same time, Boethius' transformation allegorizes the relationship between philosophy and allegory themselves. Finally, in the dialogue in Leibniz's *Theodicy*, Valla and Boethius' figures are made to speak once again as Leibniz transforms the conceptual conflict between them into the formal philosophical allegory that concludes the *Theodicy*. Building a vast structure of possibility in the form of an infinite pyramidal library, Leibniz explores the problem of how one can allegorize freedom philosophically. Ultimately, his response to and reinscription of the figures of Boethius and Valla constitute a philosophical and rhetorical method. Framing this battle between the philosopher who writes allegorically and the rhetorician who refuses allegory as the interpretive anteriority of his own philosophical discourse, Leibniz takes seriously the movement of repetition at the heart of allegorized philosophy.

DECLARING WAR ON BOOKS

Rarely discussed in contemporary philosophical circles until recently, Valla was one of the premiere rhetoricians among the Italian humanists.[20] Before coming to fame as a major voice championing the systemization of rhetorical analysis and eloquence, Valla was known for his vehement attacks on Aristotelian logic and his defense of an Epicurean conception of pleasure. These attacks, like his straightforward rhetorical work, took "eloquence" as their evaluative criteria and thus, unlike many of the more prominent forays against Aristotle by Renaissance Neoplatonists, were first and foremost aesthetic. His primary objection was that Aristotelianism (and even more so Scholasticism) depended primarily on linguistic barbarism. For Valla, language is so much a part of thought (and especially philosophical thought) that there is little distinction between concepts and the words that express them, or between determinate expressions and the determination of things.[21]

Valla's explicitly philosophical questions in *Dialogue on Free Will* are framed by concerns that may sound quaint to contemporary philosophers, structured as they are in terms of divine foreknowledge of future events and the possible restrictions it may place on human freedom. Indeed, by Valla's time, these issues already had a long history in medieval philosophical theology, framed ontologically by Aquinas, Scotus, and Ockham as the terms of a debate over the problem of God's knowledge of future contingents.[22] To this end, Valla argues that the possibility of an event does not necessarily involve its actual occurrence, and thus previous knowledge of a future event (even on the part of God), cannot be considered to be the cause of that event. What piques Leibniz's interest is that Valla introduces a distinction between a possible and an actual futurity. There is, therefore, a distinction between God's will and power (which determine the course of things) and God's wisdom (or his knowledge of that course). The second section of Valla's text asks: Do not God's will and power determine even what it is that a human being can freely will? How, then, can we reconcile God's will with the freedom of human beings? In the face of these questions, Valla makes a move that Leibniz will ultimately be unwilling to accept: he refuses to answer this question, claiming that God's will must be accepted as a matter of faith.[23] This is, of course, a philosophically disappointing answer, but it is interesting in this respect: Valla is insisting on a strict division between epistemology and ontology. *Knowing* the cause or chain of causes behind an event or state cannot be rationally reconciled with *being* that cause or chain of causes and human freedom can be recognized only in the realm of knowing, not in the realm of being. From Leibniz's perspective, a major problem with this position is that while it grants us rational freedom, ontologically speaking we seem to be reduced to little more than automata or scripted characters. This, for Valla, necessitates an ultimate recourse to faith in the form of Pauline mystery (Boethius' mistake was perhaps only that "he loved philosophy excessively") (*DF*, 156), but it is worth noting that his position also opens the door for the kind of secular skepticism that will later emerge in Montaigne and the Cartesian tradition.

Let us now examine the way that Valla constructs his dialogue and the complex artifice that frames his text. Valla's work is structured by a series of negative moments. On its most material level, of course, it takes the form of a small philosophical book. But within the pages of this volume, Valla quickly refuses both philosophy and books, first insisting that a retrieval of ancient philosophical texts has no value whatsoever—he claims that it leads good men into impiety—and second denying that reading itself is an appropriate contemplative activity. "For what should I say about books?" he writes. "Either you agree with them, then nothing further is demanded; or you do not agree with them, and then there is nothing more to be said. Yet you will see how pious and tolerable it is for you to declare war on all books, including the wisest, and not to side with any of them" (*DF*, 159). In an attempt to distance his own publication from the object of his attack, Valla frames it in the epistolary mode. The *Dialogue on Free Will* is ostensibly not a book, but a letter to Garzía Aznárez de Añón, the bishop of Lerida. The bulk of this letter, however, "reports" the words of an argument between Valla and one Antonio Glarea, "recounting them," Valla writes, "as if the affair were proceeding and not narrated, so that 'I said' and 'he said' does not need to be so frequently interpolated" (*DF*, 157). So from the opening moments of his text, Valla explicitly refuses to invoke the traditional form of the philosophical dialogue with its emphasis on the inventive possibilities of narrative. He claims instead to be a mere recorder. This dialogue is to be a literal one: the written trace of a conversation that actually took place.

However, when we turn to the contents of the conversation that Valla reports, this refusal of the dialogical form is immediately undercut. First, early in the text, the character "Laurentius" (framed, of course, as speaking for Valla himself) justifies the book's form by invoking martial metaphors in a remarkable prefiguration of

Nietzsche's insight that philosophical language is made for cutting in the knife-thrust of syllogism.[24] Valla has Laurentius' interlocutor Antonio say, "Do not expect me to give in to you so easily or to flee without sweat and blood," and Laurentius responds, "Good luck to you; let us contend closely in hand-to-hand and foot-to-foot conflict. Let the decision be by sword, not spear" (*DF*, 163). The error of the philosopher, Laurentius holds, is to engage concepts from the safe distance of an implacable and universal rationality—whether framed by a historical reactivation of the ancients and their positions, a reliance on books and their supposedly static discursive schemata, or a tentative engagement with what he describes as the bloodless weapons of analysis and synthesis. For Valla, the violent exchange of sentences and arguments in a dialogue corporealizes language and this embodiment of abstraction revitalizes what he sees as the morbidity of the written word.

A second and even more important affirmation of dialogue in Valla's text takes the form of another dialogue in the midst of the first, this time in the mythical and allegorical mode. In the middle of their discussion of the problem of freedom, Laurentius and Antonio abruptly construct a fable that includes fictionalized and invented narrative counterparts, who then proceed to advance a set of positions in dialogue with one another. Laurentius recounts the tale of the young Sextus Tarquinius (the son of the last king of Rome and the future rapist of Lucretia). Sextus is disappointed by the fate foretold for him by the Delphic oracle—"An exile and a pauper you will fall, killed by the angry city" (*DF*, 171)—and becomes furious with Apollo for divining such a wretched fate. Apollo defends himself by insisting that divine foreknowledge cannot lie, explaining, "I know the fates, I do not decide them; I am able to announce Fortune, not change her; I am the index of destinies, not their arbiter; I would reveal better things if better things awaited you" (*DF*, 170). When Sextus asks how the gods could so cruelly determine such a grim future for him, Apollo replies: "Jupiter as he created the wolf fierce, the hare timid, the lion brave, the ass stupid, the dog savage, and the sheep mild, so he fashioned some men hard of heart, others soft ... To you, indeed, he assigned an evil soul with no resource for reform. And so both you, for your inborn character, will do evil, and Jupiter, on account of your actions and their evil effects will punish sternly" (*DF*, 173).[25]

Valla interprets this deliciously biting myth within the text itself, having Laurentius explain,

> For this is the point of my fable, that although the wisdom of God cannot be separated from His power and will, I may by this device [*similitudo*] of Apollo and Jupiter separate them. What cannot be achieved with one god may be achieved with two, each having his own proper nature—the one for creating the character of men, the other for knowing—that it may appear that providence is not the cause of necessity but that all this whatever it is must be referred to the will of God. (*DF*, 174)

After this pronouncement, Valla's text effectively abandons dialogue altogether, as if the interpretation of this allegory had exhausted its possibility. What remains of the *Dialogue on Free Will* is an exhortation by Laurentius to Antonio to avoid the hubris of philosophers "who, calling themselves wise, are made foolish" (*DF*, 181). However, in the final sentences of the text, Laurentius denies even the exhortative value of this speech, explicitly describing what has just taken place as an *exhortatio* but nevertheless immediately claiming that it was made "not so much that I might move you . . . as that I might show my own disposition of mind" (*DF*, 182). Thus, Laurentius explains, the speech was meant to express his own perspective on the matter and not to persuade or exhort his now silent dialogical partner.

Where does this leave us? When the *Dialogue on Free Will* is examined, there is first, a philosophical book that opens with a declaration of war on both philosophy and on books. Second, this book is textually framed in the epistolary mode (a one-sided dialogue in which the other is incapable of offering a response). Third, this epistle is immediately transformed into a philosophical dialogue (the argument between Laurentius and Antonio) that refuses the dialogical form by determining its own reception as mere reportage. Fourth, in the midst of this supposedly unornamented description of an informal disputation, the purportedly nonfictionalized participants abruptly shift to the invention of fictional, historical, and mythological characters in an allegorical dialogue. Finally, a single character in this doubled (and doubly refused) dialogical structure acknowledges his identity as the author of the book, concluding with an exhortation against philosophy (and by extension against philosophical dialogues) that at the same time denies its own exhortative character. Given that the ultimate issue at stake for Valla is whether the actions of human beings can be reduced to their narration or fictionalization by an omnipotent and authorial divinity, these formal complications are philosophically significant. Even while Valla holds narrative, dialogue, allegory, and philosophy at arm's length, his text presents the problem of freedom as one that can be solved only with a radical alternation of voice, an ever-shifting stage play in which the human being freely articulates and fictionalizes the voices of the very divinities whose power renders articulation and fictionalization futile. His initial double refusal of the dialogical form serves as the frame on which to hang a doubled dialogue. This intricate narrative structure is itself bound up with a response to the narrative strategy of one of the philosophical dialogues *par excellence*, Boethius' *Consolation of Philosophy.*

PHILOSOPHY IN CHAINS

Valla's multiplicity of rhetorical forms and denegations become even more interesting when we consider that the *Dialogue on Free Will* is explicitly framed as a response to Boethius' *Consolation* (specifically the arguments of book 5, though it also addresses those of book 4).[26] The *Consolation* is a textual performance in which high Socratic dialogue is transformed into a confrontation between a philosopher and philosophy itself.[27] The book recounts a long conversation between an imprisoned philosopher—chained and awaiting death, accused of crimes he claims not to have committed—and the avatar of philosophy imagined on the model of the Muses. The philosopher of the dialogue, of course, is none other than a *prosopon* for its author, languishing in prison after accusations by agents of the emperor Theodoric. This identification of Boethius with the philosopher-prisoner who figures in his book takes a particularly grisly turn if we consider the *Consolation*'s repeated invocations of Diogenes Laertius' account of the fate of Zeno of Elea. Throughout the book, Philosophia approvingly reminds the condemned philosopher that in the face of torture by the tyrant Nearchus, Zeno "bit off his own tongue and spat it in the face of the enraged tyrant," the likely origin of our contemporary commonplace "a biting remark" (*Cons.*, 2, pr. 6.29). What Boethius, soon to be tortured and bludgeoned to death, has his character Philosophia carefully avoid mentioning is that in at least one telling Nearchus eventually had Zeno pulverized in a giant mortar.[28]

The *Consolation* begins with what most interpreters agree is an intentionally bad poem wherein the philosopher, taking dictation from the Muses of poetry, bemoans his sad state and blames "fickle Fortuna" for his troubles (*Cons.*, 1, m. 1.17). As the text shifts to dialogical narrative, philosophy is personified as an "awe-inspiring" woman with "burning eyes," immeasurable or indescribable by any ordinary standard. She is immensely old, Boethius writes, yet "of youthful appearance and inexhaustible vigor. It was difficult to be sure of her height, for sometimes she seemed confined to the ordinary human measure, and other times the top of her head seemed to touch the heavens, and when she raised her head even higher, she pierced them and was lost to human sight" (*Cons.*, 1, pr. 1.7–13). Her dress is of a "fine and imperishable material" that she has woven herself, with a *pi* on its lower border and a *theta* on its upper, and "between the two letters, steps rose like a ladder, by which one could climb from the lower to the higher" (*Cons.*, 1, pr. 1.13–16). The dress also "appeared enshrouded by a kind of neglect, like a smoke-covered family statue" and had been ripped to shreds (*Cons.*, 1, pr. 1.16–24). Finally, she holds books in her right hand and a scepter in her left (*Cons.*, 1, pr. 1.24–25). Her first acts are to denounce the Muses of poetry as "theatrical prostitutes" and "sirens" and to chase them from the room, replacing them with her "own" Muses, those of rhetoric and music (*Cons.*, 1, pr. 1.28–41).

What we encounter in Boethius' allegory of Philosophia is a relatively straightforward depiction whose iconography has historically been the subject of much commentary.[29] Modeled on the classical Muses and similar to Martianus Capella's allegorization of the liberal arts, a form or mode of thought is materialized in a gendered body.[30] Philosophia's "burning" and "piercing" eyes (on which Boethius twice remarks) are the visual models of speculative insight. In his masterful line-by-line commentary on the *Consolation*, Joachim Gruber traces Philosophia's *oculis ardentibus* and *toruis inflammata luminibus* (*Cons.*, 1, pr. 1.4 and pr. 1.28) back to Athena's "bright" or "blazing" eyes in the *Iliad*, so central to her personification that *glaukopis Athene* is her first Homeric epithet).[31] This is particularly significant given that in Leibniz's reconfiguration of both Boethius' text and Valla's response, he directly transposes Athena for Boethius' Philosophia. Philosophia's shifting age and height corresponds to the *Consolation*'s description of the hierarchy of modes of knowledge (the path from sensation through imagination to reason, finally arriving at *intelligentia*). The insistence that Philosophia has woven the dress herself signifies that philosophical thinking does not depend on the assumption of externally generated tools or methods.[32] The *theta*, *pi*, and ladder image on the dress correspond to Boethius' account of the Aristotelian division of philosophy into the practical and theoretical as well as the Platonic methodological ladder of contemplation leading from the former to the latter.[33] Regarding the ladder on the dress, Seth Lerer intriguingly comments,

> The flat, fallen *gradus* of the prisoner contrasts with the rising vertical *gradus* of philosophical education. The meaningful markings on Philosophy's gown (the word *insigniti*) echo the meaningless marks Boethius made in silence (the word *signarem*). Through these verbal echoes Boethius creates a unified structure of imagery that explains the prisoner's initial silence and prepares us for Philosophy's opening words. (*LB*, 98)

The disheveled state of her dress indicates that since the days of Plato and Socrates, true philosophy has been neglected. Philosophia herself blames "mobs of Epicureans and Stoics" for tearing it to shreds as they attempted to abduct her after Plato's death. "They tore off small pieces from it and left believing that they had the whole of me with them. And since they were seen wearing the vestiges of my dress, they were imprudently accepted as my followers, and were dragged down by the errors of the common multitude" (*Cons.*, 1, pr. 3.21–30). The scepter signifies the dominion of philosophy over the Muses, and the books are simply books (i.e., Boethius' Philosophia is effectively the goddess of textual materialism), though they are also the very volumes on which Valla will declare war. Despite its eminent interpretability, in this scene of the *Consolation* we also have one of the most definitive aesthetic moments for the philosophical branch of the allegorical and emblematic tradition in the Middle Ages and early Renaissance. Countless depictions of philosophy take this passage in the *Consolation* as their touchstone, personifying philosophy in much the same imagery as Boethius describes. Many even add a representation of Boethius himself in conversation with her, and some place her atop a shattered wheel, corresponding to the refutation of an allegorized Fortuna (the subject matter of the first three books of the *Consolation*).[34]

Partly due to this elaborately allegorical imagery, what first looks like a simple philosophical dialogue turns out to have a rather complex narrative structure. Boethius' *Consolation* is a fictionalized dialogue articulated by one character who corresponds directly to its philosopher-author and another whose characterization becomes the definitive allegorical and iconographic representation of philosophy itself. That is, Boethius' book confronts us with a philosophical dialogue constructed through narrative, dialectic, and allegory and also with an allegory of philosophical dialectic and of narrative themselves. Thus, Boethius' reflections on death, freedom, and divine determination are allegorized here, but so is philosophical reflection as such in its most classical narrative and iconographic genres. Several commentators have noted that the confrontation with Fortuna stages yet another allegory within the allegory, since Fortuna only appears as a mask of Philosophia, who is herself an allegorical incarnation of the prisoner's reflections, all of which, furthermore, allegorize Boethius himself writing the *Consolation*. As Jon Witman remarks,

> Boethius makes the personification of Philosophy itself fashion the *prosopon* for another personification—the very personification, in fact, who is her abstract adversary. Such a "bracketing" of one figure by another tends to subordinate Fortune logically, as well as rhetorically, to Philosophy. But this ingenious philosophic strategy is itself accomplished only by means of a rhetorical amplification. In short, Philosophy's daringly literary gesture is the very guarantee of her conceptual control.[35]

Indeed, this narrative and allegorical multiplication becomes a philosophical issue for Boethius at precisely the moment when Valla—and by extension, Leibniz—will later intervene in the *Consolation*. In the last two books, Boethius introduces a temporalized distinction between providence and fate. To grasp events under the hermeneutic of providence is to take them to be teleologically planned and determined. Providence is "the simple and immobile form of things," a realm of pure and unchanging being, and a unified whole enfolded or implicated in the divine mind. The perspective of providence is that of an eternal system of final causes. To grasp these same events as fated, by contrast, is to see them as fixed within a nexus of efficient causes, determined in their states by infinite chains of temporal consequence and eventuality. Fate is the "disposition inherent in mobile things," the realm of an ever-differing becoming, and "the unified whole distributed [*digesta*] and unfolded [*explicata*] in time" (*Cons.*, 4, pr. 6.34–57). For Boethius, as one might expect, fate is ultimately subordinated to providence. While the realm of efficient causation is necessarily included in that of final causation or teleology, elements of the teleological exceed or are unable to be captured by an efficient or mechanistic analysis. Boethius illustrates this priority of teleology with the Neoplatonic and Aristotelian cosmological figures of a set of revolving concentric circles. Providence is allied with the figure of an immobile central point while fate is associated with the revolutions of the circular periphery (*Cons.*, 4, pr. 6.65–101).

Boethius' philosopher-prisoner raises an objection to this portrayal. If the order of existence is eternally determined according to divine teleology and the sequence of events is merely the unfolding of that order in time, then it is difficult to find any room for freedom. Philosophia responds by introducing a distinction between divine and human knowledge, arguing that divine foreknowledge is a kind of vision that does not impose determination. Divine foreknowledge of a future event involves "foreseeing" (in a swift example of Boethian paronomasia, it is now *providentia* [looking forth] rather than *praevidentia* [seeing beforehand]), just as our everyday knowledge of a present event may depend on human vision without our sight being the cause of that event (*Cons.*, 5, pr. 6.69–70). Divinity (and divine teleology) is merely an eternal vision of the totality of temporal events grasped in a single glance, or put otherwise, it is an immobile image of time. Conversely, time, as in Plato's *Timaeus*, is figured as the moving image of an immobile eternity. This difference between time and eternity produces a hierarchy of knowing. While human beings are capable of sensation, imagination, and reason, atemporal entities, that is, God, have a capacity for knowledge that exceeds ours. Boethius names this knowledge *intelligentia*, an immediate, that is, simultaneous intuition of the "simple form" of what is (*Cons.*, 5, pr. 4.82–91). Different capacities for knowledge belong to different substances, and a "lower" capacity for knowledge cannot comprehend a higher. While God has command of all these forms of knowledge, human beings grasp only sensation, imagination, and reason, remaining forever barred from the eternal viewpoint of divine intelligence.

However, in the remaining claims of the *Consolation*—an investigation of the nature of the eternal and its differentiation from finite and infinite time—the prisoner and Philosophia immediately violate this strict division. Giving an account of the nature of the divine, that is, eternity, Philosophia proposes to the prisoner an attempt to "raise ourselves to the point of that highest intelligence" and seek to understand (within the limits of reason) how the problem of freedom appears from the perspective of the eternal (*Cons.*, 5, pr. 5.50–53). That is, a rational account of the nature of teleological necessity will constitute a *rational* allegory corresponding to what cannot be presented rationally. No marked change in the tone of the text occurs here, though a new language of imitation, emulation, portrayal, and resemblance is subtly introduced.[36] However, if Boethius takes seriously his own postulate that reason cannot trespass against the boundaries of the eternal, then what follows—a diachronic, rational account of eternity—can only be an allegory of philosophical reason. Rather than figures corresponding to a secret layer of conceptual meaning, here concepts refer only to other concepts, allegorizing and figuring them *as* rational. Reason itself becomes allegorical (and no less rational for that) when it reasons about that which transcends, and in transcending, defines, its limits. At the end of the *Consolation*, philosophical allegory has become the temporal method by which reason unfolds the implicated synchrony of the eternal present. In a dialogue between characters already doubly marked as allegorical, the eternal present of divine vision is ejected from the experience of duration. Temporal entities exist, strictly speaking, only in this present, but what they experience and rationally comprehend is the coming-to-be of the future and the passing away of what has been. When reason explicates its own temporality—when it seeks to reinscribe itself in the simultaneity of the eternal—it can do so only through an allegorical metamorphosis. Not only does philosophical dialectic begin to speak in allegory but it also refigures itself as the discourse of a doubly allegorized dialogue.

To summarize, in order of composition, the story begins with Boethius' *Consolation*, a dialogue whose characters are a narrated prisoner-philosopher identical with its author and an iconographic allegorization of philosophy whose "conversation" with the prisoner becomes the definitive allegory for philosophy. Not only is the dialogical character of the *Consolation* thus doubled when via its historical appropriation it becomes an allegory of an allegory, but also the theoretical content of the dialogue culminates in an account of the *necessity* of such an allegory for the rational defense of human freedom. Later, when offering a refutation of Boethius, the philosophical rhetorician Valla is confronted with the task of refuting not only a set of arguments regarding foreknowledge, temporality, and human reason, but also with a strategy for the allegorization of rational dialectic. Thus, Valla does not simply offer counter-arguments to Boethius' claims, but writes (and in writing, allegorizes and repeats) an attack on the double allegory of the *Consolation*. Valla, therefore, doubly distances himself from dialogue and the allegorical narrative it implies, but ultimately articulates that refusal through a mythological dialogue in the high allegorical style. In the same way, his confrontation with Boethius' allegorical book becomes an attack on books in their materiality as such, which is nevertheless articulated within the pages of an actual book, albeit one that goes to great lengths to deny that it is a book at all. Valla's refusals of Boethius' allegory of philosophy, the philosophical conclusions of the *Consolation*, and the materiality of philosophical books is therefore a doubled, negative repetition of the methodological and rhetorical form of Boethius' text, one that was already structured by the repetition of a doubled philosophical allegory.

THE INFINITE LIBRARY OF POSSIBILITIES

When Leibniz takes up Valla's dialogue in the *Theodicy*, it is by no means with the oppositional intent imbuing Valla's relation to Boethius.[37] Indeed, in the preface, Leibniz describes Valla as one of the writers to have "charmed" him when he "first gained some tolerable understanding of Latin writings and had an opportunity of turning over books in a library" (*Theo.*, 67).[38] Elsewhere in the *Theodicy*, he speaks of "remembering" Valla's dialogue, and thinking that quoting it in the abstract while "retaining the dialogue form" might be an "opportune" means of concluding his dissertation. He speaks courteously of Valla, claiming the *Dialogue on Free Will* "makes it plain that he was no less a philosopher than a humanist," and describing it as "excellent" (*Theo.*, 366).[39]

Nevertheless, Leibniz lodges a major complaint against Valla: because in the end, his attack on Boethius seems merely to call for a renunciation of philosophical reason in favor of a fundamentally theological affirmation of Pauline mystery, Valla has only dispensed with the problem of the relationship between divine foreknowledge and freedom instead of solving or dissolving it. Valla ultimately holds that we must take our freedom on faith. Since even the contingency of our will is determined by divine power, our ignorance of the form of this determination effectively leaves us free. This, Leibniz writes, merely "cuts the knot" and "seems to condemn providence under the name of Jupiter, by nearly making him the author of sin" (*Theo.*, 369). Rather than simply providing an alternative dialectical account, Leibniz responds allegorically and dialogically to Valla's attack on Boethian dialogue and its allegory of philosophical reason.[40] Leibniz, in fact, reassembles *all* of the characters from both Valla and Boethius (even Antonio and Laurentius), and inserts his own author-*prosopon* into their midst. The allegorical figure of philosophy incarnate was expelled from Valla's mythos. Likewise, Boethius' doubly allegorized philosopher had no place in Valla's dialogue; he was an impious and dangerous enemy whose books were to be burned or left to molder, his fate a consignment to eternal flame. Leibniz immediately returns both these characters to the fable. Like Boethius, he introduces an author-philosopher, now in the guise of a priest of Jupiter named Theodore, but like Valla, Leibniz's dialogue is one between a mortal and a divine: Theodore converses with Philosophia refigured as Pallas Athena, daughter of Jupiter, sister of Apollo, and goddess of wisdom.

Valla left us with Apollo having answered Sextus' complaint: he merely *sees* what Jupiter has determined. Extending Valla's dialogue, Leibniz sends Sextus to plead for his future at Dodona, where Jupiter offers him a choice: If he will renounce his claim to the crown of Rome, then the Fates will spin him a different destiny. Sextus, however, resists, insisting that he is free to choose to be a good king. When Jupiter subsequently condemns him to the fate Apollo had foreseen, Theodore protests to his master that the god's actions display an unbecoming cruelty. In response, Jupiter sends Theodore to Athena for a lesson in allegorical pedagogy and the architecture of possibility. Theodore journeys to Athens, where he sleeps in the Parthenon and dreaming, "finds himself transported to an unknown land," waking before "a palace of inconceivable brilliance and immense grandeur" (*Theo.*, 370). When Theodore meets Athena at the gate, she is, Leibniz writes, "surrounded by rays of dazzling majesty," and he can perceive her only after she touches his forehead with an olive branch (*Theo.*, 370). This olive branch is one of Athena's traditional iconographic traits, stemming from her victory over Poseidon in the contest of gifts to endow Athens with a name (her gift of the olive tree was prized over his of either a horse or a salty well). In explicitly naming the olive branch rather than the presumably more recognizable spear, Medusian shield or helmet, Leibniz transforms Valla's allegorical emphasis on a founding myth of the Roman Empire into an evocation of Greek antiquity. In the face of Valla's rejection of philosophy and his declaration of war on books, Leibniz repeats Boethius' retrieval of the philosophers of ancient Athens.

The same gesture that reveals Pallas Athena's visage to Theodore allows him to discern the form of the palace before which they stand. It is an infinite pyramid of possible worlds whose chambers descend in an endless chain of permutations but whose apex is occupied by the optimum—the best of all possible worlds, which for Leibniz means the compossible totality of events and things that includes the most desire, force, and variation. This pyramid is the architectural and allegorical reconciliation of finite form and infinite extension, its figure mathematically determinable (a pyramid) but its ground literally beyond measure. "The pyramid had a beginning," Leibniz writes, "but one could see no end to it; it had an apex, but no base at all; it extended continually into the infinite" (*Theo.*, 372, trans. mod.). Its form, as Athena tells Theodore, is also the locus for the determination of the real. "Jupiter, having reviewed—before the beginning of existence—the representations within its halls not only of that which happens, but also of all that is possible, classified [*digeré*] the possibilities into worlds and chose the best of them all. He sometimes comes to visit these places to give himself the pleasure of recapitulating things and of renewing his choice" (*Theo.*, 370, trans. mod.). For Leibniz, the divine power of determination is no longer allegorized as the passive gaze of a disembodied and providential eye that watches temporal entities exercise all their diachronic freedom in a single glance (as in Boethius). Neither is it the arbitrary legislation of a natural disposition that reduces freedom to ignorance of our own predestined fate (as in Valla). Instead, Jupiter—the personification of divine will and power—is a calculator and classifier of possibilities who intervenes only to establish the law that governs their systematicity. As Leibniz scribbled in the margins of one of his texts, "God calculates and thinks, and the world begins" (*GP*, 7:191).[41]

In the figure of Jupiter browsing the infinite series of possible worlds only to reaffirm his choice, Giorgio Agamben finds an allegory of tyranny and tragedy. When Jupiter takes pleasure in recapitulating his act of determination, Agamben insists, the god "must close his own ears to the incessant lamentation that, throughout the infinite chambers of this Baroque inferno of potentiality, arises from everything that could have been but was not, from everything that could have been otherwise but had to be sacrificed for the present world to be as it is" (*AP*, 266). Arguing for an inverted pyramid of potentialities, Agamben insists that the *telos* of this hierarchical arrangement of existential combinations is actually the death of possibility as such. The pyramid, he suggests, "projects an infinite shadow downward, which sinks lower and lower to the extreme universe . . . in which nothing is compossible with anything else and nothing can take place" (*AP*, 266). A more positive reading would hold that the law of systematization Leibniz invokes here is both aesthetic and mathematical. The fact of its transition from the possible to the actual, that is, the arbitrary choice of a capricious God condemning unactualized possibles to the eternal damnation of nonexistence, is not what makes one world the best of all. Rather, this categorical transformation derives from the beauty and intricacy of its infinite folds and the sheer quantitative diversity of its expression of force and striving (its *impetus* or *conatus*). This is the model that Leibniz proposes in "On the Ultimate Origination of Things," where he claims, "there is a certain urge for existence [*exigentia existentiae*] or, so to speak, a straining toward existence in possible things or in possibility or essence itself" (*AG*, 150). Identifying perfection with quantity of essence, Leibniz argues "essence in and of itself strives for existence" (*AG*, 150).[42] The transition from mere possibility to perfected actuality, then, is no transition at all, but simply the sheer quantitative extremity of a geometrical figure traced by the arrangement of possibles. This extremity is precisely what Theodore discovers when Pallas Athena leads him to the apex of the pyramidal library.

Before they arrive, however, Athena takes Theodore on a tour of the palace, showing him worlds, she says, "where you will find not completely the same Sextus as you have seen . . . but several Sextuses resembling him . . . Sextuses of every sort and of an infinity of kinds" (*Theo.*, 371). When she commences her presentation of possible worlds and possible Sextuses, the palace of destinies undergoes an allegorical transformation that adds another level to the significance of Jupiter's obsession with classification. The palace of destinies is also an infinite library, with Jupiter as its cataloger and occasional peruser and Athena as its librarian. After witnessing an abbreviated theatrical presentation of Sextus' life in one hall, Theodore notices that the walls of this chamber are lined with books, and asks about their significance. Athena replies,

> You have seen a number on the forehead of Sextus. Look in this book for the place that it indicates. Theodore looked for it, and found there the history of Sextus in a form more ample than the outline he had seen. Put your finger on any line you please, Pallas said to him, and you will see represented actually in all its detail that which the line broadly indicates. He obeyed, and he saw coming into view all the characteristics of a portion of the life of that Sextus. They passed into another hall, and lo! another world, another Sextus. (*Theo.*, 371–72)

Each hall in the palace of destinies—each possible world—is a divine reading room and the system of classification by which this library is ordered is inscribed on the very bodies of those who inhabit its shelves.[43] The philosophical interrogation of freedom has become the act of reading these bodies and of tracing the intricate structure of reference that they enfold. While each hall in the pyramidal library is first a *theatrum mundi*, it is more fundamentally a volume, a book of fates, of which every line, word, and character corresponds to some series of predicates inhering in a single concept, to some particular event which is ideally divisible to infinity, to some simple, single, partless metaphysical point on which is inscribed an infinite repetition of the totality of the real. The palace itself constitutes the divine library of these volumes, determinate and finite in form (a pyramid) but infinite in its measure (literally groundless). Furthermore, the infinite and ideal continuum of an actually divided reality is inscribed on the very body of Sextus, which is to say, an elaborate structure of ontological reference allows a singular, unified metaphysical point to express an infinity of other such points, constituting a continuum only insofar as it is the expression or speculative reflection of an entire world. The library itself—the totality of such possible points—moves beyond the realm of the aggregational to achieve an organic unity.

And yet, has not Leibniz already argued that the infinite or divine machine of the realm of the organic cannot itself be taken as a real unity, but only as an ideal continuum composed of an infinity of metaphysical points and an organically complete world inhabited by an infinity of monads? Was not this problem the very path by which the actual and the ideal became a question? Indeed, it is only at the pyramidal library's apex—which Leibniz explicitly names "the real"—that the ideal continuum of a possible world fully corresponds to both its actual infinite division and the reality of the monad, identical with what we call the "I" in Sextus Tarquinius.

When Pallas Athena and Theodore finally reach the highest hall (the apex of the pyramid), Theodore is "ravished by ecstasy" and falls unconscious. Athena revives him by placing a drop of divine liquid on his tongue and explains that they have now entered "the true and actual world" (*Theo.*, 372, trans. mod.). Here, Sextus will freely commit his crimes and be condemned. But this world—the one whose power and beauty is too great for Theodore to endure without the divine ambrosia of philosophy—is also a *mise en abîme*. *This* is the world in which Theodore will demand an explanation from Jupiter. *This* is the world in which Athena will reveal to him the pyramidal library of destinies. *This* is the world in which Philosophia and the philosopher will roam the stacks of possibility, discussing the principles of their classification. *This* is the world in which Theodore can observe himself observing Sextus and conversing with Athena, note the number inscribed on his *own* body, and consult the page that recounts this very act of reading. What renders Theodore senseless is the abrupt conjunction of the merely possible with actualized possibility, that is, the intersection of reflective philosophical abstraction and the materiality of his own body transformed into a book. Theodore loses consciousness when confronted with the identity of reading and the read and the full congruence of a philosophical allegory with what it allegorizes. Christiane Frémont argues that the *transition* from the possible to the actual is what shocks Theodore, rather than his confrontation with actuality itself (*FS*, 107). I am arguing that the operative figures here are neither transition nor confrontation but conjunction and identity. The optimum possible world does not *pass from* possibility to actuality, nor does it confront the long shadow of those worlds it condemns to darkness, as Agamben would have it (*AP*, 266). Rather, the possible world expressing the most intense or greatest striving for existence *is* the actual world, and its actualization *adds* nothing to it.

Leibniz's extension of Valla's allegorical and dialogical narrative develops a new form of philosophical allegory through its transformation of Valla's response to Boethius' allegory of reason. Conceptually, this shift subordinates "divine will" to the "strife of possibles" that people the pyramidal library of destiny. Leibniz's response to the *Dialogue on Free Will*, in other words, transforms Valla's negative repetition of Boethius' doubled allegory into an allegorical method *of* bibliographic repetition. When Boethius' mentor Philosophia reappears as Pallas Athena, where does this new goddess take our new Boethius? They visit the palace of possible fates, an eternal library housing an infinite number of possible temporal webs of efficient cause, each doubly figured as a stage play and a book. Leibniz's dialogue takes up Valla's doubled rejection of allegory and narrative precisely to allegorize the Boethian distinction between time and eternity that Valla's method was meant to refute. The divine library emerges as an allegory for the determination of the field of possibility, its infinite volumes of possible worlds themselves containing every possible allegory, every possible narrative, and every possible dialogue, as well as every possible disavowal of them. Philosophia's dress has become the mantle of a divine librarian as she offers an account of the volumes under her charge and rationally recounts what it means for wisdom to allegorically lead the philosopher through this library's infinite shelves.

In one episode that Leibniz and Valla both knew, this logic of the *mise en abîme* was already inscribed into the historical narrative of Boethius' *Consolation*. In the first book, after the prisoner has marveled at Philosophia's appearance and she has recommended that he take refuge from his cares through discourse with her and the intellectual contemplation of higher things, she asks him whether he has understood. Embarking on a lengthy oration that bemoans his plight, the prisoner—still unconvinced, refers to the already allegorical space in which their conversation is taking place. "Is my harsh treatment at fortune's hands not obvious enough?" he asks. "Are you not affected by the very appearance of this room? Do you not recognize the library, which you once chose for yourself as a secure dwelling place in my house—the very room in which you used often to sit with me discoursing on the knowledge of all things human and divine?" (*Cons.*, 1, pr. 4.7–14) The entire allegorical discourse between the personification of philosophy and the philosopher-prisoner will thus occur within a library, which doubles as the prison cell in which Boethius is ensconced while writing the *Consolation*. Philosophia responds, however, by shifting this local reference to another register entirely, such that in what will follow, their discourse will take place in the library of the mind. "I am moved more by the sight of you than of this place," she says. "I seek not so much a library with its walls ornamented with ivory and glass, as the storeroom of your mind, in which I have laid up not books, but what makes them of any value, the opinions set down in my books in times past" (*Cons.*, 1, pr. 5.20–25). Philosophia will not engage the books lining the walls of the prisoner's library-cell but the volumes stacked in the folds of his mind, that is, the notions, arguments, and affective meanings contained within their pages. At the same time, the books renounced here are not whatever material objects Boethius may have access to in his prison cell, but the wholly imaginary and allegorical books that furnish the room of the already allegorized prisoner. Philosophia insists that the prisoner—and the reader of the *Consolation*—thus walk and speak with her in an already doubly allegorized library: a library of the mind within the library of the text, both of them inscribed within the pages of a book.

This logic is recapitulated and hypostasized in an episode from the pictorial history of the *Consolation* and its iconography, though one that neither Valla nor Leibniz likely would have known. An illuminated manuscript of the *Consolation* produced in a Bourges scriptorium in 1476 contains the Latin text of the *Consolation*, several commentaries, a French translation by Jean de Meun (the continuator of the *Roman de la rose*), and an astonishing series of miniatures attributed to the illuminator Jean Colombe.[44] The first miniature in the text (Figure 1), accompanying a prologue designated as Boethius' own even though Boethius wrote no such prologue, shows an enrobed figure sitting at a sloped desk in a Renaissance library. The figure gazes at the pages of a book open before him, his fingers delicately pressed against the vellum, his left hand holding the page flat, his right guiding his eye along the column of words. Hanging by a chain on the library wall across from him is an enormous panel painting. Within the painting, the space of the prisoner's library-cell opens like a screen on which the images evoked by the words read by the man seated at the desk are visibly projected. In the painting, a figure lies in bed (sickly in comparison with his appearance in the later miniatures), simultaneously engaged in two activities.

THE ALLEGORICAL LIBRARY

Figure 1 Miniature by Jean Colombe in a fifteenth-century illuminated manuscript of Boethius' *Consolation of Philosophy*. Boethius, *De consolatione philosophiae* (Bourges: 1476), Harley 4335, f.1. © The British Library Board.

In his hands, he holds a book that he seems to be in the process of reading. At the same time, he converses with a woman dressed in white standing at the foot of the bed. Her attributes are subtle, but just visible enough for the informed interpreter to recognize her as Philosophia: the letters of *theoretica* and *practica* are faintly discernible on her dress, as is a golden pattern resembling a ladder (though it is horizontally oriented, unlike the ladder Boethius described).

Within the panel painting, Colombe has presented a prisoner who, in reading a book, has allegorically summoned Philosophia to converse with him in his sickbed. He reads the physical book he holds in his hands and discourses with the figure who will lead him out of bed, away from books, and into the library of his mind. We should recall, however, that the book in this painted prisoner's hands is *not* a physical book. It is an allegorical image of a book depicted in an imaginary panel painting hanging on the wall of a fantastic library painted on the pages of an illuminated manuscript, which, as long as it is being read, lies before the gaze or in the hands of a reader. This manuscript, in turn, relates the story of a prisoner in a library, who in conversing with a personification of philosophy is told to abandon physical books and turn to the volumes housed in the library of his mind.

Of course, only one place remains for the prisoner in the panel painting to travel when he exits his cell—a library of allegorical images and philosophical discourse. He will emerge from the surface of the painting hanging on the wall of the Renaissance library, but remain ensconced within the page of the manuscript illuminated by Jean Colombe. He will enter the very library where perhaps Colombe himself sits at the sloped writing desk, caressing with his fingertips the volume of Boethius' *Consolation* he is soon to illuminate. Perhaps this figure is not Colombe but Jean de Meun, perusing the Latin text as he prepares the translation to be illustrated by Colombe. Or—and this is the possibility that pushes this visual *mise en abîme* of a textual *mise en abîme* to its limit, perhaps when the panel painting's prisoner leaves his sickbed to enter the library of his mind, he will encounter, as does Leibniz's Theodore at the apex of the pyramid, no one other than himself. Thus, in rising from his bed to exit the library of books and enter the library of his mind, the prisoner steps through the surface of the panel painting and finds no one but Boethius, ensconced in his library cell, reading his book, in dialogue with philosophy.

My claim is that, in Leibniz's text, Theodore is shocked out of his journey through the infinite library at the precise point of coincidence between the possible and the actual (its apex). At this instant, the discursive understanding that our philosopher has allegorically achieved is frozen in an abyss of self-reflection. In grasping that within the order of the real he can read himself reading himself in an infinite regress, Leibniz's allegory is momentarily unchained from reason. Or rather, the successive narrative duration of Theodore's journey is interrupted by the simultaneity of an infinitely self-reflective subject. But the potion that revives Theodore is the ambrosia of Philosophia's reminder that there are other texts to read, or that an interiority of infinite self-reflection is not the only figure in which philosophy can appear. The freedom of philosophical allegory is the interpretive liberty to read texts other than the self. It is also the freedom to allegorize the reading-self by congealing a set of historically interpenetrating texts and allegories of philosophical reason. Leibniz displays Valla's double methodological refusal of allegory and dialogue as if in a stage presentation and finds a number inscribed on the forehead of the rhetorician. Consulting the book of fate that contains the history of the world in which Valla is writing, and looking in the place this number indicates, he reads of Valla reading Boethius, and watches as Valla allegorically refuses Boethius' double allegory of philosophy. A dialogical repetition of a dialogue within a dialogue and an allegorical repetition of the allegory of an allegory, Leibnizian dialectic remains a theoretical and philosophical language but its contact with the allegorical has transfigured its conceptual content. What we are left with is a philosophical allegory and an allegory of philosophy: a conceptual discourse about repetition that repeats the history of its own dialogical and allegorical conceptualization.

BIBLIOGRAPHICAL *APOKATASTASIS*

While the pyramidal library of the *Theodicy* provides a key to reconciling the determination of possibility (the ideal modalities of the actual) and its intensive repetition in an immanent absolute (the actual division of the real), it takes a toll: the labyrinthine repetition of singularity is subordinated to a bibliographic principle of the optimum. While this optimum is by no means the cheery oblivion mercilessly skewered by Voltaire, it may nevertheless too neatly sidestep the problems of repetition inherent in the ideal and the actual, quickly delivering them over to the twin solutions of theological selection and the exigency of existence. With its recourse to the best of all possible worlds, this library provides a map for the unity of the organic and the problem of textual repetition, but its golden thread of optimism has not yet led us through the singularity of the simple substance and labyrinth of the monad.

The divine library of possible worlds with which the *Theodicy* concludes ultimately takes the optimum as its principle of organization. Without seeking to minimize the importance of this principle for Leibniz, I will now turn to another of his infinite libraries, one that paradoxically begins with a declaration of its own finitude. If the singularity of the monad is to be maintained, then this library must be infinite in precisely the sense of Leibniz's actual metaphysical points. The murmuring volumes shelved within its walls must not merely compose the ideal continuum of a total library containing every possible book, but they must each *be* this continuum. They must express not merely the mathematical divisibility of the realm of the ideal (where each book could become any book, the many letters of Leibniz's *Sämtliche Schriften und Briefe* reconfigured and permutated until they express several sets of Descartes' *Oeuvres*) but the actual infinity of the real: the structure of each book actually expressing the infinite structure of the library, the real parts of an organic whole, composing an ideal continuum only insofar as they each *are* the total and infinite library.

In a series of essays, each a revision of the last, Leibniz returns to his obsession with the permutation of possibilities and the infinite division of the real, now in the form of a second library: the library of the history of eternity. "One can determine the number of all possible books of a definite length," Leibniz writes in "Apokatastasis panton," "formed of meaningful and meaningless words," adding in a draft "this number thus includes all books *having a meaning.*"[45] Leibniz clarifies:

> I call "a book of a definite length" a book that consists of a definite number of letters. Take for example a folio book formed of 10,000 pages, each page of 100 lines, each line of 100 letters: it would be a book of 100,000,000 letters. Now the number of books of this length—which can be formed of 100 million letters of the alphabet—is finite, and one can obtain this number with the calculus of combinations. (*H,* 60)

It follows, he adds, "that all possible shorter books are at the same time contained in these longer ones" (*H,* 60). Leibniz goes on to present the apotheosis of metaphysical repetition in the form of the eternal library of possible books, each of its volumes figuring as the annals of a possible year in the history of the world. Given that the number of possible books in this library is finite, the history of the world, of a single being, of a word, or of an image (the structural description of any given metaphysical point) finds itself locked in a great Platonic year of return (*reditio*), regression (*regressio*), and repetition or anaphora (*repetitio*). The finitude of this library portends the infinite and eternal repetition of the world, as Leibniz writes in "Demonstrationes de Universo immenso aeternoque,"

> ... such that in the course of a whole century exactly the same sensible things happen that had already happened in another century; for all the affairs of a century could be held by a vast fact and the history of a whole century by a single great utterance; these same affairs in their turn necessarily repeat themselves, or exhaust themselves, that is repeat themselves again after exhaustion. (*H,* 58)

Once the librarian of eternity has consulted the entire collection of the universal library, the same volume will necessarily be pulled off the shelf once again, the same histories will recur, the same years and days will return eternally, and the same absolutely singular metaphysical points will not only repeat the ideal continuum of which they are the parts, but will themselves become subject to the law of repetition.[46]

In a brief treatment of this figure in Leibniz, Agamben brings it together with the infinite pyramidal library of the *Theodicy,* claiming that Nietzsche's experience of the eternal return is "only an atheistic variation" of the fable in Leibniz's book (*AP,* 268). But the figure that Leibniz is invoking here—*apokatastasis panton*, or universal restitution—is a concept that can be traced at least as far back as the third century neo-Platonic theologian and philosopher Origen. In his writings, *apokatastasis* referred to a quasi-Platonic doctrine of eternal creation and cyclical repetition, *apokatastasis panton* naming the cycle or phase in which the order of things attains perfection. Theologically, this implies a moment when every created being attains salvation and evil simply ceases to exist.[47] However, Leibniz's version of *apokatastasis* is decidedly nontheological in character. It implies nothing about perfectibility, but takes up only those metaphysical aspects of the doctrine that allow for the infinite repetition of possible combinations to be enclosed within the finitude of a bounded cycle.

Leibniz does not end his considerations with a universal library that contains all possible histories of a year of the world's existence. He recognizes the objection that its texts could never be more than the briefest of sketches, outlines so general that their repetition remains utterly trivial. The number of "all possible books of a definite length" will remain an indeterminate variable, since neither the number of characters nor the expanse of the history to be recorded is ultimately relevant. If one-hundred million characters are not sufficient for the singularity of a year in the history of the world, then we should let a book of the same length (or any other) be devoted to each week of each year; if not a week—it follows in principle—then a day; if not a day, then an hour; if not an hour, then an instant. If even this should not suffice (and it will not), then the same space will be devoted to each single being and a year (resulting in a ten million page history of the world composed of a hundred thousand million trillion characters), or the same space to a month, to a day, or to an instant. A library of books that consist of *any* definite number of letters will bring on the Leibnizian *apokatastasis* of repetition.

Those who pursue this game (Lull and his *magna arcana,* Mill and his fear that all possible musical combinations would have already been played by the end of his century, Lasswitz's Epicurean library) can be charged with transforming philosophy and literature into a mere play of combinations. However, these denunciations provide a key to unlocking what is most magnificent in this moment in Leibniz. The Leibnizian repetition inherent in the labyrinth of the actual is not the function of a mistaken and monstrous obsession with a progress *ad infinitum*, but the formulation of its problem as a methodology, and an essential chapter in the history of repetition. To put it differently, what is important and fascinating about this figure of the infinite library, the eternal regression of history, and the depletion of the finitude of possible books is not the laborious exhaustion of possibilities and the Eleatic finitude of language and motion that it implies. Leibniz goes on to offer a refutation of his own project, claiming that no finite text, no aggregation or series of characters, however long they may be, suffice to record, describe, or represent the smallest historical particle of the structure of the partless monad;

and this, whether the substance in question be that of a stone, a leaf, a book, or a philosopher. He writes in "Apokatastasis":

> Even if a prior century returned in that which concerns sensible facts, or what the books could describe, it will not return completely in every respect. For there would always be distinctions, although imperceptible, which would not be able to be described by any book, because the continuum is divided into an *actual* infinity of parts, so that in each part of matter there is an infinity of creatures which could not be described by any book, no matter how long. (*H,* 72)

The infinite division of the divine and organic machine into an infinite totality of metaphysical points, along with the relationality of the spatial and the temporal, ensure that the philosophical library (and the labyrinth hidden among its many leaves) will itself be the site for the inscription of the infinite within the finite, the modalization of the absolute, and the formulation of the rationality that is a *ratio* of inscribed repetition. The distinction between the book and the library as the structure that houses and organizes the totality of possible books disappears here, since one must recognize, as do Borges and Foucault, that the figure of the library is interchangeable with that of a single volume of infinitely thin pages, rather inconvenient to handle, each apparent page unfolding into other analogous ones, the inconceivable middle page having no reverse.[48] Thus, from the ideal unity of the infinitely and actually divided continuum, Leibniz is brought to the paradoxical and self-refuting structure of the universal library, each of its volumes reflecting an absolutely singular metaphysical point, and each of these itself a repetition of an entire world. The problem is not that of a difference in kind between the histories promised by the universal library, on the one hand, with its volumes recording the minute, tortuous, and passionate details of their own structure, and on the other hand, the force, desire, and passion of the monad. Rather, the ultimate failure of the infinite repetition of the real allows us to glimpse the utter singularity of any given substance, idea, instant, or world in its repetition of the whole. A methodological labyrinth is built on the ruins of the infinite library and of the labyrinth of the composition of the continuum: it becomes the site, not of problems of ideality, priority, temporality, continuity, or succession, but of the labyrinthine singularity of the real.

CHAPTER 2

ENCYCLOPEDIC METHOD AND THE UNINTERRUPTED OCEAN

Encyclopedias trouble themselves a great deal about words fallen into disuse, never about words still unknown, burning to be uttered . . . If it were possible for us to catch, be it only in snatches, the language that is yet to come, we would immediately become men of more than one time, as the polyglot is a man of more than one land. This enterprise will appear foolhardy to some, but since it is by no means proven that that which must be *does not already exist and that the division of time into past, present, and future is not due solely to our present incapacity to embrace everything in a single glance, the method we envisage is perhaps an expedient, a short cut, which will enable us to reach where other more ambitious disciplines are incapable of leading us.*

> Georges Ambrosino, Georges Bataille, André Breton, Jacques Brunius, Jacques Chavy, René Chenon, Marcel Duchamp, Charles Duits, Jean Ferry, Jean-Jacques Lebel, Robert Lebel, Emmanuel Peillet, or Isabelle Waldberg, "Encyclopedia" entry in Encyclopaedia Da Costa *(1947)*[1]

FROM THE LIBRARY TO THE ENCYCLOPEDIA

Leibniz set himself the task of elaborating the language that was yet to come in the introduction to one of his many abandoned encyclopedias. In "Preface to a Universal Characteristic" (c. 1679), he recounts his youthful proposal for the construction of "a certain alphabet of human thoughts" and his notion that "through the combination of the letters of this alphabet and through an analysis of the words made by them, all things can both be discovered and judged" (*AG*, 6–7). This alphabet, a project that Leibniz traces as far back as his 1666 *Dissertation on the Art of Combinations*, was to be composed of a finite set of signs, each corresponding to one particular primitive concept.[2] These concepts were then to be the basis for the analysis of any proposition or set of propositions through a logical calculus, the grammatical rules of the "universal characteristic." The value of such a system was to be an indisputable clarity of thought and the elimination of the uncertainty of communication; not only was it to increase the power of our minds via the transformation of language into a clarity-machine, but also to eliminate the vagaries of rhetoric and the practical barriers of dispute.[3]

The 1679 version of this project was to involve two operations: the reduction of complex propositions to their constituent simple elements and the discovery of the syntax governing the possible relations among them. These operations required, according to Leibniz, only four simple steps: (1) take a set of propositions or things and imagine a corresponding series of numbers or signs to be given (the letters of the alphabet of human thoughts); (2) observe a general property to be true of the propositions; (3) arrange the imagined numbers or signs in an order consistent with that property; (4) use this order and structure (which has been arbitrarily assigned and has no truth value in and of itself; the signs or numbers are utterly empty of content) to "demonstrate all the rules of logic through numbers, and show how we can know whether arguments are well formed" (*A*, 6.4-a:26). Leibniz was not naively suggesting that the resolution of concepts into their constituent elements would be easy to perform, though he did claim that it would require little more effort than was being expended by his contemporaries on writing encyclopedias, such that, "a few able men would be able to finish it in five years; in two through an infallible calculus they could produce the doctrines most frequently needed in life, that is, morality and metaphysics" (*A*, 6.4-a:268). Leibniz's real proposal is not for a device that relies on success in working out the correspondences of this language, but for a textual and linguistic structure that is able to bring its syntax into effect prior to the discovery or invention of its semantic content. Even in the absence of a readymade lexicon of primitive concepts, the first stunning effect of Leibniz's clarity-machine would be to give an *a priori* proof for its own possibility.

Leibniz, of course, never completed the construction of this alphabet, but he also never stopped evoking its power. As his thought matured, his concern with structures for the organization of knowledge shifted away from the manipulation of linguistic and numerical systems and toward, among other things, general methodological approaches to the construction of encyclopedias.[4] One of Leibniz's richest reflections on the "foolhardy" enterprise of encyclopedism articulates an important connection between philosophical method and what I will call the problem of repetition. The formal concept of repetition has taken on varied forms in the history of philosophical and theoretical discourse: the great Platonic year; Origen's *apokatastasis;* its role in the formation of Hume's "custom"; Hegel and Schelling's competing notions of philosophical systematicity; Kierkegaard's ethical, aesthetic, and religious despair; Nietzsche's eternal return; Freud's repetition-compulsion; Borges' library of Babel; as well as the transformations of the concept by Foucault, Derrida, and Deleuze.[5] For Leibniz, the problem has two versions. First, Leibnizian metaphysics posits that singular things are ontologically identical to the whole of the universe of which they are a part. Leibniz provides an account of individuals, maintaining both that they are absolutely unique entities lacking real relations to other existent things and that their conceptual structures (the arrangement of predicates inhering in their subjects or the order of the qualities modifying their essences) are expressed by all the others. Thus, each thing is absolutely singular but is also repeated within the structure of every other singular thing. This apparent paradox lies at the heart of Leibniz's account of metaphysically real entities, and his solution to it—a perspectivism in which what it means to be a substance is to express a unique viewpoint on the universe—is one key to understanding how he confronts and mobilizes repetition in less directly metaphysical contexts.[6] Second, Leibniz's metaphysical notion of repetition is put to work when he confronts the project of establishing a static taxonomy of human knowledge in the face of its fluidity and mutability. Leibniz holds that most methods for the formation of classificatory structures implicitly depend on an exclusion of the possibility that the terms to be classified appear in more than one category. The difficulty that Leibniz's reimagining of the encyclopedic project activates is that the arrangement of the propositions of human knowledge under an exhaustive organizational system (e.g., within an encyclopedia) provokes their repetition in category after category.[7]

A consideration of Leibniz's reflections on methods for constructing an encyclopedia in *New Essays on Human Understanding* (finished in 1705 but only published posthumously in 1765) will show that Leibniz's engagement with the latter version of this problem (encyclopedic taxonomy) depends heavily on his solution to the former (the metaphysical identity of the singular and the multiple). First, Leibniz's encyclopedism is contextualized and his project is introduced in terms of both early modern and contemporary theoretical concerns. Next, Leibniz's critique of Locke's proposal for an encyclopedic system is examined and an explanation is given of why Leibniz thinks that it results in the dissolution of categorical boundaries via the repetition of each element of knowledge at every systematic location. The third part of this chapter follows Leibniz's explication of alternative methodological strategies for the systematization of knowledge and examines his scheme of cross-referencing and inventory. Leibniz is interested in a system of references, I argue, not only insofar as they provide a practical means for the organization of an encyclopedia but also in that they constitute a metaphysical solution to the two versions of his problem of repetition. The fourth section elucidates this metaphysics of cross-reference by comparison with a hypothetical Newtonian encyclopedia and a consideration of Leibniz's shift of theoretical attention from the content of the encyclopedia to its form. Finally, this move from content to form is reframed in terms of Leibniz's break with Cartesian serial rationality and its impact on the development of a Leibnizian concept of method. Rather than simply discovering a method for the organization of knowledge, Leibniz sees it immanently developing out of the failure of other strategies.[8]

BORGESIAN TAXONOMIES

Despite the general polemic surrounding its reception and evaluation, one of the touchstone interpretive works dealing with the taxonomic obsession in early modernity remains Michel Foucault's *The Order of Things*. Foucault mentions Leibniz only in passing, but in the preface he describes the origin of his own project in the shattering laughter provoked by a now-famous passage by one of Leibniz's intellectual heirs, Jorge Luis Borges (*OT*, xv–xix). The passage, from Borges' essay "John Wilkins' Analytical Language," presents the impossible taxonomy of an imaginary Chinese encyclopedia entitled *The Celestial Emporium of Benevolent Knowledge*. In the decades subsequent to Foucault's book, in theoretical circles at least, this reference has become the best-known quotation of that master of fantastical citation. Despite its familiarity, it is worth repeating:

> In its distant pages it is written that animals are divided into (a) those that belong to the emperor; (b) embalmed ones; (c) those that are trained; (d) suckling pigs; (e) mermaids; (f) fabulous ones; (g) stray dogs; (h) those that are included in this classification; (i) those that tremble as if they were mad; (j) innumerable ones; (k) those drawn with a very fine camel's-hair brush; (l) etcetera; (m) those that have just broken the flower vase; (n) those that at a distance resemble flies.[9]

The only real competing image from Borges that obsesses philosophers and theorists is Jean Baudrillard's paraphrase of Borges' "Of Exactitude in Science." This short piece famously includes a description of a map of an empire so detailed that it coincides with the territory it represents, its frayed and ruined remnants blowing through a dusty landscape while locals make use of its fibers for the construction of shelters. Baudrillard proclaims that the hilarity of this abstraction has "today" (i.e., by the mid-1970s) become trite. To we apparently post-Buñuelian thinkers who live in the realm of the hyperreal, "Of Exactitude in Science" expresses nothing but "the discrete charm of second-order simulacra."[10] Like many readers of Borges, Baudrillard neglects the context of the imagery. "Of Exactitude in Science" is one of a number of quotations "collected" pseudonymically by Borges and Adolfo Bioy Casares under the heading "Museo" and first published in 1946. The supposedly fragmentary quotation is attributed to one nonexistent J.A. Suarez Miranda in book 4, chapter 14 of his never-written *Viajes de Varones Prudentes* (Lérida, 1658, supposedly). The image is in fact a reconfigured version of Josiah Royce's illustration of self-representative systems in his 1899 *The World and the Individual* (Borges cites a small portion of Royce's figure in "Partial Magic in the Quixote"), which was in turn probably inspired by a similar figure in Lewis Carroll's 1893 *Sylvie and Bruno Concluded*.[11] The Borges-Casares text is thus an imaginary recasting of a citation of a citation that itself is presented in the form of citation.

Just as Borges' passage in "Of Exactitude in Science" was "extracted" from a text that never existed, so too was the one referring to the Chinese encyclopedia. The context of the "citation" is interesting both in its own right and in relation to early modern taxonomy. Not from one of his metaphysical fictions, Borges' fantastic image appears in an essay on John Wilkins, the seventeenth-century philosopher, theologian, taxonomist, and linguist whose *An Essay Toward a Real Character and a Philosophical Language* (1668) is both a masterpiece and a *reductio* of the impulse to provide an overarching taxonomy and systematic description for all that exists.[12] In his book, Wilkins attempts to construct a written language capable of capturing every nuanced detail of reality within a vast symbolic terminology. His project is in many ways typical of other early modern attempts to construct a universal language, but it exceeds them in its obsession with the possibility of mapping a universal taxonomic structure. Wilkins' "language" is in fact an enormous system that attempts to classify all objects of perception and expression within a single synoptic table, including the denotation of all possible predicates and their modalities. Thus, like more directly philosophical thinkers of his day, Wilkins was involved with the construction of an encyclopedia of simple concepts and their reduction to a system of arbitrary signs. Borges' evocation of this project (as well as the Chinese encyclopedia) is what fascinated Foucault and led to his obsession with mapping the *episteme* of the tables, schemes, and other practices of classification in the so-called classical age. As a brief aside, it is strange how many readers and critics of Foucault fail to realize (1) that Borges' encyclopedia is a fictional construction, and (2) that Foucault is quite aware of this. Foucault's account contains, of course, documented historical flaws. Naiveté is not among them.[13]

As Foucault demonstrated, this early modern fascination with taxonomy is above all an obsession with the nature of methodological thinking, which he interpreted specifically in terms of a shift toward representational and reflexive theories of the sign. More generally, in Descartes' early work we can already see methodological reflexivity begin to take its definitive rationalist form: an immanent self-constitution of method that results when method takes itself as its own object, repeating its own structure as the first task of its self-articulation.[14] Philosophical method, on this model, emerges precisely out of its repetition of itself; it arises from the methodological investigation of the nature, status, and form of rule-governed thinking. For Leibniz, by contrast, this methodological reflexivity is a result of thematizing the encyclopedia. The encyclopedia was to be both a comprehensive and generative text, its categorical structure not merely recording scientific, intellectual, historical, and literary achievements but functioning as a philosophical machine for the production and organization of knowledge. Repetition becomes a philosophical problem for Leibniz in the sense outlined earlier and is then investigated through its differentiation into a struggle among competing encyclopedic methodologies.

Peter Remnant and Jonathan Bennett, the English translators of Leibniz's *New Essays on Human Understanding,* claim that his use of *encyclopédie* should be rendered as "the realm of knowledge" so as not to invoke anachronistically what they call its "twentieth-century sense." Their claim is somewhat supported by the etymology of the word as well as its general usage at the time. "Encyclopedia" derives (via an error in a humanist transcription of Quintilian) from *enkyklios paideia,* the circle of arts and sciences of ancient Greek education.[15] Both Antoine Furetière's 1690 *Dictionnaire universel* and the 1694 *Dictionnaire de l'Académie française* use similar definitions, the former giving "Universal science, collection or linkage of all the sciences together" and the latter "Linkage or circle in which all the sciences are enclosed."[16] Therefore, when Leibniz writes of the rules for the construction of the encyclopedia, he has in mind the vast epistemological project of weaving the multilayered structures of human knowledge into a single, systematically unified tapestry. However, as early as 1620 our contemporary sense of the term—a printed referential artifact containing the whole of human knowledge and not just reflecting its structure—had begun to appear in book titles.[17]

Leibniz, for example, was familiar with the *Encyclopaedia septem tomis distincta* (1630) of the Herborn philosopher and Calvinist theologian Johann Heinrich Alsted, an earlier and less elaborate version of which was one of the first modern works to use the word in its title.[18] Alsted's *Encyclopaedia* is a systematic work presenting the structure and content of 37 disciplines in seven volumes divided into more than 1,000 chapters of definitions, propositions, commentaries, compiled textual extracts, and Ramist tables. Leroy Loemker argues that the Herborn encyclopedists were influenced by Baconian science and its emphasis on the apprehension of particulars together with positing the unity of human knowledge, while still remaining "Ramist in procedure." Thus, as Loemker cites Leibniz, the encyclopedists put the classificatory methods of Peter Ramus to work in the metaphysical interpretation of the particulars of natural philosophical investigation by way of "joining method to things."[19] There is a strong sense in which Alsted's *Encyclopaedia* can be seen as one culminating example of the Renaissance encyclopedic ambition to capture and organize the totality of human knowledge within a single, complex printed artifact. The *Encyclopaedia* is dominated by a comprehensive collection of structural tables establishing disciplinary boundaries and thus encyclopedic organizational categories. These categories, in turn, map an encyclopedic content taking the form of conceptual definitions extracted from the writings of suitable authorities, synthetic discussions of the rules or propositions that can be formed on the basis of those definitions, and extensive commentaries on the implications of the rules. In its attempt to manifest a perfected and comprehensive structure of all possible terms, Alsted's work is the realization of the legacy of that aspect of Renaissance encyclopedism driven toward the synoptic stabilization of the totality of human knowledge. In actualizing, after a fashion, the dream of a comprehensive and unchanging printed structure mirroring the totality of what is, what is known, and what is done, Alstedian encyclopedism aspires to provide a comprehensive micro-representation of the totality of the real.

At the same time, Alsted's *Encyclopaedia* inherits a second thrust of the Renaissance encyclopedic tradition: the drive to produce a textual and conceptual machine for the production of knowledge rather than its merely passive reflection. While the definitions it contains and the rules and commentaries that follow from them function as a compendium—often reproducing precise textual extracts from authorities in the particular discipline under consideration—its Ramist structure is meant to provide a didactic and pedagogical edifice that makes it possible for readers to trace new paths through the conceptual and disciplinary framework, to generate new forms of human knowledge, new accounts of natural phenomena, and indeed, to discover new instances of the things themselves. In this sense—linked inescapably to its inclusion of an elaborate theory of combinatoric circular models in the strangely unsystematic "mixed disciplines" section—Alsted's encyclopedia is a further development of the Lullist tradition that sought a means of dynamic visual and textual combination that would generate new modes of knowing. Although Alsted's combinatoric theory of *cyclognomonica* remains marginal to the work as a whole, Howard Hotson has provided a fascinating account of the epistemological abysses that open when the Alstedian combinatoric is applied to the categories of the *Encyclopaedia* itself.[20] I mention the combinatoric element of the text here simply to point out that even while Alsted's encyclopedia can be understood as one culmination of the desire of Renaissance encyclopedism to capture a stable textual structure corresponding to the unchanging series of essences that constitute the real, it also gestures toward the mobilization of the encyclopedia as a site of productivity and dynamism capable of generating new forms of knowledge.

As William West has argued with particular reference to the *Margarita Philosophica* (1535), although the primary sense of encyclopedism in early modernity was that of the construction of a space for the preservation and discovery of knowledge, many such texts mobilized the encyclopedic project in such a way as to transform it into a method for the production of truths rather than the mere reflection of their structure.[21] At the very least, by the seventeenth century the project of constructing the material apparatus that would house, generate, organize, and present the fully schematized linkages of human knowledge had already begun. Leibniz's references to constructing, writing, and publishing an encyclopedia make it clear that this is the sense he has in mind. His encyclopedia project is indeed a realm of knowledge that encircles or encloses all the sciences, but it is also a text, an apparatus, a machine, and a book.

THE UNINTERRUPTED OCEAN

In its initial stages, Leibniz's encyclopedia was humbly revisionist. The project he proposed in 1671 was to be nothing more than a modernization and expansion of Alsted's encyclopedia.[22] Leibniz would exchange its already expansive textual reliance on Scholastic and Ramist metaphysics and natural philosophy for a broader collection of texts that would take account of the fruits of the "new philosophy": Hobbes, Galileo, and Huygens with Aristotle in the physics, Jungius and the Arnauldian Port-Royal school in logic, Descartes and Digby in pneumatology, etc. After assembling copious notes with proposed definitional and propositional substitutions, Leibniz abandoned the project, only to continue to produce a myriad of unfulfilled proposals and theoretical introductions to never-realized encyclopedias throughout his life. As Leibniz's notion of encyclopedism developed, however, he began to see the Alstedian project of assembling a compendium of texts structured by a disciplinary conception of knowledge as doomed to failure. His reasons for this had nothing to do with practical problems of magnitude or extent; instead, they revolved around a developing critique of the model of disciplinary conceptual knowledge on which Alsted's project (along with much of the Renaissance encyclopedic tradition) depended.

By 1690, the metaphysical and epistemological problems inherent in an encyclopedist approach had moved to the forefront for Leibniz. The problem facing any attempt to deal with human knowledge as a systematic totality, Leibniz writes in the fragmentary preface to *De l'horizon de la doctrine humaine,* is that "the entire body of the science can be considered as an ocean, continuous everywhere, without interruption or break, though men conceive parts in it, and give them names according to their convenience" (*H,* 35). Chapter 1 used this and associated texts to bring together a Leibnizian conception of textual repetition with his figure of the infinite and total library. Leibniz returns to the problem of figuring the totality of human knowledge in his *New Essays*. He wished to engage in a public debate with Locke, either in the pages of one of the learned journals with which Leibniz was involved (probably the *Le Journal des savants* or *Acta eruditorum*) or in some other form of collaborative writing. In the absence of an answer (or even acknowledgment) from the author of *An Essay Concerning Human Understanding* (1690) to critical remarks sent by post, Leibniz began crafting the *New Essays*, hoping to provoke a response. Never one to let mortality stand in the way of a good philosophical argument, when Locke died in 1704 (9 months after Leibniz had completed his first draft), Leibniz transformed the whole of the text into a massive exercise in prosopopeia, framing it as a dialogue between Philalethes (who has read Locke's *Essay* and will argue on his behalf) and Theophilus (who largely articulates Leibniz's positions, or at least those presumably cast as such).[23] Together they consult a copy of Locke's book, with Philalethes for the most part simply articulating Locke from beyond the grave by reading passages from his work aloud.

In the final chapter of the *Essay* (IV.21), Locke proposes a threefold division of the sciences into physics, ethics, and semiotics.[24] Leibniz responds in the final chapter of the *New Essays* where the issue at stake is precisely that of the division of knowledge and the construction of an encyclopedia. His attack on Locke's scheme is notable not only for its stringent criticism of the imprecise nature of the latter's concepts of *logos* and *semiotikos*, but also for its discussion of the possibilities for division and classification of concepts in general.[25] Noting that Locke's proposal corresponds to an ancient version of the division (physics, ethics, and logic, a system that can be traced, via Diogenes Laertius, to the Platonic-Stoic tradition), Leibniz argues that its chief defect is that "each part appears to devour the whole" (*A*, 6.6:522).[26] A full and encyclopedic elaboration of natural philosophy will include an account of living beings with understanding and will, and thus of the whole of the logical and ethical systems that govern their structure. Likewise, because "everything is useful for our happiness," the category of practical philosophy extends its hold over every segment of human knowledge. Most important, the same holds for logic, insofar as any analysis or knowledge whatsoever has the form of a set of words or characters and is thereby governed by the science of sign and signification. "So here are your three great provinces of the encyclopedia," Leibniz writes, "continually at war because each is always usurping the rights of the others" (*A*, 6.6:523).

After establishing what he sees as the ineptitude of the ancient and Lockean divisions to maintain their boundaries, Leibniz offers two possible explanations. A nominalist stance would claim that every particular truth provokes a corresponding particular science; therefore, the great genetic groups of the division are merely the imposition of some meddlesome categorizer and bear no intrinsic relation to the sciences themselves. The holist approach, by contrast, would reject this particularization of the sciences in themselves and disrupt the identity of truth and knowledge (*A*, 6.6:523). While in this context Leibniz clearly has more sympathy for the descriptive validity of the holistic strategy, he holds that it alone is not enough to avoid the dissolution of categorical thinking. The problem with both approaches is that these modes of the division of knowledge guarantee that each proposition or truth will appear more than once and that each will be repeated in different divisions or even within the same division many times. Under the rule of either of these potential encyclopedic methodologies,

> An anecdote [*histoire memorable*] may be placed in the annals of universal history, and in the particular history of the country where it happened, and in the history of the life of a man who was concerned with it. And suppose that it has to do with some fine

moral precept, some military stratagem, or some invention useful for the arts which serve the convenience of life or the health of men; then this same story will be usefully attached to the science or art that it concerns, and one could even mention it twice within that science; namely, in the history of the discipline it concerns, in order to recount its effective development, and also in that discipline's precepts, in order to confirm or clarify them through examples. (*A*, 6.6:523)

We are faced, in other words, with a quandary of multiplication and repetition. If the disciplinary boundaries of knowledge turn out to be arbitrary, whether following from classical, Lockean, nominalist, or holist grounds, then any given proposition will necessarily be repeated throughout the system meant to organize and classify propositional knowledge as such. At first, Leibniz's discussion appears to indicate only that this repetition of propositions throughout the classificatory systems in which they are located may pose a practical problem. It quickly becomes apparent, however, that he takes the impasse to be far more general, in that it generates potentially devastating implications for the project of the classification and systematization of knowledge. The logic of Leibniz's position indicates that the multiplication and repetition of terms throughout encyclopedic systems is generated not by the insufficiency of the notions of conceptual division and organization in themselves, but by their strategic reliance on the *content* or *meaning* of the terms to be divided. Insofar as an encyclopedic system of classification organizes propositions by virtue of their content, those propositions will never find their home in a proper categorical locus or encyclopedic term. Instead, each position will belong to many categories, and the more rigorously we examine its connections and internal structure, the more we will find it implicating still other propositions and demanding its repetition in the context of *their* encyclopedic location. In other words, the problem is not simply that the vagaries of language require each proposition to include reference to others, but that classification of propositions on the basis of their content will result in an infinite proliferation of terms and thus fundamentally weaken the classificatory categories themselves.

This means that the repetition of a single truth within a classificatory division renders that category incapable of doing more than distinguishing its members from the members of other divisions.

Within their own division, these members can no longer be meaningfully distinguished from one another; bodily organs are now merely "organs," no longer livers, hearts, and spleens. Natural philosophy is nothing more than the set of all truths that fall in neither practical philosophy nor logic. Conversely, the repetition of the truths of a particular division within the set of its competing divisions renders their very organizational boundaries meaningless. The class of ethical concepts can no longer be described as a meaningful category when all of its members also appear in every other category. The result of pursuing classification on the basis of propositional content is that a division of knowledge becomes a set of propositions that repeats its members indefinitely and that is itself repeated in all other divisions. A single proposition, in other words, comes to occupy every possible categorical location, and the classificatory scheme lies in ruins.

In the *Discourse on Metaphysics* (1686), Leibniz provides a theory of individual substances that helps to explain his thinking here. In that text, singular things are understood to be beings with "a notion so complete that it is sufficient to contain and to allow us to deduce from it all the predicates of the subject to which this notion is attributed" (*AG*, 41). The "predicates" that can be truly said of the notion of an individual substance include all the events and actions connected to it, such that (to use Leibniz's example) the notion of the soul of Alexander the Great includes *les restes* of everything that has happened to him, *les marques* of everything that will happen to him, and *les traces* of all that occurs in the universe: not just that he vanquishes Darius and Porus, but also that Leibniz uses him as a philosophical example in the seventeenth century (*AG*, 41; *A*, 6.4-b:1540–41). Understood on this model of individual substances, the notions of the encyclopedia's propositions include not just the predicates related to their own specific referents—the particular qualities of the things they are supposed to explain—but also traces of every proposition in the classificatory universe of knowledge. Thus, taken purely in terms of their content and organized according to the classical, Lockean, nominalist, or holist schemes, each proposition in the encyclopedia is completely identical to all the others. The identification of their proper classificatory location is not merely complex, but impossible.

The crux of the problem is that these schemes are incapable of grappling with what Leibniz would describe as the unique perspective that differentiates and individuates singular things. If real things are understood merely in terms of their content (as heaps of qualities or predicates), he argues, they lack a principle of individuation. What makes them unique, he proposes, is that "each singular substance expresses the whole universe in its own way" (*AG*, 41). While each singular thing is the same as all the others—it "is like a complete world and like a mirror of God or of the whole universe" insofar as it includes "all its events, along with all their circumstances, and the whole sequence of exterior things"—its uniqueness is constituted by the singular perspective from which it represents this totality (*AG*, 41). Just as each urban dweller possesses a unique point of view on and situation within the city that she inhabits, so each individual substance expresses the totality of the universe in its own way (this is another of Leibniz's examples) (*AG*, 42). Classifying propositions according to the encyclopedic schemes hitherto considered is like forgetting that without their individuating perspective (something that has nothing to do with their content), these propositions are all identical. Since they attempt to organize propositions according to their content, under these schemes the encyclopedic imagination generates a classificatory text consisting of the interminable repetition of the same infinitely long and unpronounceable word.

REFERENCE AND INVENTORY

Leibniz is not satisfied with the metaphysically and epistemologically incoherent result generated by the traditional strategies for the division of knowledge, and he proposes and evaluates several more methods of arrangement. He quickly discounts the "civil" method, which consists of nothing more than a historical refinement of the Platonic-Stoic division (physics, ethics, and logic) through the medieval system of trivium (grammar, logic, and rhetoric) and quadrivium (geometry, astronomy, arithmetic, and music) into the early modern classification by faculties (theology, jurisprudence, medicine, and philosophy). While Leibniz allows that this method is deserving of pedagogical respect, it in no way escapes the problems of Locke's original division. The first meaningful procedure that he identifies is the "synthetic and theoretical" method. It consists in arranging propositions or truths according to the order of their proof, such that "each proposition comes after those on which it depends." The second is the "analytic and practical" method that "begins with the goal of human beings, which is to say with the goods whose fulfillment is happiness, and conducts an orderly search for the means which serve to acquire these goods and to avoid their contrary ills" (*A*, 6.6:524).[27] Even using both these methods in tandem for the construction of the encyclopedia, however, Leibniz thinks one cannot avoid the same problem of repetition and dissolution of categorical boundaries described earlier. Both methods still rely on the content of a proposition to furnish its systematic location, and thus both are susceptible to the same topical explosion that destroyed the original divisions of the sciences. Finally, Leibniz points to a new possibility with consequences that turn the entire problem of encyclopedic propositional repetition on its head. He postulates, "in writing the encyclopedia following both these methods together, one may take referential measures in order to avoid repetitions." These *mesures de renvoi* constitute another form of ordering altogether: what Leibniz calls "disposition by terms" and the subsequent generation of a systematic inventory (*répertoire*) (*A*, 6.6:524). Rather than a repetition of terms in their content, meaning, and sense, these references send us back to the single and simple occurrence of truths or propositions via a series of arbitrary signs.

There is nothing mysterious about Leibniz's innovation. The *mesures de renvoi* that he proposes are nothing more than the use of a system of cross-referencing footnotes and the generation of an index.[28] At the same time, the notion of organizing and sustaining a work through a structure of numbered marginal references not reducible to a series of external commentaries on a main text was something fairly new in this period. Anthony Grafton has suggested, for example, that the origins of the modern historical footnote can be found in Pierre Bayle's *Dictionnaire historique et critique* (1697 and 1702). The *Dictionary*—to which the next chapter will turn directly—is an enormous work originally intended to be a catalog of the errors and omissions in contemporary reference books and histories, which becomes an enormous biographical-historical-philosophical dictionary supported by an elaborate system of notes.[29] It is, in fact, a vast assemblage of articles, remarks, and marginal notes, each displacing the priority of the others, each referring to an almost infinite set of marks within its many pages, as well as to the thousands of external works its articles, remarks, and marginal notes cite, quote, or paraphrase. Indeed, the vast majority of Bayle's text—both its literal instantiation on the page and its conceptual content—is located in its complex layers of citation rather than in the articles that provide its architectonic. The folio pages of its volumes (two in 1697, three by 1702) are given over primarily to the remarks, the primary set of which run in two columns occupying the bulk of most pages, complemented by two (and sometimes three) sets of marginal notes to the columnar remarks and primary article. Often, as one might expect, these remarks refer the reader to other remarks in other articles, which in turn contain remarks referring to still further articles, and so on.[30]

Consider, for example, the structure of Bayle's article on Jerome Rorarius, the site of his most explicit engagements with Leibniz in the *Dictionary*. In the 1702 edition of the *Dictionary*, the last published during Bayle's lifetime, the article spread over 14 pages in folio, with the article text including a mere 25 sentences accompanied by 4 marginal notes denoted by symbols. This text is "supplemented," however, by 11 lengthy, lettered remarks running in columns over the bulk of the page, their 162 lettered and numbered marginal notes, as well as 5 marginal headings. As Figures 2 and 3 should make evident, the bulk of Bayle's articles are devoted to this so-called supplementary material. Only a few lines of the article itself appear on most pages, often merely fragments of sentences in slightly larger typeface (only 3 pages include more than 2 typographic lines of article text), while the complex remark and citation structure constitutes approximately 95% of the page space and the conceptual-critical content of the "Rorarius" text as a whole.

It is not that Bayle's complex *mise en page* and referential system is something entirely new. The *Dictionary*, after all, in some ways bears a resemblance to the work of Alsted and other Renaissance encyclopedists and polyhistors, despite the fact that its primary principle of encyclopedic organization is alphabetical rather than disciplinary or structural. Scribal practice was, of course, rife with a variety of systems for the juxtaposition of text and glosses, including the use of readers' marks that could key one element of text or commentary to another elsewhere in the work as well as marginal commentary columns that resemble Bayle's.[31] Renaissance editions of ancient and classical texts also frequently made use of marginal commentaries and notational devices in many forms. By the early modern period, printed notation had proliferated into what we may retrospectively recognize as a standard typographical practice: the marginal space of the page became an integral part of the visual scheme of the printed book.[32] William Slights, for example, has undertaken a massive survey of English books printed between 1525 and 1675, and

Figure 2 Page including the end of the "Roquetaillade" and the beginning of the "Rorarius" article in the extended 1702 edition of Pierre Bayle's *Historical and Critical Dictionary*. Portions of 5 lettered remarks are visible, along with 4 symbolic marginal notes to the article-text and 13 lettered marginal notes to the remarks. Pierre Bayle, *Dictionnaire historique et critique*, 2nd edn. (Rotterdam: Leers, 1702), 2599. © John J. Burns Library, Boston College, Chestnut Hill, MA.

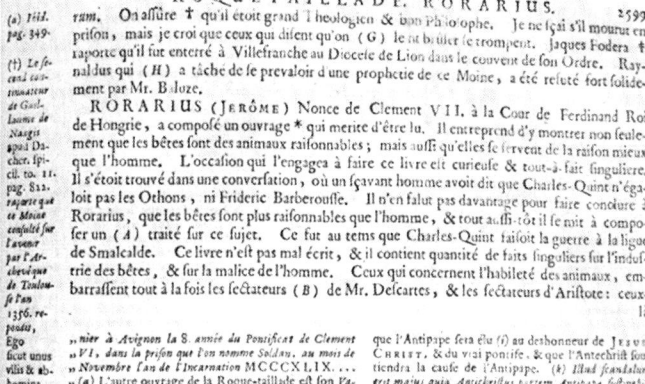

Figure 3 Detail of Figure 2 emphasizing the diversity of the marginal notation and the paucity of article text. Pierre Bayle, *Dictionnaire historique et critique*, 2nd edn. (Rotterdam: Leers, 1702), 2599. © John J. Burns Library, Boston College, Chestnut Hill, MA.

concluded that the majority include printed marginal notes. When counting only large format books (like the folios of Bayle's *Dictionary*), Slights claims that close to 80% contain such notes.[33]

Even beyond texts requiring commentary and supplement, the diversity of Renaissance typographical conventions often differentiated the printed page into multiple layers of referentiality. Henri-Jean Martin's comparison of French editions of Thomas Aquinas' *Summa theologica* from a 1471 incunabula through mid- and late-sixteenth-century printings, for example, displays the evolution of a single text from a simple set of columns into a typographically complex artifact that visually distinguishes questions, articles, conclusions, and marginal references to other sections of the work.[34] Further, Alsted's 1630 *Encyclopaedia* does not entirely eschew systems of internal textual reference, and, as Hotson has pointed out, its typographical variations are deliberately arranged to reflect its methodological structure.

With Bayle's *Dictionary*, something fundamental has changed. First, for Bayle, the master text to which marginal glosses are appended as interpretive or contextual supplements has effectively disappeared—or, rather, it has been replaced with a rapidly proliferating series of texts, each of which refers its readers to a further series, none remaining even as stable as a fragmentary text in an encyclopedic compilation. Here, any or every text can be taken to be the central one that grounds the systematic *ordinatio* of the work, yet the collective and encompassing *copia* encyclopedia model has at the same time been left behind. This master text can be Bayle's article itself, the text that is the source of the commentary in that article, the discursive remarks to Bayle's text (individually or as a whole), the quotations or references located in the margins of *either* Bayle's article text or his remarks, and so on. Furthermore, no longer bound by a disciplinary framework of the trivium and quadrivium or Ramist structural entablature, readers of the *Dictionary* are faced with a massive and unprecedented freedom with regard to construing the methodological order of the work and to constructing the function of a system of reference and commentary. At the very least, they are invited to develop a new set of capacities for orienting the text according to their reasons for reading it or for orienting their reasoning according to the order they discover within it.

Second, in several respects (explored in Chapter 3), the *Dictionary* is an encyclopedia of *error*, assembling concepts, stories, fables, arguments, and figures so that its remarks delimit a negative space within the vast maelstrom of texts and words circulating with ever increasing speed in the Republic of Letters. In order to formulate a coherent structure of definition and identification for the figures it addresses, the *Dictionary* composes a vast system of evidence via citation and quotation, intended to trace the differential outlines of everything that these figures are *not*. Thus, the *Dictionary* is not a vast compendium of all the things known to the late-seventeenth-century mind; it is a comprehensive critical account of a historical void teeming with language, a self-consciously textual abyss on the margins of which knowledge slowly accretes. In this sense, the *Dictionary* is an encyclopedic anti-encyclopedia.

Finally, mitigating against the new form of encyclopedic readerly freedom offered by Bayle's system of multilayered referential disposition, the *mise en page* of Bayle's *Dictionary* presents us with a good example of the way that the materiality of early modern textual organization is capable of channeling its readers in particular ways while also opening up unique forms of conceptual encounter through processes of juxtaposition and reference both within and among articles, their remarks, and cross-references to texts inside and outside the work.

Before composing the *New Essays*, Leibniz himself had appeared as a figure in this system of reference. In his entry on Jerome Rorarius, Bayle devoted remark H (as well as its marginal notes and the secondary set of citations attached to them) to a discussion of Leibniz's *New System*. Leibniz responded with private letters and articles in learned journals, and Bayle included portions of these responses (along with his own counterresponses) in a further remark to this article in the 1702 edition of the work (remark L, its marginal notes, and their secondary citations).[35] While Leibniz himself offered suggestions to Bayle regarding the organization of his work through referential marginal citations, it is clear that Bayle's actual practice of mobilizing citations and notational commentary far exceeded the recommendations of his correspondent (*GP*, 6:16–20). I should note that Leny Van Lieshout suggests that it is unclear whether Leibniz's letter to this effect ever actually reached Bayle.[36] In this letter, Leibniz is responding to Bayle's preliminary *Projet et fragmens d'un dictionnaire critique* (1692) which experiments with multiple forms of citation and typographical arrangement throughout its articles. Only the form of the last article in the collection, on Zeuxis, the Greek master of mimetic painting, directly resembles the notational methodology Bayle uses in the *Dictionary* itself.[37] By the 1697 and 1702 editions, the type of explosive *mise en page* described earlier (Figures 2 and 3) has come to fully structure Bayle's textual production. This is especially significant, given that this equivalence of citational and referential organization comes to characterize Leibniz's own metaphysics of encyclopedic reference. The typographical explosion of notes and references on the pages of Bayle's *Dictionary* may be what eventually convinced Leibniz to radicalize his conception of encyclopedic referentiality, transforming his *mesures de renvoi* from a simple textual addendum into a metaphysical theory of encyclopedism.

Since Leibniz never published an encyclopedia and never actually used such a system of references despite his dozens of introductions and schematic plans, the actual technique of his references is not what interests me here. More important is the crucial role played by Leibniz's theoretical system of textual cross-referencing in the formation of his encyclopedic methodology. In the 1755 article "Encyclopédie" appearing in the fifth volume of the *Encyclopédie ou Dictionnaire raisonné des sciences*, Denis Diderot describes analogous techniques of cross-referencing as "the most important part of our encyclopedic scheme," which would "give to the whole . . . that unity so favorable to the establishment of truth and to its propagation," so that "the work as a whole should acquire an internal force and secret efficacy, the silent results of which will necessarily be felt with the passage of time."[38] Explicitly acknowledging his formal debt to Bayle, implicitly and inadvertently Diderot is tracing the genealogy of his system of encyclopedic reference back to Leibniz. In contrast to Diderot, however, Leibniz does not simply propose that references are an essential element of an encyclopedic scheme. Instead, Leibniz claims that the very notion of an encyclopedic method structured by cross-referencing emerges out of a philosophical consideration of the other options for constructing a total system of knowledge. He argues that the particular way in which other encyclopedic methods fail produces the concept of textual reference. Moreover, this failure is not primarily a practical one. The problem, as we have seen, is not simply that other methods for the encyclopedic organization of knowledge are clumsy. Rather, something about the nature of propositions, the fluidity of knowledge, and the project of organizing it into a total system actually brings about the failure of these methods. Leibniz is not so much interested in proposing a practical model for the organization of encyclopedic texts as he is in grasping the metaphysics of a referential system and the philosophical methodology that it demands.

REFERENCE, REPETITION, AND THE NEWTONIAN ENCYCLOPEDIA

The simple and common predicates Leibniz uses in his *mesures de renvoi* form the structure of a system of reference confronting the problems of repetition found in all other methods of classification. Leibniz frames encyclopedic reference, that is, as both contrary to and the solution for the problem of encyclopedic repetition. Where arbitrary division, synthetic arrangement, and analytic ordering all generate the *aporia* of repetition that destroy their very structure, cross-reference and its inventory constitute the circle of human knowledge as a coherent and consistent totality. Put another way, Leibniz articulates *two forms of repetition*, standing in radical opposition: the iterative power of categories that explodes the encyclopedia's propositional structure and the return or sending back of cross-reference that constitutes its possibility. What is it about Leibniz's method of referential return that avoids the dangers posed by repetition? What exactly is the difference between the two movements of repetition? How is it that the method of classification by terms and the inventory it generates manage to maintain the stability of categories and organization where synthesis and analysis fail?

Both the synthetic and analytic methods depend on the linear motion of an intellect scanning the order of a series, the former rising from the order of proofs and the latter retracing a path of causes. A synthetic and theoretical method arranges its encyclopedic categories by beginning with the simplest and most fundamental concepts and then tracks the way their possible conjunctions and disjunctions generate a further series of complex notions. Thus, the method of synthesis focuses on the notional origins of encyclopedic terms, arranging its entries according to the order by which they can be generated. An analytic and practical method, by contrast, locates complex concepts at the root of encyclopedic terms and simple ones at their endpoints, arranging its entries according to the logic by which the former can be unfolded in a logical series from the latter. Here, the encyclopedia is structured by the way general categories can be broken up into their constituent elements. The assumption both these procedures share is that encyclopedic classification requires tracing a conceptual series. For Leibniz, however, this figure of the series fails to comprehend the ultimate circularity and referential totality that constitute the form of human knowledge and encyclopedic systems. Insisting that the content of a concept determines its place in an ordered line of classification, both methodological approaches dissolve in the face of the problems of repetition discussed earlier. For the system of cross-reference, however, the *form* of the concept, truth, or term is what gives it its categorical location, rather than the way the content of propositions can be serially arranged in order of their generation or dismemberment.

One way to explain this shift of emphasis from the content of encyclopedic concepts to their form is by casting it in the terms of Leibniz's 1716 correspondence with Samuel Clarke. That exchange is a battle by proxy with Isaac Newton, largely devoted to arguments regarding conceptions of space and time.[39] Clarke, following Newton, holds that space and time are containers and measures for the objects that appear within them, while Leibniz argues that they are phenomenal orders of existence that are real only insofar as they are representative expressions of things. In other words, for Clarke, space is an empty and absolute field in which things appear and relative to which they take up a position, while time is a measure of motion across this field. Most crucially, for Clarke, space and time are both independent of the bodies that have positions and coordinates within them. For Leibniz, by contrast, space and time are merely "well-founded phenomena," the former in the perceived simultaneous coexistence of things and the latter in their perceived sequentiality. This means that for Leibniz, space is simply the way we perceive things to be arranged in relation to one another, while time is a condition of perceptual confusion that results from our inability to conceive an ultimately simultaneous reality. The most important contrast to Clarke's Newtonianism here is that Leibniz holds that space is perceptually constituted by perceived relations of things, and thus depends on those perceptions. With regard to time, Leibniz's position relies on an account of the constitution of "apperception" through an infinity of confused and unconscious microperceptions *(petites perceptions)*. As he puts it in the *New Essays*, "there are a thousand signs [*marques*] leading us to judge that at every moment there is an infinity of perceptions within us, but without apperception and without reflection; that is to say, of changes in the soul itself of which we apperceive nothing, because the impressions are either too small and too great in number, or too uniform, so that they are not sufficiently distinctive on their own. But joined to others, they nevertheless make their effect and make themselves felt, at least confusedly in the assemblage" (*A*, 6.6:54). Where for Clarke, being and events unfold in time, for Leibniz, as for the authors of the *Encyclopaedia Da Costa*, the division of time into past, present, and future is due solely to our present incapacity to embrace everything in a single glance.

Based on this fundamental philosophical difference between Clarke's Newtonianism and Leibniz's phenomenalism, we can propose a Newtonian model of encyclopedic classification and explain the Leibnizian model by contrast. Our imaginary Newtonian encyclopedia would be organized by the notion that the classificatory space of its pages and volumes is absolute and empty, ready to receive its content from the substance of particular truths. No matter which propositions those truths may be, the classificatory system awaiting them is understood to be already given. More important, the "terms" of a Newtonian encyclopedia—the "truths" or "propositions" to be organized—*occupy* a location within that classificatory space. These terms are the content of the encyclopedia, arranged according to a scheme that bears in itself no intrinsic relationship to them. The Newtonian encyclopedia, that is, has the form of an absolute conceptual container within which content is arranged and according to which it is measured and understood. A Leibnizian critic of this Newtonian encyclopedia would insist that insofar as the encyclopedia as a whole is understood to be a conceptual structure by which propositions are arranged according to their content, it dissolves before the force of the repetition of those terms as they reappear in multiple classificatory locations simultaneously. If the content of a single substantial truth expands into the totality of human knowledge—each page unfolding in all pages, the least scientific treatise or moral tract becoming a comprehensive encyclopedia of human knowledge—then the Newtonian encyclopedia lies in ruins.

Only the method of reference is adequate to the uninterrupted ocean of knowledge, Leibniz thinks, because only referential return can tame the danger of the repetition of terms. Sending its terms back through each of their iterations, the method of reference models the encyclopedia on Leibniz's answer to Clarke: classificatory space is a relational totality of simultaneous coexistents. This means that on the Leibnizian model, the terms of the encyclopedia are understood through their formal structure of reference to all other terms rather than through their role as the content of an already given structure. Thus, the infinitely complex and mutually implicated relationships reflected in the structure of each of the terms are what generate the categories of the encyclopedia. *Because* every substantial proposition contains an entire world—because every truth mirrors the universe of knowledge from a particular perspective—the repetition of all truths in every truth and every truth in all truths does not destroy the system. Leibniz holds, in other words, that the system of classification through reference is itself constituted by the infinite repetition of terms that destroyed the previous alternatives. Rather than seek a model for the encyclopedia that avoids the problem of repetition, the Leibnizian encyclopedia takes conceptual repetition as its organizing principle.

LEIBNIZ AGAINST CARTESIAN FORMALISM

To review, Leibniz holds the position that a self-undermining conceptual repetition results from approaches to the construction of an encyclopedia that depend on the arbitrary imposition of classificatory categories (the classical, Lockean, nominalist, and holist models), from strategies that rely on the serial arrangement of the content of terms according to their origins or ends (the synthetic and analytic models), and from procedures in which each term is a type of content to be located in an absolute classificatory space (the Newtonian model). These methods of organization generate a situation in which the propositions of human knowledge overflow their classificatory boundaries, reappearing within all other classifications and destroying the structure of the encyclopedia as such. Leibniz, by contrast, proposes a method of formal cross-reference and inventory in which the terms to be classified are not separable from the structure of their classification. According to this approach, the particular form of repetition that constitutes a term's structure of reference to all other concepts (i.e., to the conceptual universe of which it is the expression) is what makes it the concept that it is. Insisting that through the system of cross-referencing each proposition must be "sent back" to the whole of which it is a part, Leibniz allows the formal referential structure of concepts to determine the encyclopedic categories themselves.

If the Leibnizian model of the encyclopedia is to rely on and be generated from the explosion of its terms throughout its classificatory space, how will these terms be distinguished from one another? What is it that constitutes the identity or singularity of a given "entry" within the encyclopedia? If we maintain fidelity to Leibniz's model of individual substances as outlined earlier, then for one encyclopedic term to stand in the same relation to the whole of human knowledge as another (for two truths to occupy the same part of a classificatory space, in the terms of the Newtonian encyclopedia) is simply impossible for the Leibnizian concept. In a statement of the principle of the identity of indiscernibles in the same part of the *Discourse on Metaphysics* discussed earlier, Leibniz holds that "it is not true that two substances can resemble each another completely and differ only in number [*solo numero*]" (*AG*, 41–42). Put positively, this means that any two individual substances possessing the same predicate structure are in fact one and the same substance; two conceptually identical things are one and not two. If Leibniz's method of encyclopedic cross-reference embraces the repetition of every conceptual term in each encyclopedic category, then it would seem that all of these categories would possess the same conceptual structure. Leibniz's principle of no difference *solo numero* would demand, it seems, that there be only one encyclopedic category. If there is no difference among the categories, then the categories are identical; and if the categories are identical, then they are one and the same. At the limit of the formalization of encyclopedic terms, writing the encyclopedia again seems to be impossible.

Thus, with the generation of encyclopedic structure by way of reference and inventory, the full problem of the organization of knowledge has by no means been solved. Leibniz's move from the content of propositions to their formal repetition has provided a general structure for the classification of any and all human knowledge. If this structure is to be filled—if the repeated encyclopedic terms are not all to be identical and if content is to be provided for Leibniz's formal encyclopedic structure—then this reversal through content to form must itself be repeated. This second reversal is, for Leibniz, a reiteration of the problem of classificatory repetition and can be elucidated by way of comparison with Descartes' project for the self-certification of knowledge in order to ground its formal certainty.

In important ways, Leibniz has remained Cartesian up to this point. As for Descartes, the moment of certainty for the foundation of a system of knowledge is the discovery of an empty and formal point. Leibniz's move to an absolute formality of thinking via an encyclopedic method of reference parallels the following way of reading the foundational moment of Cartesian metaphysics. Readers familiar with Descartes' *Meditations on First Philosophy* (1641) will recall his famous account of the Cartesian meditator's skeptical "general demolition" of his opinions in the search for a certain and indubitable foundation for knowledge (*scientia*) in Meditation One, as well as the subsequent discovery of a "necessarily true" proposition that can serve as such a foundation in Meditation Two. What tends to be forgotten is that the order of reasons in the argument of the *Meditations* is different from that found in the *Discourse on Method* (1637) and the *Principles of Philosophy* (1644). While in the latter two texts the indubitable proposition Descartes discovers is the famous "I think, therefore I am" in the form of *Je pense, donc je suis*

(*AT*, 6:32) and *Ego cogito, ergo sum* (*AT*, 8:7), in the *Meditations* its form is simply "I am, I exist" *(ego sum, ego existo)* (*AT*, 7:25).[40] While Descartes tempts his readers to conflate these notions by arguing from "I am, I exist" to "I am, then, in the strict sense, only a *res cogitans*," these claims nevertheless have a very different status in the unfolding of his methodological thinking (*AT*, 7:27; *CSM*, 2:18). What distinguishes the *ego sum, ego existo* from the totality of dubitable propositions tested in Meditation One is neither the immediacy of the ego to thinking nor the instantaneity of its utterance and conception (though "this proposition . . . is necessarily true whenever it is put forward by me or conceived in my mind") (*CSM*, 2:17). While the activity of thinking is indeed the guarantor for the certainty of this proposition, the empty formality of *ego sum, ego existo* is what constitutes its indubitability. The certainty of "I am, I exist" does not immediately refer to what I am (my nature or essence, my quiddity), but merely to *that* I am (my existence). In the order of Descartes' *Meditations* argument, even while *that* I am has been firmly established, *what* I am still remains to be seen. As Descartes puts it after claiming certainty for his "thatness," "But I do not yet have a sufficient understanding of what this *ego* is, that now necessarily exists"(*CSM*, 2:17). Not until three full paragraphs of philosophical meditation later—a methodological eternity for the scriptive self—is the meditator able to claim that he knows with certainty that he is, in fact, a *res cogitans*.

Given this reminder, it is plausible to claim that the dubitability of each opinion Descartes' meditator examines in Meditation One is not the result of his failure to dig far enough into the soil of hyperbolic doubt, but rather of the way he posits the *content*—the "whatness"—of any given proposition as that which is to be tested. The mechanics of Descartes' argument thus turn on the way propositional content as such always fails to attain indubitability before the test of hyperbolic doubt and its personification in a supremely sly and powerful deceiver. What this deceiver does not and cannot destroy is the formality of the proposition as such, because even his deception has a propositional form; I only escape his clutches by positing something absolutely emptied of content: "I am, I exist." It is of course true that all such "positing" turns out to be a kind of thinking and that "he will never bring it about that I am nothing so long as I think I am something" (*CSM*, 2:17). It is still, however, the pure propositional formality of *ego sum, ego existo* rather than its content that renders it indubitable. In these terms, the gradual evacuation of all propositional content is the target of the meditator's general demolition of his opinions.

For Descartes' hyperbolic theatrics of the subject, Leibniz substitutes an equally exaggerated and analogous staging of the encyclopedic system. Just as the Cartesian meditator gradually eliminates all propositional content by way of an exaggerated method of doubt in order to arrive at a self-certifying, foundational, and purely formal claim, so too is Leibniz's philosophical consideration of encyclopedic methodology a reversal through content-oriented systems of organization to the absolute propositional formalism required by the method of reference. The metaphysics of the Leibnizian encyclopedia, however, is eventually forced to leave this formality behind. It does so by substituting the circular conception of encyclopedic categorization for the seriality of Cartesian rule-governed thought. For Descartes, the absolute certainty of the empty and formal proposition establishes a foundation on which the meditator can build a system of knowledge. Once the cornerstone of this foundation is laid, however, the meditator slowly retraces the serial dubitability of Meditation One and supersedes it with serial clarity and distinctness. He (or she) will once again distinguish his dreams from his waking hours; the existence of his body will be reestablished; he will rely on his senses once more; and he will go on to investigate scientific, philosophical, and theological problems of all sorts.

For the Leibnizian encyclopedist, however, the reversal from pure formality back into conceptual content is instantaneous and total. First, the consideration of content-oriented methods for constructing an encyclopedia shows that they dissolve before the repetition of propositional content throughout their classificatory systems. Second, the failure of these methods prompts the generation of an inventory and the development of a new method depending entirely on the establishment of terms through a formal structure of cross-reference that replaces propositional content. At the limit of this empty methodological formality, each "term" to be organized and classified within the encyclopedic structure is in fact nothing more than a referential reflection of the totality of that structure. In this way, encyclopedic cross-reference does not do away with the repetition of each element of human knowledge in every conceptual category, but instead provides a method for incorporating repetition into a stable systematic structure. Finally, while at the level of pure formality each of these referential structures reflects the entirety of the encyclopedic system—both its classificatory framework and the totality of its terms—each is also individuated by way of the referential and perspectival expression of the total conceptual universe of the encyclopedia. The "thisness" or "haecceity" of an entry in the Leibnizian encyclopedia consists in its being a particular and unique point of view on the infinite system of cross-referencing that structures the work as a whole. Every concept includes a reference to every other, but each is also a unique pattern of that total system of references.

Put another way, the individual substances of Leibniz's *Discourse on Metaphysics* are each structurally and formally identical to the totality of which they are a part ("complete worlds," "mirrors of God or of the whole universe") (*AG*, 41). At the same time, they are absolutely individuated by virtue of their singular perspective on that whole ("each singular substance expresses the whole universe in its own manner" and "each substance is like a world apart, independent of all other things outside of God") (*AG*, 41 and 47). Analogously, each term in the Leibnizian encyclopedia is an absolutely self-contained and singular text. At the same time this singularity is constituted precisely by its status as an elaborate and total system of cross-reference to every other concept, the unique order of these references constituting its identity. At the limit of the formality of categorical organization, the shimmering surface of the Leibnizian encyclopedia refigures the depths of human knowledge as a unique and total set of internal references.

It may be tempting to take Leibniz's hypostatization of encyclopedic referentiality as a useful model for thinking about our contemporary electronic information networks. It is easy enough to imagine an idealized version of the internet where meaning is constituted purely through the network of relational linkages rather than the more commercialized content they actually tend to string together. Certainly, the general encyclopedic dream of a machine or text in which the totality of human knowledge is assembled and organized resembles the hyperbole surrounding the possible futures of the internet. Furthermore, it is certainly the case that the entries in the Leibnizian encyclopedia—as complexes of total internal relations—bring to mind the sudden and surprising sequence of connections that can unfold in online experiences.

My inclination, however, is to propose that such parallels posit a series of structural continuities where there are primarily superficial resemblances. What is most interesting about the *mise en page* of Bayle's *Dictionary* is not the way it resembles, for example, medieval Talmudic commentaries and gloss editions of Aristotle, but rather the way that its mobilization of notational structure makes possible conceptually unique ways of reading. In the same sense, the more general aspects of Leibniz's theory of encyclopedism can capture the way only a few clicks through URL links may connect sixteenth-century linguistic theory with the details of a teenage pop star's recent fashion purchases. To focus on this, however, is to miss the philosophical originality of Leibniz's notion. Furthermore, it seems to me that Leibniz's presentation of encyclopedic notions as absolutely referential and indexical terms is a way of imagining a structure far more variegated than the online world we encounter. Our current reliance on search engines, at least, means that the "reflections" of the totality of the universe of knowledge we encounter are structured not by the unique point of view on the whole that individuates a Leibnizian encyclopedia entry, but rather by the vagaries of fashion as inscribed by proprietary algorithms of usage, volume, and traffic, not to mention sophisticated techniques of niche-marketing and surveillance.

In this chapter, I have suggested that the Leibnizian encyclopedia constitutes a theoretical framework for reflection on one form of the problem of repetition. It is a proposal for the reconciliation of a formal taxonomy with a totality of human knowledge that refuses to submit to organizational stasis. In practical and even physical terms, of course, it is an impossible project. Our Leibnizian encyclopedia would be an infinite set of volumes containing entries for every particular concept and entity, these entries each consisting of nothing more than an infinitely complex pattern of reference to every other entry. In his critique of Lockean categories and the ancient division of knowledge, Leibniz first articulated a problem of repetition: concepts cannot be contained within the bounds of such a structure but are repeated at every categorical location within it. The only possible adequate method for categorizing concepts, Leibniz argues, is a method of metaphysical cross-reference that develops out of the failure of the analytic and synthetic attempts at arrangement, replacing an emphasis on the content of concepts with a consideration of their formal structure. This method ultimately breaks with the seriality of Cartesian thought and replaces it with the circularity of a referential system that is able to encompass rather than reject the methodological alternatives and problem of repetition with which it struggled. Ultimately, it arrives at a substantial ontology of concepts and an imaginative vision of the entries in a total encyclopedia for words still unknown and still burning to be uttered.

CHAPTER 3

THE MATERIALIST ENCYCLOPEDIA

What is this "completeness"? It is a grand attempt to overcome the wholly irrational character of the object's mere presence at hand through its integration into a new, expressively devised historical system: the collection. And for the true collector, every single thing in this system becomes an encyclopedia of all knowledge of the epoch, the landscape, the industry, and the owner from which it comes.

Walter Benjamin, The Arcades Project

Several times Pierre Bayle referred to his philosophical-textual project in terms that make direct contact with the thematics treated in the previous chapters. Two years after the publication of the first edition of the *Historical and Critical Dictionary* he described his writings as engaging his readers "in a labyrinth." Seven years earlier in an August 28, 1692 letter to Vincent Minutoli, shortly after publishing a schematic theoretical plan (complete with exemplary articles) for the still unwritten *Dictionary*, Bayle described his project as "a stormy sea without bottom or bank."[1] The previous discussion of Leibniz's project for a metaphysical encyclopedia introduced a series of marginal considerations of the *mise en page* of Bayle's *Dictionary*. I began to argue that the structure by which Bayle's text is typographically framed on the page presents a good example of the way that the materiality of early modern textual organization is capable of channeling its readers in particular ways while also opening unique forms of conceptual encounter through processes of juxtaposition and reference both within and among Bayle's articles, their remarks, and their cross-references to texts inside and outside the boundaries of the work. Extending and continuing that exploration, the current chapter will use Bayle's text to refine this account of early modern textual ontology. I will initially describe the implications of the citational structure of Bayle's *Dictionary* with respect to its status as a critique of *error* rather than as an attempt to present a positive account (or rather, an almost uncountable series of positive accounts) with respect to philosophical and intellectual controversies. The second half of the chapter will turn to a very specific series of engagements with the history of the metaphysics of materialism within the pages of the *Dictionary*. While Bayle himself can no more be directly described as an Epicurean materialist thinker than Leibniz could, a series of articles that engages major figures in the materialist tradition allows him to frame that discourse in a unique and productive way. While he will criticize certain foundational atomist hypotheses (the role of chance in the encounter of bodies and the fully secularized account of the generation of the world), he will nevertheless accept its general program. That is, even while Bayle will reject propositions such as the fundamentally random nature of events in the corporeal world, he will both affirm the irreducibility of real parts of matter and develop a position uniquely located to provide a protohistory for the force of seventeenth-century materialism. While he does not, in the end, explicitly affirm its truth (indeed he rarely makes such a move for any of the positions he considers), Bayle nevertheless gives materialism an aesthetic and conceptual coherency that most other early modern accounts of the Epicurean revival lack. Finally, this chapter will demonstrate that Bayle frames this coherency as a confrontation with two specific books. In what may initially appear to be a strange textual choice, Bayle's confrontation with two poems provides a major site for this engagement with materialism: Lucretius' *De rerum natura* and Ovid's *Metamorphoses*.

BAYLE, SKEPTICISM, AND PHILOSOPHY AS A CORROSIVE POWDER

Thomas Lennon has described one of the major difficulties facing interpreters of Bayle's work as a confrontation with a Bakhtinean dialogical polyphony of voices and positions that makes it extremely difficult to nail down what Bayle actually held to be the case, or better, that makes Bayle's own positions far more complex than the simple assertion or denial of a series of immobile philosophical premises or conclusions.[2] Rather than seeking to quell this dialogicism by purging our interpreted "Bayle" of all conceptual contradiction, which Lennon describes as the dominant strategy in the secondary literature, he argues that it may be helpful to reorient our reading toward the question of how and why Bayle's considered theoretical position is so difficult to identify—be it skepticism of a Pyrrhonist or mitigated brand, fideism, atheism, materialism, Calvinist antirationalism, Cartesianism, etc. (*RB*, 17).[3] A dialogical approach to Bayle's texts is justified, Lennon argues, not merely due to the inherent virtues of this methodology, but also because it is closely akin to the strategy that Bayle himself uses when approaching the vast field of writers, texts, and positions.

The interpretive field Lennon addresses from this perspective is exceedingly diverse. Bayle in some places appears to define himself as a weak skeptic in the tradition of Montaigne, and in others as a fideist who merely uses philosophical skepticism as a tool to undermine the efficacy of reason in favor of a faith grounded in revelation. Bayle thus argues against those theologically inflected seventeenth-century thinkers who see even a mitigated Pyrrhonism as an irreducibly dangerous position. Instead, Bayle holds that the domains of revelation and philosophy are fundamentally distinct, as the former concerns a "supernatural" order and the latter a "natural" one (*Dict.*, exp. 2). This insistence leads some readers of Bayle to follow the lead of his major twentieth-century interpreter, Elisabeth Labrousse, who emphasizes the fundamentally religious context in which Bayle's work must be understood. In this vein, she claims that the Enlightenment reception of Bayle as a skeptic, crypto-atheist, and materialist was primarily due to the anachronistic and culturally displaced expectations of his early-eighteenth-century French readers. Though initially published in relatively censorship-free Rotterdam, later French readers assumed, she argues, that the *Dictionary* must be read according to the conventions adopted by authors surreptitiously espousing positions banned under the censorship regime associated with the royal privilege-to-publish structure operative in France.[4]

Nevertheless, I suggest Bayle's distinction between the domains of religion and conceptual analysis has less to do with the objects of his interrogation than with the ways they are approached and received. Philosophy, Bayle holds, ought not seek to pass judgment on matters of revealed religion, because where a philosophical approach touches on the reasonableness or meaningfulness of possible answers to a question under consideration, theology deals only with acceptance and obedience to the word of God, regardless of the manner in which it is comprehended (*Dict.*, exp. 2). In practice, Bayle frequently places himself in the position of developing merely hypothetical discussions of positions he clearly endorses but refuses explicitly to affirm.[5] In other cases, he denies these positions in what amount to brief asides following extensive theoretical discussions that display remarkable philosophical and rhetorical enthusiasm. For example, his treatment of Zeno of Elea—discussed at length by Thomas Holden—updates Zeno's arguments against motion to take account of seventeenth-century developments in mathematics, physics, and debates over the nature of matter.[6] Pursuing this line, Bayle presents several arguments he claims a modern-day Zeno could make in the face of the assertion of the reality of motion. The most important of these are aimed against the reality of extension as such. If the existence of extension can be refuted, Bayle holds, then *a fortiori* a refutation of the motion of extended bodies will follow (*Dict.*, art. "Zeno of Elea," rem. I). At the same time, in related articles he affirms the actuality of the infinite parts of bodies against the merely possible infinity of parts of the continuum defended by Aristotelians (*Dict.*, art. "Leucippus" and "Spinoza"). In other words, without actually embracing Zeno's antimotion position, his engagement with it results in the presentation of a series of arguments that actually have the effect of reinforcing its philosophical power.

More generally, Bayle's "critical" and "historical" approach to major philosophical disputes does not involve the production of positive, definitive answers to historically controversial questions. Rather, it is framed as a process for the discovery of all errors in the entire field of positions taken on any particular question. Thus, he at least acts the part of the classical skeptic, offering a series of reasons to reject a wide variety of affirmative propositions, though without ever fully embracing the *epoche* that is supposed to follow. At the same time, Bayle vehemently rejects skepticism when it turns its sights on the propositions affirmed by revealed religion (*Dict.*, exp. 2). Thus, Richard Popkin asserts that Bayle is a skeptic in the classical Pyrrhonian vein, though one who takes skepticism to constitute a prolegomena to a faith that derives exclusively from revelation. Bayle's skepticism, on Popkin's reading, thereby constitutes a critical attack on the power of reason and its dogmatic pretensions.[7]

Jonathan Israel, by contrast, insists on Bayle's contribution to what he has named "the radical Enlightenment," pointing out that

Bayle's resistance to arguments that an "unbroken chain of tradition" provides the historical veracity of revealed Christianity and his defense of the notion of the "virtuous atheist" put him totally at odds with the leading fideists of his day (Jacques-Bénigne Bossuet and Pierre-Daniel Huet).[8] Rather, Israel insists,

> Contrary to what is often said, Bayle is strictly speaking neither a skeptic nor a "fideist." His position is that philosophical reason is the only tool we have to separate truth from falsehood, the only secure criterion, and that consequently, by its very nature, religious faith can never be based on reason . . . But the ultimate paradox in Bayle is not that faith can never be explained or justified by reason, but that what is chiefly opposed to reason in his philosophy, namely, "superstition," is indistinguishable from faith. His principles irreducibly render one man's faith another's "superstition" with no rational grounds or criteria being provided to differentiate the one from the other.[9] (*RE*, 338)

Even further to the left of Labrousse than Israel lies Gianluca Mori, who rejects Labrousse's position wholesale and argues for Bayle as an implicit but committed proponent of a "critical" or "speculative" atheism. Arguing on a strictly textual rather than biographical and cultural-historical basis, Mori proposes that Bayle's work progressively abandons all but a nominal commitment to Christianity as its trajectory approaches the constitution of the *Historical and Critical Dictionary*. In the face of passages difficult to reconcile with this position, Mori argues persuasively that Bayle's texts are "coded" in exactly the sense that Labrousse rejected.[10]

Hence the most paradoxical aspect of Bayle's stance with regard to philosophy and skepticism is that at times he seems to hold that the latter is the unavoidable result of the former, especially when philosophy is forced to its limit. Thus, despite providing a vigorous defense of the philosophical endeavor against its theological critics, Bayle also reserves some of his most vitriolic rhetoric for philosophy. For example, in a well-known passage from his article on Uriel Acosta, he writes,

> One can compare philosophy to those powders so corrosive that, after having consumed the infected flesh of a wound, eat into living flesh, rot the bone, and penetrate all the way to the marrow.

Philosophy at first refutes errors, but if it is not stopped at that point, it attacks truths: and when one leaves it to its fantasy, it goes so far that it no longer knows where it is and can no longer find a resting place. (*Dict.*, art. "Acosta," rem. G)

Philosophy is thus the only discourse capable of providing rational answers to questions concerning the nature of things, but that capacity itself presents a real danger. When it moves beyond the critical refutation of error (as Bayle thinks it inevitably must) it begins to dissolve the very grounds of its own approach to the natural world. A related methodological difficulty in reading Bayle philosophically is his reliance on the variegated levels of citation that permeate the *Dictionary*. In other words, the question of Bayle's skepticism, atheism, or fideism may turn in part on how a reader of the *Dictionary* might distinguish between instances when Bayle is writing in his own name and those when he mobilizes the proper names and—more importantly—texts and arguments of others. Even these extra- and intertextual references are problematic, as they allow Bayle to both *mine* and *mime* the positions of thinkers with whom he may or may not agree. Thus, in what follows, my primary concern will not be to stake out a definitive position on the traditional question of Bayle's ultimate stance with regard to fideism or philosophical skepticism. Instead, I will ask what the form and evidentiary practice of the *Dictionary* may be able to tell us about its textual function at the end of the seventeenth century, and more broadly about the practice of using textual citation *as* evidence. If Bayle's skepticism—however it fits our methodological typologies—rejects the straightforward philosophical project of the discovery of truths (at least those beyond what Bayle designates, in Cartesian fashion, as irreducibly simple clear and distinct truths of reason), then with what does he replace it? If the *Dictionary* disavows philosophy taken to its limit as a dangerous oxidizing agent that moves too far in the right direction and ultimately consumes the frame of the soul, then what does Bayle's arsenal of citational evidence mobilize in its stead?

EXPLOSIVE CITATION AND THE CRITIQUE OF SIMILITUDE

These questions will be approached by way of the materiality of Bayle's text and his mobilization of figures of textual inscription. In order to develop the account of the textual materiality of the

Dictionary initially presented in the previous chapter and to display more directly the oddity and philosophical relevance of its format and citational structure, I will return to the "Rorarius" article where Bayle stages his confrontation with Leibniz. A significant portion of the "Rorarius" article is dominated by remark D, which is appended to the article sentence, "For a long time people have maintained that the souls of animals are rational." The content of this remark—the evidence for this claim—is an extremely long string of citations, quotations, and discussions of various authors who have endorsed animal rationality since antiquity. These are the authors, in the order discussed by Bayle: Strato and Aenesidemus (as cited via Plutarch, Diogenes Laertius, and Isaac Vossius' citation of Sextus Empiricus), Parmenides, Empedocles, and Democritus (as cited via Sextus Empiricus and Strobaeus' citation of Plutarch), Anaxagoras (cited via Vossius' citation of Aristotle), Virgil, Philo (as cited by Eusebius), Galen, Lactantius, Arnobius, Xenocrates of Carthage, Clement of Alexandria, Pliny the Elder, Dion, all the early Platonists (at least as described by Paganinus Gaudentius), Solomon (though, Bayle insists, despite his explicit endorsement in *Ecclesiastes* of the proposition that the souls of animals and men have the same nature, he actually must have meant something else), "several rabbis" including Maimonides (as discussed by Antoine Arnauld), and the Socinians (according to Wolfgang Franzius). Among the moderns, Bayle cites Lorenzo Valla, Antoine Cittadin, Etienne Pasquier, Montaigne (who has "taken such care to defend this opinion that he seems to have designed that the apology for Raymond Sebond should partly serve as one for brutes"), Pierre Charron, and finally, one "Mr. de la Chambre, Médecin de Mr. Seguier Chancelier de France." Remark D also includes four references to other articles and their remarks (*Dict.*, art. "Pereira," cit. 38; art. "Galen"; art. "Sennertus," rem. D; and art. "Sennertus," rem. E) where Bayle provides discussions of those who hold that the souls of beasts are spiritual (whereas in remark D to "Rorarius" he has discussed only those who endow them with reason).

The context for these citations is the attempted refutation of Leibniz's account of the sensation of pain that Bayle undertakes in remarks H and L in terms of the mechanism of the body and its complex relationship to an incorporeal yet sensate mind. In the broader field of a remark clearly geared toward this engagement with Leibniz, Bayle's argument accords equal weight to an incisive and extended discussion of the history of the reception of Cartesian mechanism (*Dict.*, art. "Rorarius," rem. C and G) and the remark D discussion of textual *loci* like this well-known and hilarious passage from Pliny on the cultural and religious mores of elephants:

> Elephants are the greatest of animals, and come nearest to human sense: for they understand the language of their country, obey commands, remember the offenses done to them, and have the pleasure of love and glory; so too (which are rare even in men) probity, prudence, equity, religious regard of the stars, the worship of the sun and the moon. It is reported that when the moon is waning in the forests of Mauritania they go down to a certain river called Amelio where they purify themselves by sprinkling themselves with water in a solemn manner, and, after worshiping the moon, return into the woods while carrying their tired young. And set to cross the seas, it is said that they will not go aboard a ship until they have obtained their master's oath to bring them back. And, when worn out with sickness (to which these bulky animals are also subject), they have been seen lying on their backs and throwing herbs into the air as if thereby to atone to the heavens.[11] (*Dict.*, art. "Rorarius," rem. D)

What exactly do the affective and religious customs of elephants have to do with Cartesian mechanism or the Leibnizian theory of preestablished harmony? On one level, the relation is obvious. Descartes proposed that we could understand animals as mere machines lacking a rational soul, and Leibniz was concerned with establishing a new theory of the relationship between the physical forces governing a mechanical nature and the metaphysical laws governing thought and final causes. Pliny's account, along with those of the authors Bayle cites around him, provides an alternative perspective to Cartesian mechanism. But things, of course, are not that simple.

Why not merely state (as Bayle does in the body of the article) that various people have held a position different from the Cartesian one? Why engage in an exhaustive listing of every author—ancient and modern—whose remarks on animal consciousness Bayle could find cited anywhere? Why accord equal argumentative weight and page space to such citations as to his explicitly philosophical engagement with Leibniz's ideas and arguments? Exactly what kind of evidence does this structure of wild, excessive, and exhaustive citation provide?

To begin to deal with these questions, it may help to consider the structure of Bayle's *Dictionary* in terms of the broader context of early modern citational practice. At the core of Foucault's discussion of the differences between the epistemic frameworks of the sixteenth and seventeenth centuries is a distinction between a regime of resemblance and a system of representation (*OT*, 17–77). In the Renaissance system of resemblance and similitude, the language of things is inscribed in their very being as a system of hieroglyphic signs that point to the way that *res* may be lodged within the unitary fabric of a semantic network connecting them to the world. In the late-sixteenth-century history of dragons and serpents by Ulisse Aldrovandi, to use Foucault's example, the chapter "On the Serpent in General" is arranged under topics dealing with the meaning of the word "serpent," its etymologies, explanations of serpent anatomy, descriptions of their nature and habits, their modes of copulation, death and wounds that serpents can cause, remedies to poisonous bites by serpents, serpents' roles in omens, monsters and mythological beings related to the serpent, emblems, heraldic devices, and coins on which serpents appear, allegories, proverbs, and fables featuring serpents, historical events in which serpents have played a role, recipes for cooking serpents, and so on (*OT*, 39–40 and 129).[12] For Aldrovandi, all the forms of similitude by which the serpent can be related to any other existing thing are inscribed in its history. Identifying the various ways in which it resembles everything else related to it is the key to grasping its nature.

In the shift to the seventeenth-century system of representation and eventually to the eighteenth-century discourse of natural history, Foucault argues that this sense, that a mystical language and the resemblances it articulates are lodged *in* the world of things, disappears entirely. A framework of representation replaces it, as discourse and signification become more and more a function of the distance between the observer and the phenomena, and knowledge is understood to require a set of reflective distinctions predicated on the *uselessness* of similarity. To Aldrovandi he contrasts the naturalist Georges Buffon, who in the eighteenth century finds nothing but a hodgepodge of legends in Aldrovandi's work, and demands that natural history take the form of an experiential method that will construct a series of claims about nature based on empirical observation (*OT*, 40).[13] Foucault's point is not that Buffon is a better naturalist than Aldrovandi. Rather, Buffon's practice is articulated by another set of epistemic rules entirely. Most important among these rules is that, in early modernity, the structures of similitude that underlie Renaissance discourse have not so much disappeared as been refigured as a problem that knowledge must seek to rigorously circumscribe. For early modern writers, resemblance has been hypostasized such that every thing resembles every other, and thus the similitude that grounded Renaissance claims about nature becomes the mark of error, which must be guarded against. Foucault's point is thus not that Buffon relies on more stable and rigorous evidence than Aldrovandi, but that *the rules of evidence have altogether changed* in the period that separates them.

I have rehearsed Foucault's familiar position because it seems to me that Bayle's *Dictionary* offers a particularly subtle example of how the history of epistemic shifts and evidentiary frameworks can be understood not so much as the narrative of how one set of rules gets abandoned or evolves into another, but as the way in which supposedly obsolete forms can be completely recast in the service of an entirely different set of projects and assumptions. Bayle's *Dictionary*, in fact, seems to bear a great resemblance to the histories of nature written by Aldrovandi and his Renaissance contemporaries, just as its form resembles the texts of Renaissance encyclopedists and polyhistors. A single article in the *Dictionary* assembles in its notes all the accounts, legends, biographical claims, philosophical arguments, literary and culinary references, art historical depictions, political and theological controversies, jokes, etc. that bear even the most distant relationship to the subject of the article in which they appear. Like Aldrovandi, Bayle's vast network of citations, remarks on citations, notes on the remarks on citations, and descriptions of the cultural and historical milieu in which those citations were written together weave the discursive space in which the subject of the article is defined—be it Manichaeism, Spinoza, ancient skepticism, or Ovid.

The previous chapter discussed the sense in which Bayle's citational practice was fundamentally different from that of scribal, medieval, and late Renaissance encyclopedic cultures. There is a second sense in which his evidentiary citational practice is fundamentally new. Recall that in a fundamental way Bayle's *Dictionary* is a structure of error, assembling these stories, fables, arguments, and images so that its articles construct a negative and differential framework within the storm of language that constituted the early modern Republic of Letters. The history of the compilation, organization, and production of the *Dictionary* may help to illuminate this issue.

In 1689, the *Dictionary* began as a series of notes intended for use by Dutch printers preparing an emended edition of Louis Moréri's famous *Grand Dictionnaire historique* (1674).[14] By 1690, the printers have chosen the cheaper option of a reprint, and Bayle realizes that his notes have, in any case, become an attack on errors within the entire field of historical-philosophical dictionaries, lexica, and Renaissance encyclopedias. He reconceptualizes his project accordingly, and an announcement appears in the *Histoires des ouvrages de savants* for a *Dictionnaire critique*, "wherein one will find the correction of the infinity of mistakes found in dictionaries and other books."[15] An extended promissory note (ostensibly a preface and description) for this *Dictionnaire critique* entitled *Projet et fragmens d'un dictionnaire critique* is published anonymously in 1692, including 38 pages of introduction followed by 400 pages of sample articles experimenting with the mobilization of remarks, page space, and conceptual explanation. Though many of the articles are quite different in content and form from those that would later appear in the *Dictionary* proper, the penchant of Bayle and his printer for forceful and complicated typographical structure is already obvious.

The *Projet* receives a lukewarm reception, the most frequent complaint being, as Leibniz put it, that a work correcting errors would be much more interesting than one merely cataloging them (*GP*, 6:6.16–20). Bayle takes this criticism to heart, and by the time the first edition of the *Dictionary* itself appears in 1697, it has become an enormous compendium of scholarship and original theoretical work.[16] Bayle has radically revised his concept of critique, such that the text is now an apparatus of conceptual, historical, and philosophical remarks that virtually supplant the content of the "purely historical" articles, taking the form of what Bayle describes as "a great commentary, a mélange of proofs and discussions, wherein I have inserted a censure of many faults" accompanied by a "tirade of philosophical reflections" (*Dict.*, pref.).

What for a figure like Aldrovandi would be the linguistic marks left by the thing itself in the world of signs, for Bayle are negative spaces of error left absent by the thing remaining merely and only what it is. After pages and pages of citation, argumentation, and criticism, how after all, does the "Rorarius" article end in the 1697 edition? "To get back to Rorarius," Bayle writes in its final sentences, "I do not believe that I am mistaken in giving my opinion that he was born in Pordenone in Italy. I wish I could have read the speech he made in favor of rats. It was printed in the country of Grisons in 1548. There is something like this in the writings of Président Chassanée" (*Dict.*, art. "Rorarius"). Thus, despite the shift away from its original project of cataloging the mistakes in Moréri, the *Dictionary* is not a positive collection of facts, figures, and claims that comprehends the totality of the universe of linguistic knowledge or a systematization of the resemblances among all extant things. While it does methodologically feign and structurally evoke the dream of total encyclopedic assemblage and a system of virtual resemblance, each of the printed markers it arranges or refers to are present only to be subject to critique.

Bayle himself, both as the author-assembler of the *Dictionary* and as the editor of the intellectual journal *Nouvelles des république des lettres*, did not play a merely negative role vis-à-vis the maelstrom of printed language his project was meant to arrange and critique. Both the *Dictionary* and his journal helped determine the form of the discourse produced in his day, shaping it (in ways both intentional and unintentional) into a framework amenable to historical criticism. Both can be seen as part of an explosion of discursive technology taking place near the end of the seventeenth century, which allowed the formation of a fundamentally new intellectual milieu not directly under the control of government or church, and which allowed the texts of philosophers, scientists, theologians, literary figures, etc. to reach one another with a speed and breadth of dissemination hitherto unknown.[17] By transferring intellectual debates out of the relatively closed circles of official royal societies and informal networks of recognized correspondents, and by providing more easily digestible encapsulations of difficult works and complex controversies, these texts transformed the world of inquiry and debate into a kind of public spectacle that could be enjoyed by those not directly participating in it. In a sense, the energy of obscure philosophical, scientific, and religious debates became a kind of fashionable commodity for the first time, easily and cheaply accessible for anyone who cared to read.

One might propose that journals like Bayle's and the *Dictionary* itself performed an essentially conservative function by pointing out (as does Israel) that they were often sharp in their condemnation of philosophically or politically radical ideas (*RE*, 151–52). But at the same time, the journals and the *Dictionary* provided those ideas with a far wider circulation than they had hitherto seen. What young philosopher of good sense, for example, would not secretly yearn to peruse a black-market copy of Spinoza's *Ethics* (suppressed even under the liberal publishing regime in Holland) after reading the following in one of Bayle's remarks?

> Here is a philosopher who is pleased to make God himself the agent and patient of all the crimes and all the miseries of men. If men hate one another, if they murder one another in the forest, if they assemble into armies to kill one another, if the victors sometimes eat the vanquished, this can be understood, because it is supposed that they are distinct from one another, and that "mine" and "thine" produce contrary passions in them. But that there should be wars and battles when men are only modifications of the same being, and if, consequently, only God acts, and if the God who modifies himself into a Turk is numerically identical to the God who modifies himself into a Hungarian, then this surpasses all the monstrosities and all the chimerical derangements of the craziest people who have ever been shut up in madhouses. (*Dict.*, art. "Spinoza," rem. N)

Furthermore, would that philosopher not have been led immediately to Bayle's own set of texts, upon seeing the *Dictionary* denounced again and again in learned reviews for its frequent lewdness and obscenity, coupled with review after review praising it as the most important and comprehensive intellectual work to be produced in recent memory? Even in its most rhetorically excessive denunciations of philosophical positions, then, the *Dictionary* often functioned as an agent for the dissemination of at least some version of their arguments and implications, thus carving out a niche (and sometimes even a market) for their broader circulation in late-seventeenth-century printed discourse.

Finally and most importantly, Bayle's work depends on carefully and accurately tracking the origin and authorship—as far as possible—of all the negative attributions, accounts, tales, and fables related to his figures, so that they can be subjected to a skeptical and critical evidentiary analysis. There is a kind of irony that, on the one hand, Bayle engages in a historical critical analysis of the way that a given figure has been immersed in a vast and undifferentiated sea of discourse, and on the other that in order to function in a truly critical manner, the analysis requires the stabilization of words by collecting and nailing down everything relevant that has been written about his figures to proper names, particular contexts, and thereby (in many cases) a set of internal, psychological motivations. Evidence of authorship for Bayle, in other words, is the condition for the subjection of history to criticism.

This figure of the author as an individual, creative mind who has produced a delimited piece of written language and who can therefore be held responsible for it is a relatively new one in Bayle's time (as Foucault initially theorized and as a variety of historians of reading have more recently substantiated and placed on a firmer historical ground).[18] The point is that Bayle's project of the critical and negative delineation of historical evidence not only depends on the reality of the authorial attributions it requires, but also plays a role in the realization and stabilization of the figure of literary and conceptual authority as such. But again, somewhat ironically, this figure of the author plays primarily a negative role, as the producer of words that distort the truth about the figure in whose article they appear. At the same time, the authority of the historical critic increases insofar as these authors' proper names recede into the now radically differentiated field of statements and their citations that has been organized into the critical archival structure of the *Dictionary*.

This attribution of authorship to a text at sea in an ocean of discourse is also what leads to Bayle's image of philosophy as an intellectual oxidant with the power to corrode the language of truth. For Bayle, when one leaves philosophical argumentation to its fantasy, it becomes the project of the dissociation of words from texts, the transmutation of claims in books into universal notions unmoored from the site of their articulation. The highest aim of a philosophy that has exceeded its proper limits, thinks Bayle, is to render language unattributable, thus uncitable, and therefore unassailable by historical critique. Both in developing its methods for accessing *a priori* forms of rationality and in extending its machines of skeptical demolition beyond the bounds of the possible experience of history, philosophy corrodes the nature of evidentiary discourse and practice as such. Its project, in Bayle's view, is to provide irrefutable evidence for a set of claims that will thereby be grasped as truth. But if, as Bayle holds, the true nature of evidence and the character of irrefutability are mutually exclusive, then this project, philosophy, is doomed to failure; or rather, it threatens to eat into the living flesh of the history of discourse. In order to count *as* evidence, the possibility of the negative work of the historical and critical delimitation of error must remain. This delimitation is precisely what the *Dictionary* is to carry out. As the next section will demonstrate, however, this does not prevent Bayle from engaging in serious attempts to philosophize. Given his critique of the philosophical endeavor, I will show that his approach to the problematics of materialism, in the end, results in a judgment framed simultaneously on aesthetic and conceptual grounds.

CHANCE AND THE DISCORD OF BODIES

For some scholars, consideration of the materiality of text-objects requires a ritual renunciation of metaphysics in general and ontology in particular. This is a mistake, especially if we consider early modern philosophical and scientific thought to encompass more than the repeated denunciations of metaphysics by the relatively small group of thinkers who saw a turn to the material world as inimical to ontological consideration. Instead, the revival of Epicureanism, the rise of the mechanical and corpuscular philosophies, and the increasing centrality of experience and experiment included an attempt to reinvent ontology in various forms, under the imperative of adequately accounting for a materiality that was something more than a passive formless substrate awaiting its activation by an external formal principle. As the Scholastic-Aristotelian language of *potentia* and *dynamis* is reinscribed within a vocabulary of force and power organized by the newly emerging science of dynamics, a fundamental metaphysical shift takes place. While several terms of the vocabulary remain the same, their significations change. What for the Scholastics designated the essential passivity of matter in contrast to its activated form or the various modalities of its operation, becomes a systematic language for describing a world of bodies in motion that is fundamentally and fully active. This transformation of vocabulary means that seventeenth-century materialisms writ large (thus including, for example, antimaterialist adaptations of atomistic arguments, as detailed with respect to Leibniz in Chapter 1) do not seek to escape from metaphysics as such, but rather to transform it. Not only have some of the so-called empiricists often been misread here, but even a philosopher like Descartes—who for many strands of contemporary continental philosophy embodies a figure of pure *mathesis* unmoored from corporeality—was interested above all in providing an adequate account of the parts of the extended world and their motion, built on a metaphysical foundation identifying matter with extension.

Bayle—intimately familiar with the continental scientific and metaphysical debates in the second half of the seventeenth century (though admittedly behind on his British corpuscularists and even more so on Newton)—stands not only as a participant in this discussion, but also as a retrospective and encyclopedic historian of the complex of arguments about the ontological status of matter that wracked the early modern period. To refer to Bayle's *Dictionary* as a "materialist encyclopedia," as does the title of this chapter, is not to attribute to Bayle a position he clearly did not hold, namely, that existing things are fully conceptually reducible to a subtending series of material parts. Rather, it is meant to draw attention to several specific aspects of his project. First, it emphasizes the sense in which Bayle's text constantly and consistently engages a broader conception of metaphysical and natural philosophical materialism, specifically that family of philosophical accounts that might be described as "configurationist" or "dispositional" conceptions of nature. It identifies, that is, those philosophical accounts that understand, in the wake of the revival of Epicureanism, structures of physical nature to be determined by the patterns in which their parts are arranged or by the relatively constant complex patterns of motion through which those same parts are combined and recombined. Second, attributing to Bayle a "materialist encyclopedia" draws attention to the way that the textual configuration of the *Dictionary*—the formal structure or pattern of its typography and the role of this structure in determining the way that it is perused or consulted—bears on the positions it articulates or criticizes.

In what follows, I will bring my initial presentation of the material form of Bayle's textual ontology together with one of his key reflections on the nature of matter itself. To do so requires what may seem to be a strange textual choice, namely an investigation of the remarks attached to Bayle's article on Ovid.[19] Just as with the "Rorarius" article, the real action in the "Ovid" article takes place almost entirely within the remarks. Like "Rorarius," it is 14 pages in folio. Only a few typographical lines of its 35 sentences appear on most pages, though they are accompanied by 15 marginal notes. Indeed, the 1702 edition relegates 98% of the page space in the article to its 18 remarks, including their 167 marginal notes and their 6 marginal headings. This article, I will demonstrate, is built around the transformation of the poet into a metaphysician (albeit, technically an ancient one) and a subsequent materialist critique of the ontology that results.[20] In the *Dictionary*, Ovid stands metonymically for the new physics of aggregational corporeality subject to laws of motion. In particular, Ovid embodies those atomist-inspired accounts of matter that swerved away from the *clinamen* by relying on the intervention of a formal, teleological, divine principle to bring the world into being.

OVID FOR PHILOSOPHERS, OR HOW NOT TO READ POETRY

As readers of Ovid will recall, in the opening lines of the *Metamorphoses* the poet promises to tell of bodies changed into new forms.[21] Rather than launch immediately into tales of the transformation of humans into animals, plants, or geographical features, he begins with the transmutation of the disordered world of primal bodies into an ordered universe. In the beginning is chaos, "a rough and undigested mass of things, nothing at all save lifeless bulk and warring seeds of ill-matched elements heaped into one" (*Met.*, 1.7–9). Notice, as Bayle does, that Ovid explicitly invokes Lucretian terminology here. To speak of bodies is to speak of the seeds of things (*semina rerum*) possessing mass and weight (*moles* and *pondus*), and all of these terms appear frequently throughout *De rerum natura*. "No form of things remained the same; all objects were at odds, for within one body cold things strove with hot, and moist with dry, soft things with hard, things having weight with weightless things" (*Met.*, 1.17–20). This chaotic strife of elemental bodies is then composed by a god, who performs a series of distinct operations:

1. Severing (*abscido*) things from one another and thus releasing the elements from the "blind heap of things" in which they begin (sky and sea from land, the ethereal heavens from denser liquidity), which is also described as resolution or unrolling (*evolvo*) and cutting or reduction (*seco*).
2. Binding (*ligo*) each thing in its proper place (the vault of the heavens above the air, the earth below them, and beneath all, the waters), also called disposing or distributing (*dispono*).
3. Several forms of reflexive collecting or driving together (*cogo*) of things into forms (the earth into a sphere, the waters around the

shores and riverbeds of this sphere, the plains stretching out between the waters, the valleys sinking and the mountains rising from the plains, etc.).
4. And finally, various acts of enclosing (*includo*) and dividing (*dissaepio*) things within determinate limits (the climates to their zones, the winds to their directions, lightening and thunder to the sky, etc.) (*Met.*, 1.24–69).

Thus, through a series of intentional acts of severing, binding, collecting, and enclosing, a peaceful and harmonious order composed of insensible elemental bodies is brought forth from their original chaos, a harmony from disharmony, a coherent world from the incoherent strife of contending corporeality.

This description of Ovid's prologue must strike many readers, of course, as a rather poor way to read the *Metamorphoses*: a mere reduction of the poem's language to a catalog of the individual actions mentioned in a brief mythopoetical cosmogony that serves as the prolegomena to a far richer collection of interlocking tales of desire, betrayal, mythological allegory, and bodily metamorphosis. This, nevertheless, is an important part of the way Bayle inscribes Ovid into his encyclopedic scheme in the *Dictionary*. At stake in Bayle's philosophical interrogation of Ovid (much of which sets the *Metamorphoses* against Lucretius' *De rerum natura*) is the question of the emergence of order from corporeal discord. Bayle's own position is that precisely the opposite must hold in order to explain both the disposition of nature and the constitution of the human as a "perpetual warfare of antagonistic principles" and a "theater of vicissitudes" riven without cease by the discord of bodies (*Dict.*, art. "Ovid," rem. G). The Ovid that materializes in Bayle's remarks, in other words, is as hybrid a creature as those of the poet's own creation, part literary and part philosophical, part mythologist and part physicist, an amalgamation of Hesiod and La Fontaine on the one hand with Lucretius and Descartes on the other.

Similar metamorphoses take place when Bayle's remarks confront major figures in the materialist philosophical tradition, ranging from its ancient and classical champions (Anaxagoras, Epicurus, and Lucretius, of course, but with Aesop playing a key role) to the contemporary avatars of the mechanistic, corpuscular, and neo-atomist new philosophies of early modernity (Gassendi, Hobbes, Descartes, Spinoza, Lamy, etc.). Running through the remark structure of the

Dictionary is an encyclopedic presentation of what amounts to the first critical history of early modern materialism. This is a history that explicitly refuses to take disavowals of materialism at their word (neither Descartes nor Spinoza, for example, assent to the thesis that the fundamental level of existence is populated exclusively by bodily things), instead emphasizing the ubiquity of the transformative, dispositional, and configurationist corporeal theses at the heart of the Lucretian and Epicurean model found among many more early modern philosophers than would admit to their allegiance.

Bayle, furthermore, is far less interested in evaluating the coherence and natural philosophical veracity of the cosmogenesis he finds in Ovid than he is in attempting to draw out its implications for an aesthetic and affective evaluation of the supposedly ordered world of bodies in which we live. What at first looks like a rather inept attempt to reduce the poetical philosophizing of Ovid to its conceptual framework and then to evaluate the soundness and coherence of the positions it articulates, in fact turns out to be an aesthetic critique of the moral worlds with which the work's poetics and poetic philosophy are infused.

Bayle's article, though devoting much of its space to Ovid *qua* poet and historical author, focuses its most extensive remarks on the transformation of Ovid into a philosopher and on a critique of the ontology and natural philosophy that results. Here is what Bayle tells us in the article itself about the first book of the *Metamorphoses*: "It is a description of chaos and the manner in which the universe was formed out of it. Nothing could be clearer or more intelligible than that noble description, if we confine ourselves only to the poet's phrases; but if we examine his doctrines, we shall find them incoherent and contradictory" (*Dict*., "Ovid"). Remarks G and H, which with their marginal subnotes, quotations, and text headings, comprise almost 45% of the whole article, deal with a critical examination of what Bayle identifies in printed marginal notation as Ovid's "doctrine of chaos" (Figure 4). In these remarks, Bayle is extremely self-conscious about the way that he is structuring his text and using his remarks, referring to his *mise en page* here more explicitly than usual. Also note the reflexivity of Bayle's criticism. Ovid's mistake is that he describes chaos far too chaotically: "From which it is manifest that the description of chaos and its development is composed of propositions more opposed to one another than were the elements during the chaos" (*Dict.,* art. "Ovid," rem. G).

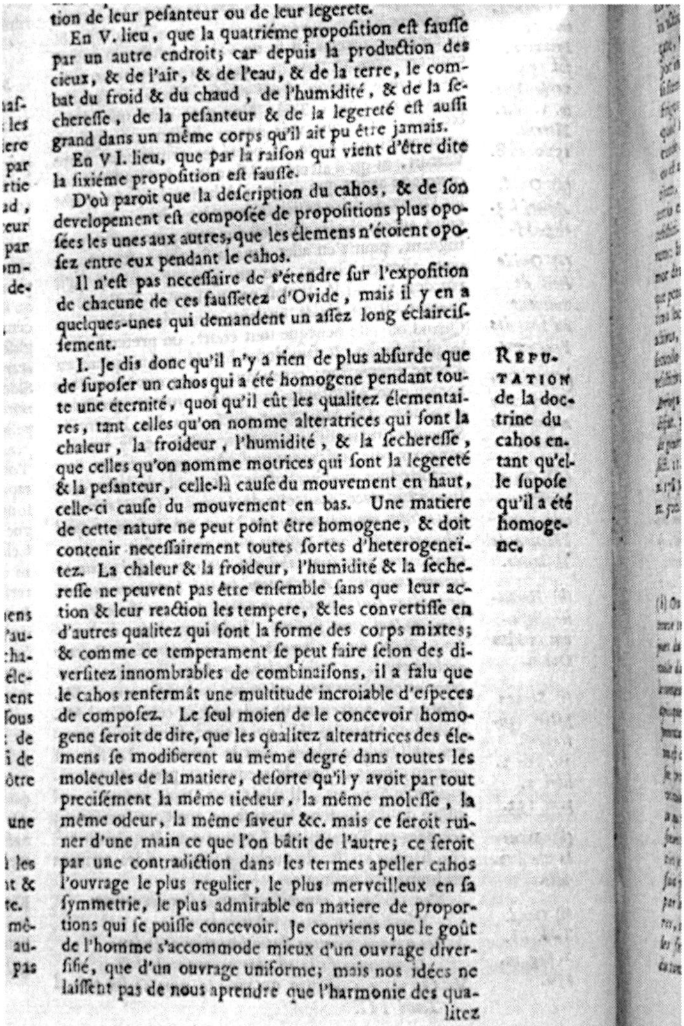

tion de leur pesanteur ou de leur legereté.

En V. lieu, que la quatriéme proposition est fausse par un autre endroit; car depuis la production des cieux, & de l'air, & de l'eau, & de la terre, le combat du froid & du chaud, de l'humidité, & de la secheresse, de la pesanteur & de la legereté est aussi grand dans un même corps qu'il ait pu être jamais.

En VI. lieu, que par la raison qui vient d'être dite la sixiéme proposition est fausse.

D'où paroit que la description du cahos, & de son developement est composée de propositions plus oposées les unes aux autres, que les élemens n'étoient oposez entre eux pendant le cahos.

Il n'est pas necessaire de s'étendre sur l'exposition de chacune de ces faussetez d'Ovide, mais il y en a quelques-unes qui demandent un assez long éclaircissement.

REFUTATION de la doctrine du cahos entant qu'elle supose qu'il a été homogene.

I. Je dis donc qu'il n'y a rien de plus absurde que de suposer un cahos qui a été homogene pendant toute une éternité, quoi qu'il eût les qualitez élementaires, tant celles qu'on nomme alteratrices qui sont la chaleur, la froideur, l'humidité, & la secheresse, que celles qu'on nomme motrices qui sont la legereté & la pesanteur, celle-là cause du mouvement en haut, celle-ci cause du mouvement en bas. Une matiere de cette nature ne peut point être homogene, & doit contenir necessairement toutes sortes d'heterogeneïtez. La chaleur & la froideur, l'humidité & la secheresse ne peuvent pas être ensemble sans que leur action & leur reaction les tempere, & les convertisse en d'autres qualitez qui font la forme des corps mixtes; & comme ce temperament se peut faire selon des diversitez innombrables de combinaisons, il a falu que le cahos renfermât une multitude incroiable d'especes de composez. Le seul moien de le concevoir homogene seroit de dire, que les qualitez alteratrices des élemens se modifierent au même degré dans toutes les molecules de la matiere, desorte qu'il y avoit par tout precisément la même tiedeur, la même molesse, la même odeur, la même saveur &c. mais ce seroit ruiner d'une main ce que l'on bâtit de l'autre; ce seroit par une contradiction dans les termes apeller cahos l'ouvrage le plus regulier, le plus merveilleux en sa symmetrie, le plus admirable en matiere de proportions qui se puisse concevoir. Je conviens que le goût de l'homme s'accommode mieux d'un ouvrage diversifié, que d'un ouvrage uniforme; mais nos idées ne laissent pas de nous aprendre que l'harmonie des qualitez

Figure 4 Detail of Pierre Bayle's "Ovid" article showing the marginal subheading that marks the beginning of his "refutation of the doctrine of chaos, insofar as it is supposed to have been homogeneous." Pierre Bayle, *Dictionnaire historique et critique,* 2nd edn. (Rotterdam: Leers, 1702), 2273. © John J. Burns Library, Boston College, Chestnut Hill, MA.

Identifying the distinct operations preformed by Ovid's god, Bayle reduces the poet's account of the emergence of order to six propositions:

1. Before sky, earth, and sea, nature was a homogeneous whole.
2. This whole was a heavy mass without symmetry, containing things only in a confused and discordant fashion, each thing bearing contrary properties.
3. Contradictory elements struggled in the same body; lightness and weight were identical.
4. God ends this war by separating the combatants.
5. God orders them according to the intrinsic lightness and weight belonging to each.
6. God forms an appropriate relationship between them.

Before moving into the generalized "refutation" of Ovid's doctrine, Bayle provides preliminary objections to these propositions, built on progressively articulating a series of contradictions he finds embedded within them. First, he argues, Ovid's two initial propositions are inconsistent. If a whole is homogeneous as the first proposition claims, then its "seeds" cannot bear contrary principles as the second suggests. Here, Bayle is again invoking his stance on the doctrine of actual parts. The relevant classical argument for the real existence of these parts is that any substance lacking such parts cannot be the bearer of contradictory accidents, that is, properties that exclude one another cannot belong to the same substance at the same time. If such contrary qualities belong to a substance, therefore, that substance must be an aggregate of real parts that can bear one or the other of these qualities but not both.[22] Prior to the ordering gestures of Ovid's divinity, then, chaos can either be homogeneous, or it can be composed of asymmetrical and discordant elements, but not both. Bayle also claims that the second and third propositions are inconsistent: "We cannot call that whole a mere heavy mass, in which there is as much lightness as gravity." Again, the presence of elements of a contradictory nature precludes their unification under one term of the opposition. Third, such a heavy mass cannot be conceived as an "inactive weight," because it contains a mixture of contrary principles without symmetry. These contraries must in fact be locked in a struggle with one another for primacy (the light parts attempting to rise and the heavy parts attempting to fall), which would be a strange description of "inactivity." Fourth, were the first three principles accepted, then the fourth and fifth would be "superfluous." Chaos would be disentangled simply by virtue of the elementary qualities (which "are a sufficient force") without the intervention of an external cause (i.e., God). I will return to this objection shortly, as it is crucial to Bayle's more developed "refutation" of Ovid's full "doctrine." Finally, the fourth and sixth propositions are false, "for since the production of sky, air, water, and earth, the struggles of cold and heat, moisture and dryness, heaviness and lightness would remain as great in the same body as they ever could have been before." Bayle's position here is that the end of elemental conflict is not the coming-to-be of an ordered and harmonious world, but the development of a dynamic system of tensions and conflicts (*Dict.*, art. "Ovid," rem. G).

After quickly presenting these "defects" in Ovid's propositions, Bayle supplies five "refutations" that develop them at length in relation to the doctrines of the atomists: (1) a refutation of the notion that chaos can be homogeneous, (2) a refutation of the eternal endurance of chaos prior to its ordering, (3) a refutation of the idea that a god is needed in order to disentangle chaos, (4) a refutation of the notion that the ordering of chaos signifies the end of the war of elements, and (5) a refutation, with special reference to human moral psychology, of the notion that the war of elements has ever, in fact, ended. In what follows, I will focus on the third and fourth of these.[23]

MATTER, MOTION, AND THE GENERATION OF WORLDS

The full refutation of Ovid's "doctrine of chaos" involves several distinct arguments, only a few of which I will discuss here. One of these critiques (the third) argues that Ovid is wrong to assume that the intervention of a god, or any equivalent external cause is necessary to disentangle it. Rather, the inherent energy generated by the natural antagonism of primordial bodies—the simple fact that they are in motion—is quite enough. Echoing the thesis that Descartes presents in both *The World* and the *Principles of Philosophy*, Bayle holds that given insensible material bodies in motion, and given the natural laws governing that motion, the world as we know it will emerge without any need for divine intervention. In an earlier refutation, Bayle extends this Cartesian position in his critique of Ovid, comparing the chaos of elemental bodies to a new wine in fermentation. Just as such wine requires only a mixture of differing bodies with differing qualities closed in a bottle to separate elements of the solids, vapors, and liquids and to ultimately produce wine of a complex bouquet, so too would the sheer flux of chaotic primordial bodies "ferment" over a finite duration into an emergent and complex world. But what is the Cartesian perspective that Bayle is working with here?

In *The World*, Descartes insists that God should be conceived as "the efficient cause of all things" and in the *Principles* that "God is the primary cause of motion" (*CSM*, 1:86 and 1:240). While this position (and its metaphysical extension in the *Meditations*) would be developed by Malebranche into a full-fledged doctrine of occasionalism, for Cartesian natural philosophy the proposition need not stretch so far. What about God as primary and efficient cause? Insofar as a Cartesian natural philosophy would refer to God at all, it would require *only* a "continuous and uninterrupted action" or "regular concurrence" of the conservation of the motion of matter. In other words, God as the efficient cause of all things means merely *that the motion of matter persists over time, subject to physical law*. Or perhaps even more specifically, we can conceive of God's action as a conservation of the regularity or rule-governed nature of the motion of matter. God's "action" here consists merely in ensuring that the motion of matter will continue to be governed by the laws of nature. This "action" is, if you like, simply the imputation of principles of regularity to a potentially chaotic world, and thus much more an Emedoclean or Hesiodic gesture than a Christian one.

Indeed, in Descartes' discussion of the "imaginary" and "hypothetical" world in *The World*—the clear locus of Bayle's considerations here—Descartes is clear that we need not even impute to God the injection of orderliness and regularity into the parts of matter themselves, but only the conservation of the natural laws governing the motion of matter as such:

> For God has established these laws in such a marvelous way that even if we suppose he creates nothing beyond what I have mentioned, and sets up no order or proportion within it but composes from it a chaos as confused and muddled as any the poets could describe, the laws of nature are sufficient to cause the parts of this world to disentangle themselves and arrange themselves in such good order that they will have the form of a quite perfect world—a world in which we shall be able to see not only light but also all the

other things, general as well as particular, which appear in the real world. (*CSM*, 1:91)

For Descartes, God creates only "so much matter all around us that in whatever direction our imagination may extend, it no longer perceives any place which is empty" (*CSM*,1:90), and he specifies further that this matter bears no qualities other than those of sheer extension (dimensionality, divisibility, shape, and diversity of motion conceived in terms of speed and directionality) (*CSM*, 1:90–91). In the Cartesian context, we need God to create matter, set it in motion, and establish the laws of nature governing that motion. Consider what this tells us about Descartes' attitude toward the orderliness of the world. Natural order need not be due to the perfection of the created world; after all, God could have created a chaotic mess, Descartes points out. Instead, all we need is extended matter in motion and the persistence of "ordinary laws of nature." Together these generate an orderly and regular world.

The way these claims impact Bayle's critique of Ovid's reliance on an ordering divine intervention is subtler than it first appears. Apparently unwilling to let himself slide into a naturalized atheism, Bayle's criticism is not so much that Ovid relies on the action of a divine principle, but rather that he locates that principle in the wrong place and makes it responsible for doing the wrong things. Ovid's mistake, that is, is to allow his god to find the basic elements of materiality already there before him, to make a series of ordering gestures—severing, binding, collecting, and enclosing—and thereby to impart motion to matter. Bayle instead insists that God must be the "author" of matter. But why?

It would be easy enough to claim that Bayle, like Descartes, remains fundamentally committed to a Christian theism, and that he sees Ovid's account as illegitimately rendering materiality coeval with divinity. But Bayle seems to have something more philosophical in mind. His real point—this holds true for Descartes as well—is not simply the onto-theological insistence that God must have created matter and must constantly intervene in the world to preserve its existence, but rather the natural philosophical claim that the existence of matter cannot be understood apart from its motion. Motion, as Descartes put it in *Principles*, is a primary mode of extended substance, as really inseparable from bodies as their extension itself, though dependent on that substantial extension (*CSM*, 1:232–33).

Bayle's argument works like this: if the organization of chaos involves God imparting motion to matter that already exists by severing, binding, collecting, and enclosing primordia, then the natural state of matter must be one of repose. But if matter is naturally at rest, then not only will we fail to understand how even a god could move it (since it is not ontologically dependent on this god, why should it not be capable of infinite resistance?), but more fundamentally, even if that god were able to intervene by imparting motion to matter, this would be a *disordering* of bodies and not their coherent resolution into a world (*Dict.*, art. "Ovid," rem. G).

Indeed, Bayle is quite clear elsewhere about the nature of his precise problem with the atomists. He rejects their assertions of the fortuitous origin of the things in the world and of the indestructible nature of *concreta*, but the world being given (and, for Bayle, authored by some external creative principle), in all other respects he takes the atomist analysis to be correct. In his "Leucippus" article, for example, he claims that "The epithets 'madman,' 'dreamer,' and 'visionary' are due to anyone who imagines that a fortuitous encounter of an infinity of corpuscles produced the world and is the continual cause of generation." Nevertheless, "If we give the same names to those who maintain that the diverse combination of atoms forms all the bodies that we see, we manifestly discover that we have neither taste nor any idea of the true physics" (*Dict.,* art. "Leucippus," rem. D). I will later return to this curious assertion that one who denies the reality of an atomistic physics is lacking in taste, but for now suffice it to say that Bayle holds that the division of complex bodies into irreducible material parts and the development of an account on that basis is correct, as long as it is shorn of the Epicurean reliance on the origins of the world in the chance encounter of bodies.[24] The same article asserts that this atomic basis for sensible entities is—most interpretations to the contrary—one shared by Cartesian natural philosophy. Indeed, the doctrine of the actual existence of materials parts of bodies (as opposed to their merely potential status, asserted by Aristotle and embraced by the Scholastics) was, in the late seventeenth century, generally shared by the major competing systems (though obviously rejected by Leibniz). As Thomas Holden puts it, for example, Cartesians and Newtonians "shared a doctrine concerning the status of material parts, holding that the undetached parts of material bodies are actual *concreta*, and not merely possible or potential beings. Each part exists as a concrete independent entity embedded in the architecture of the whole. So these undetached parts are actual parts: they are distinct beings, each of which exists even prior to any act of division. Although we may sometimes talk loosely of division as if it involved the creation of several things from one, in metaphysical rigor it is really just a separation or unveiling of so many pre-existent entities" (*HB*, 145).

To put this back in the context of Ovid's exordium, Bayle's critical position is that given that matter continues to move independently of prodding by God or any other external cause, given that it has many shapes, and given that its direction is not uniform (all of which Ovid admits), then there is no need for a god at all in order to understand the order of things. What begins by looking like a clumsy and illegitimate philosophical intervention into the cosmogony of a Latin poet by a committed Christian theist ends with the position that Ovid, as Bayle writes, "employs God needlessly and to no purpose in the construction of the world" (*Dict.*, art. "Ovid," rem. G). Ovid, that is, didn't need a god, and should have been more like Lucretius, who denied that the gods played any role in creation, who began only with insensible primordial bodies of different shapes possessing an inherent power of motion, subject to the vicissitudes of chance in the form of the Epicurean swerve, and which without the intervention of any external cause, collide, adhere into compounds, dissolve other compounds, and generally strive in a universal discord, all while producing the natural world in all its beauty, complexity, and horror.

THE THEATER OF VICISSITUDE

Bayle, of course, will not accept the Lucretian position wholesale. As mentioned earlier, he reserves a role for a theistic principle in his account of the nature of things. At the same time, he radicalizes Lucretius' philosophical melancholy into a continuum of antagonism, dissolution, and voraciousness that runs from insensible bodies to human sociality. Cartesian natural philosophy minimized the role of God to the creation of disordered and insensible bodies inseparable from a single and continuous action that conserves the sum of motion in the universe. Bayle—engaged in an energetic correspondence with Leibniz—reduces it even further to the selective emergence of the disorder that leads to *this* particular world rather than any other that could result from the chance encounter of bodies. While effectively accepting the fundamental principles of atomism by which nature is understood in terms of the discord of insensible *primordia*, and furthermore embracing the melancholic aesthetic of finitude reflecting a violent world shorn of the illusion of transcendental significance articulated by Lucretius, Bayle nevertheless rejects the role that the classical atomists reserve for chance in the tale of the emergence of the complexities of the extant universe. Even while describing the hypotheses of the Epicureans as "foolish and extravagant," Bayle writes, "All that could be denied them is that chance could produce such an assemblage of bodies as our world is, where there are so many things that persevere so long in their regularity, so many animated machines [*machines d'animaux*] a thousand times more industrious than those of human art." Rather, the production of such assemblages "necessarily requires an intelligent direction" (*Dict.*, art. "Ovid," rem. G).

On the one hand, this is nothing more than a pedestrian cosmological proof for the existence of God in the form of an argument from design, mobilized against the universalization of chance. On the other hand, even in this context, Bayle is clearly entranced by the subtlety of the Lucretian position. He recounts, for example, the answer given by the late-seventeenth-century atomist physiologist-philosopher Guillaume Lamy (in his Lucretian *De principiis rerum*) to the classical objection that since a random conjunction of characters would never produce Homer's *Iliad*, a chance clash of atoms could never produce a world.[25] Lamy argues that these cases are incomparable. Chance is unlikely to hit upon the particular conjunction of characters necessary to produce the *Iliad* among an infinity of other possible books. The construction of worlds requires no such precision, and by implication, while random printed characters will not produce the *Iliad*, they will produce *a* book, just as atoms will produce *a* world. To the objection that words formed by chance have no meaning, Lamy answers that the signification of words is a matter of convention and has no effect outside the institutions of language; but randomly conjoined atoms, being independent of such conventions, produce "considerable effects" in whatever arrangement they may stand (*Dict.*, art. "Ovid," rem. G). In response, Bayle points to a minor claim made by Epicurus and Lucretius—that their nonintervening, noncreating, and nonprovidential gods resemble men—and claims that this would require a *coup de hazard* as unlikely as the chance composition of the *Iliad* or a child scribbling a portrait of

Caesar with the skill of Michelangelo. Bayle's more extensive philosophical criticisms of Lucretius—whose poem he regards both as a literary masterpiece and the primary coherent foundation of the new natural philosophies—touch on similarly minor claims. They mainly serve to reinforce the sense in which Bayle's project involves the radicalization of Lucretian materialism and its dispersion among even avowedly non-atomist philosophers, rather than its nullification.[26]

For example, remark F to the "Lucretius" article begins by looking like a vituperate attack on Lucretius' denial of providence. However, Bayle's central complaint is that the philosophical poet's exemplary use of the fall of the mighty and the reversal of fortunes suffered by the elite ought to be more general. It is not only princes and admirals, seemingly secure in their good positions, who suddenly find themselves cast down by fortune, but all human beings, so "That which is most conspicuous in the history of man is the vicissitude of exaltation and abasement" (*Dict.*, "Lucretius," rem. F). Thus, immediately after claiming that the atomists are wrong to have attributed the origin of world to chance, Bayle himself universalizes fortune, arguing simply that Lucretius understood its bounds too narrowly. Where Lucretius sees the undetermined swerve of primordial bodies as allowing for the chance composition of the world and providing a mechanical foundation for understanding freedom, Bayle affirms the providential nature of the initial coming-to-be of the world, but then elevates the fortuitousness of the clash of natural bodies to the principle that governs all their subsequent activity.

Against the divine determinists and defenders of theodicy he points out that attributing this cycle of universalized indignity to a pedagogical God is incoherent. Not only are the innocent "punished" as often as the guilty, but history demonstrates that if there is supposed to be a hidden moral lesson for humanity here, then we are evidently incapable of learning it. While holding that grasping the relationship between fortune and providence is a better topic for theologians than philosophers or poets, Bayle nevertheless proposes an atomist solution which he claims Lucretius should have embraced. Even while denying that the gods concern themselves with our affairs, Lucretius could have supposed "that certain collections of atoms, to which he could give whatever names he pleased, were capable of jealousy with respect to man, and also of laboring invisibly in ruining exalted fortunes" (*Dict.*, art. "Lucretius," rem. F). In other words, the theses of Lucretian atomism ought to lead to a generalized pantheism, where the chance conjunctions of atoms are just as likely to produce invisible, sensate, intelligent, and malicious complex bodies as those of human beings.

A SLIT AS SMALL AS THE HUMAN MOUTH

I return now to Bayle's refutations of Ovid's exordium in order to show the deep sense in which he both incorporates and radicalizes the Lucretian aesthetic and account of the natural world. Where the refutation of the "doctrine of chaos" discussed earlier was aimed at the notion that the resolution of chaotic disorder required the intervention of a teleological principle exterior to the system of elemental bodies, Bayle's fourth refutation is aimed at Ovid's "thesis" that harmonious elemental aggregation would in fact follow from any disentanglement of chaos. This refutation is particularly significant for the way it moves rhetorically from the discord of elemental corpuscles and the voraciousness of time to the human, understood as an extreme example of natural violence and insatiable gluttony. Even while framed in Anaxagoran elemental terms, Ovid's own poetic language explicitly associates his primary natural principles with Lucretius' atomistic and indestructible *semina rerum*. Effectively, Bayle follows the logic of this association by substituting for the harmony-out-of-chaos thesis from Ovid's book 1, the metaphysics of ineluctable metamorphosis from Pythagoras' speech in book 15, built around a pursuit of an account of *quae sit rerum natura*—what the nature of things is (*Met.*, 15.60–478). This allows Bayle to pass, as does Lucretius, from elemental bodies compounded out of indestructible, insensible parts to the complex compounds of body and void engaged in the inexorable warfare of natural things. Beginning with the strife of inorganic compounds (crashing into one another, sticking together or repelling each other, augmenting or destroying complexes of bodies and void), he moves to their absorption in living bodies, those bodies themselves animated by the same fundamental principles of conflict as the inorganic, and eventually from insensate organisms to animals, and from animals to the human.

What we find in Bayle's Lucretian response to Ovid, then, is something akin to a metaphysical continuum of being. This continuum, however, is not fixed by a shared expression of energy, activity, or teleology, let alone a theological hierarchy of divine proximity. Rather, every level in the continuum is animated by the strictures of a natural mechanics of discordant corporeality, governed by what Bayle describes as ineluctable principles of action and reaction, all aimed at understanding metamorphosis and generation as processes of destruction, corruption, and disincorporation. Rather than recoiling from the melancholic bleakness he finds in Lucretius' poem—think, for example, of its grim end with a detailed description of the bloated rotten corpses littering the streets of Athens after the 430 BC plague (*DRN*, 6.1138–286)—Bayle insists that this is the fundamental aesthetic and conceptual expression of the poetics of the new philosophies of early modernity. He takes this stance not to censure Descartes, Gassendi, Boyle, and the rest (though he does of course criticize elements of their systems, just as he does with Lucretius), but rather as a fundamentally accurate description of their emerging modernity.

Thus, Bayle sees the exordium of Ovid's first book as standing in direct conflict with the metaphysics of vicissitude articulated in its last. Where Ovid writes, "O Time, thou great devourer, and thou, envious Age, together you destroy all things: and, slowly gnawing with your teeth, you finally consume all things in lingering death!" (*Met.*, 15.234–36), Bayle comments that this inevitable withering and destruction "has no other foundation than the conflict of bodies" (*Dict.*, art. "Ovid", rem. G). The world is an "engagement," in his terms, where "clemency or pity have no place," an "internecine war" among bodies of differing nature and quality, voracious in their appetites. Thus, against Ovid, Bayle writes, "nothing could be more improper than to present the four elements in a state of peace," because a cessation of chaos would set them against one another rather than reconciling them. Referring explicitly to Lucretius' account of change as death, Bayle writes,

> It is through their [bodies'] combat that nature becomes fertile; their concord would render her sterile, so that without the implacable war which they unleash wherever they encounter one another we should see no generation. The production of one thing is always the ruin of another. *Generatio unius est corruptio alterius.* That is a true philosophical axiom. (*Dict.*, art. "Ovid", rem. G)

This last passage is enmeshed in a web of intertextual citation, recitation, and printed marginal inscription. *Generatio unius est corruptio alterius* is a Scholastic commonplace adapted from

Aristotle's "The passing-away of one thing is the coming-to-be [*genesin*] of another thing, and the coming-to-be of one thing is the passing away of another thing."²⁷ Bayle, however, frames it as a paraphrase of Lucretius' often-repeated, "Whatever by being changed passes outside its own boundaries, at once this is the death of that which was before" (*DRN*, 1.670–71, repeated at *DRN*, 1.792–93, 2.753–54, and 3.519–20), even explicitly quoting Lucretius in marginal note 62. Thomas Lennon points to another somewhat sarcastic adaptation of the phrase by Bayle (*RB*, 178). When criticizing Molière's tendency to produce neologisms Bayle writes, "the birth of one word is commonly the death of the other" (*Dict.*, art. "Poquelin," rem. D). It is furthermore significant that this line is inscribed almost immediately after two quotations of Lucretius on the problem of inventing new Latin terms to translate Epicurus' and Anaxagoras' Greek (*DRN*, 1.137–39 and 1.830–33), and is coupled with yet another explicit citation of the *generatio unius* phrase (*Dict.*, art. "Poquelin," rem. D, cit. 25). Bayle's "true philosophical axiom," then, relies for its veracity on a complex series of textual repetitions and contextual displacements.

In accordance with the continuum of discordant bodies outlined earlier, Bayle thinks that all this is just as true of living bodies as of the quasi-atomic elements with which Ovid's exordium deals. The legacy of Lucretian atomism combined with Ovid's principle of incessant mutation constitute, for Bayle, a voracious metaphysics, the only one adequate to describe on the same discursive plane atomic bodies, elemental aggregates, material complexes, organic life, and human existence. Just as Bayle argues that Ovid was mistaken to think that cosmogenesis involves the orderly disposition of the elements of the world and the hierarchical stratification of a primordial chaos, so too does he insist that constant destructive and dissoluble becoming ought to have been the principle governing Ovid's account of living organisms. "Living bodies act in accordance with the order to engage in mutual destruction that Ovid should have supposed to be given by the author of the disentanglement of chaos," Bayle writes. "For it is true to the very letter that they feed only upon destruction: everything that serves for the support of their life loses its form and changes it state and its kind." This notion that at a fundamental level the very existence of living bodies depends upon patterns of strife and mutual disincorporation runs directly from plants through animals to the human.

Vegetables destroy the constitution and qualities of all the juices they can attract. Animals commit the same ravage upon all the things that serve them for food. They eat one another, and there are many kinds of beasts that make war upon one another for no other end but to devour such of their enemies as they shall happen to kill. In some countries men follow the same course, and everywhere they are great destroyers. (*Dict.,* "Ovid," rem. G)

Indeed, Bayle insists, the very abundance and seeming orderliness of commodities produced by the rise of urban-based mercantile capitalism provides the prime illustration of the voracious nature of corporeal existence itself:

I do not speak here of the carnage arising from ambition, avarice, or cruelty, or from the other passions as are the causes of war; I speak only of the effects of the care we take to feed our bodies. In this regard, man is a principle so ruinous and so destructive that if all other animals did as much in proportion, the earth would be incapable of furnishing them with sufficient provisions. When we see in the streets and markets of the great cities this prodigious multitude of vegetables and fruits and an infinite number of other things destined for the nourishment of the inhabitants, would not we say, here is enough for a week? Is it imaginable that this display is to be renewed every day? Would we believe that a slit as small the human mouth were a gulf, an abyss, which would devour all in so short a time? Nothing but experience can persuade us. (*Dict.,* "Ovid," rem. G)

Bayle would, like Lucretius, go on to speak of the "carnage arising from ambition, avarice, or cruelty, or from the other passions as are the causes of war," though his approach to the conflict of bodies which he sees as governing human sociality and history, is one never fully articulated. I will only mention that the next extended remark to the Ovid article deals at length with the insatiable conflict of the elements that constitute the human psyche, and what Bayle sees as the fundamental inability of reason to master the passions (*Dict.,* art. "Ovid," rem. H). Given this lack of restraint, the human is itself a further proof against the thesis that chaotic disordered antagonism has been resolved in an act of harmonious creation. Thus, the voraciousness that renders the slits of our mouths abyssal gulfs is not directly articulated in the spirit of social critique. It is rather, for Bayle, a proposition of descriptive ontology and natural philosophy. The principle of Ovid's "Time, thou great devourer" is located, for Bayle, at the heart of matter, running its course from insensible *primordia* to the complexity of human bodies (*Met.*, 15.234).

What is the relationship between this ineluctable ontology of vicissitude and the material form of Bayle's own encyclopedic text? On the one hand, we find a materialist cosmogony constantly at war with itself, insisting first on the necessity of an authorial God responsible for the existence of matter, but second, separating that creative act from the subsequent motion, agglomeration, and conflict that produce a world. The motion of matter is a metaphysical bearer of fortuity responsible for the universalization of chance, but also governed by the iron necessity of mechanistic physical law. The complex textual structure within which this ontology is presented, meanwhile, simultaneously models, activates, and resists these metaphysical principles. The sheer materiality of its typographical structure involves complex layers of textual disposition and contraposition that open multiple paths of reading, constructing a seemingly infinite series of channels through which its patterns of reference and critique can freely flow. The same elements of the material apparatus of the book that in principle force readers into inescapable, teleologically determinate paths through a text instead turn the *Dictionary* inside out, such that the edges of its pages expand to encompass the horizons of the Republic of Letters. Where typographical form is the material bearer of the metaphysical principle of necessity inherent in the act of reading, in the *Dictionary* it is fundamentally grounded on chance juxtapositions, aleatory connections, and even fortuitous readerly glances (whether our own as we peruse its pages, or Bayle's as he manipulated and organized the textual traces embedded in his library and commonplacing). Where we might think of the constitution of a philosophical text as the process of intervening in a chaotic conceptual world and imposing various forms of harmony and order upon it—philosophy, after all, is for some the language game of dematerialization *par excellence*—Baylean encyclopedic textual ontology insists that we conceive the result of a conceptual event (a philosophical cosmogony, if you like) as the emergence of living disorder from tranquilized harmony, a process that subjects the necessity of thought to the vicissitudes of matter.

CHAPTER 4

READING AND REPETITION

It is probable that the notions of singular and regular, distinctive and ordinary, have for philosophy an ontological and epistemological importance much greater than those of truth and falsity in relation to representation; for what is called sense depends upon the distinction and distribution of these shining points in the structure of a given idea.

Gilles Deleuze, Difference and Repetition

One of the extrinsic reasons for the success of René Descartes' *Meditations on First Philosophy* is the way it demands, especially in Mediations One and Two, that its readers approach it as an experiential and experimental process. In doing so, the *Meditations* calls attention to the physiological situation of the act of reading and writing a philosophical text as well as to the materiality of the page before its readers' eyes. This strategy constitutes a corporeal framework that is quickly overcome through a radical skeptical reduction of all sensible knowledge, adjudicated by the criteria of indubitability. In one of the most celebrated and disputed passages of the *Meditations*, even in the face of the disappearance of the veracity of external sensation, the meditator considers whether corporeality may still have its epistemological day. Sitting before a fire in his dressing gown, the meditator asks whether the sensations of his own body, its location, and its corporeal activity are something of which he can be certain. Pointing not only to his sense of his own clothed body and the warmth of the fire by which he sits, Descartes points to the very manuscript pages on which he is inscribing his meditative narrative, and presumably to its printed and bound instantiations in the hands of his readers. The corporeality of philosophical writing and reading thus becomes one more locus of skeptical interrogation that, like all the others in Mediation One, fails to withstand the destructive procedure of hyperbolic doubt. Madmen, after all, believe certain things to be true based on a performatively analogous set of evidence and, leaving aside the vigorous debate between Foucault and Derrida regarding the exemplary status of this stage of the reduction, the meditator points out (and Descartes clearly expects his readers to confirm this experience) that he is accustomed to dreaming nightly. In such dreams he is susceptible to deceptions identical to the corporeal situation he is now evaluating with respect to its indubitability. "How often, asleep at night, am I convinced of just such familiar events—that I am here in my dressing gown, sitting by the fire—when in fact I am lying undressed in bed!" (*CSM*, 2:13). Briefly he considers whether the physical sensation of paper constitutes an exception to the dreamer's world—"Yet at this moment my eyes are certainly wide awake when I look at this piece of paper" (*CSM*, 2:13)—but of course it does not. So much, it seems, for the ineliminable nature of scriptive corporeality in Cartesian philosophy.

Despite Descartes' urge to dematerialize the site of conceptual writing, figures of philosophical inscription nevertheless play a crucial role in the constitution of the Cartesian project. First, focusing on Descartes' manipulation of writing material I demonstrate that especially in the context of his account of corporeal and intellectual representation he constantly relies on images of paper, pen, and ink. Turning to Descartes' account of philosophical reading, I then explore both his critique of the book as a source of intellectual understanding and his apprehension before a community of readers who take up his texts in ways other than those he desires. Descartes simultaneously denigrates reading as a proper avenue for methodological thinking and imposes a method *for* reading on those who encounter his work. Finally, moving away from Descartes' own articulation of the figure of the book, I turn toward a set of problems that follow from the fragmentary textual status of one of his major works on philosophical method, *Rules for the Direction of Mind*. Focusing on metaphysical and epistemological problems of exemplarity and repetition as well as on the extravagant interpretive practices these have provoked in the text's twentieth-century reception, I argue that the logic of a set of rules governing practices of philosophical reading necessarily demand that a text purporting to be about method submit to the very methodological rules that it articulates. This demand is in fact levied by Descartes' own text, that is, it is an intrinsic scriptive element of Cartesian methodological thought as such.

PAPER, PEN, AND INK

Figures of paper, pen, and ink return in at least four contexts in the body of Descartes' philosophical writing: (1) the rejection of the notion that representative signs must resemble their sensory objects, (2) the articulation of a theory of communication without transmission in the account of the mechanics of sensation, (3) the intellectualization of scriptive figuration, and (4) the radicalization of the classical memory-prosthesis trope. The first of these is essential for Foucault's account of a key epistemic shift marking the distinction between what he identifies as the Renaissance and the Baroque *epistemes*: Descartes' general critique of iconic systems of resemblance and similitude together with their differentiation from the logic or semiotic of ideational representation (*OT*, 50–70). In a *locus classicus* for the development of anti-similitude, representationalist semiotics, in *The World* Descartes writes of words in general:

> Words, as you well know, bear no resemblance to the things they signify, and yet they make us think of these things, frequently even without our paying attention to the sound of the words or to the syllables . . . Now if words, which signify nothing except by human convention, suffice to make us think of things to which they bear no resemblance, then why could nature not also have established some sign which would make us have the sensation of light, even if the sign contained nothing in itself which is similar to this sensation? (*CSM*, 1:80)

In his many other attempts to argue that ideas—whether purely intellectual or derived directly from sensible things—need in no way resemble that which they represent, he consistently makes reference to the very pen with which his arguments are inscribed on the manuscript page (or, as I will discuss in the following section, the pens with which he encourages his readers to mark in the margins of his books). Against the Scholastics, Descartes holds that the stimulation of an external sense organ and the subsequent stimulation of the brain need involve no transmission of a sensible *species* shaped like or similar in any other way to the object or objects perceived. Nor, in the milieu of a post-Galilean mechanism, must the transmission of sensible motion from the object through the sense organs to the *sensus communis* in which they are united involve an unmediated transmission of a given movement.[1]

It is true that nothing but motions of the body are required in order for a diversity of sensations and feelings to be produced in the mind, but these ideas "have no likeness to the movements in question," as Descartes puts it in the *Principles of Philosophy* (*CSM*, 1:284). Ink, pen, and paper function as the primary examples of a causal locus for the production of nonresembling images and affects:

> If the tip of the pen is pushed across the paper in a certain way it will form letters which excite in the mind of the reader thoughts of battle, storms and violence, and emotions of indignation and sorrow; but if the movements of the pen are just slightly different they will produce quite different thoughts of tranquility, peace and pleasure, and quite opposite emotions of love and joy. (*CSM*, 1:284)

These affective sensations are excited when the local motion of the sensory organs of our bodies is impacted by the local motion of external bodies, and, in Descartes' example, the efficient cause of that external motion is the tip of the pen scraping slowly across the surface of the paper.

This motion, of course, does not pass directly through empty space between the paper and the eye, as Descartes' identification of space with extended corporeality leaves no room for the void this would require. Rather, it is the motion of the extremely fine and slippery corpuscles that Descartes postulates constitute light, which produce motion in the eye when they impact it. These motions, moreover, do not need to form a motive image that resembles their cause (the pen corpuscles, the ink corpuscles, the paper corpuscles, the aggregate corpuscular text they constitute). "We must at least observe," Descartes explains in the *Optics*, "that in no case does an image have to resemble the object it represents in all respects, for otherwise there would be no distinction between the object and its image. It is enough that the image resembles its object in a few respects. Indeed, the perfection of an image often depends on its not resembling its object as much as it might" (*CSM*, 1:165). His example here is of the image produced by an engraver's burin. Engravings consists "simply of a little ink placed here and there on a piece of paper" yet just as in the *Principles* "they represent to us forests, towns, people, and even battles and storms" (*CSM*, 1:165).[2] These engravings evoke a multitude of objective qualities, yet the only sense in which the ink-and-paper image resembles the objects it represents is with respect to shape. Descartes is quick to add, however, that the "resemblances" of the shapes in the engraving to the shapes of what they represents are in fact mediated (seemingly beyond all direct resemblance) by the flatness of the paper and the distorting projections the rules of perspective require. Note that even the qualifications Descartes reserves in the *Optics* for the nonresembling, nonpictorial representational process involved with an engraved image (it need not resemble its object "as much as it might" or "in all respects") are superseded by the parallel figure in the *Principles*, where the letters formed by the nib of the pen scraping across the page resemble in *no sense at all* the representations they produce.

Descartes not only holds that representational ideas need bear no significant resemblance to their *ideata*, but also that the language of the "transmission" of representations is fundamentally flawed, whether in the form of sensible *species* for the Scholastics or of atomic *eidola* sloughed off by the edges of compound bodies for the neo-Epicureans. Again, the argument is articulated through figures of pen, paper, and ink. In *Rules for the Direction of Mind*, Descartes argues that the stimulation of an external sense organ is conveyed to the *sensus communis* not by way of the propagation of motion along some imagined corporeal path, but immediately and "without an entity passing from one to another" (*CSM*, 1:41). He goes so far as to specify that this propagation of motion should be understood to be a form of virtual inscription on the sensitive faculty:

> I understand that while I am writing, at the very instant when singular characters are printed [*exprimo*] on the paper, not only does the nib of the pen move, but the slightest motion of this part cannot but be received simultaneously by the whole pen. All these various motions are traced out [*designo*] in the air by the end of the pen, even though I do not conceive anything real

passing [*transmigrare*] from one end to the other.³ (*CSM*, 1:41; trans. mod.)

The connection between the parts of the body's sensory apparatus (i.e., any given sense organ and the *sensus communis*) is as tight as that between the two ends of the pen during the act of writing. Thus, just as nothing (even motion) is transmitted from one end of the pen to the other while I write on paper, so too does nothing "pass" from the affected sense organ to the brain. Rather, a motion in one is a motion in the other.

This single motive event (affection of the organ : reconfiguration of the *sensus communis* :: pen nib marking characters on paper : pen end tracing motions in the air) involves a multiplicity of "alphabets" of sensation that submit to the prohibition on the resemblance or similitude of representations and their objects. Despite nothing being "transmitted" from one end of the pen to the other and despite the inseparability of the movement of the one from the other, "the pen as a whole does not move in exactly the same way as its lower end; on the contrary, the upper part of the pen seems to have a quite different and opposite movement" (*CSM*, 1:42). The nib of the pen expresses the characters of the alphabet of the affection of the sense organs on the paper of the extended body, while the end of the pen (or the feather of Descartes' quill) traces the ethereal yet sensible characters of cognitive representation on the folded surfaces of the brain.

Of course, Descartes will insist against the Aristotelians that not all that is intellect was first in the senses. His classic example for this is the intellectual nature of our ideas of geometrical figures. In Mediation Five, Descartes claims "figures such as geometers study" do not even exist in the extended world, "except perhaps ones so small that they cannot in any way impinge on our senses" (*CSM*, 2:262). His explanation of this claim is tightly folded into the figure of paper and the images drawn upon it. Most geometrical figures are constructed with straight lines, yet "when we examine through a magnifying glass those lines which appear most straight we find they are quite irregular and always form wavy lines" (*CSM*, 2:262). Thus, our experiences with "triangular figures drawn on paper" cannot have been the basis for our formulation of the true idea of any geometrical figure. Rather, the idea of a true triangle, for example, must have already been innate in us such that it actually guided and directed our sensible apprehension. The power of the ideas innate in the Cartesian mind allow it to render the body of the paper triangle invisible, shining through it so intensely with the natural light of the intellect that the irregular and wavy lines of ink on its surface become ordered and regular geometrical abstractions. The paper and its figure disappear entirely. When we gazed at it, "we did not apprehend the figure we saw, but rather the true triangle" (*CSM*, 2:262). Paper and ink return, but only on the far side of a deduction that begins with the geometrical idea, as Descartes claims that it is the idea of the perfect triangle, which serves as the condition for my recognition of the imperfect ink-and-paper figure.[4]

Figures of paper, pen, and ink have a final major locus in Descartes' work: memory. In many of his texts, Descartes recapitulates the standard link between writing and memory: the practice of writing functions as a supplement and corrective to memory. This notion is neither original to Descartes nor particularly interesting in itself. What is fascinating, however, is the extremity to which Descartes is willing to take the usefulness of paper and writing conceived as a mechanical memory prosthesis. In the *Rules*, for example, Descartes recommends that we use paper to evacuate our memory of everything not absolutely necessary to the methodologically structured attempt to discover certain truths.[5] Proposing the development of a concise mnemonic alphabet, he claims, "we shall leave absolutely nothing to memory but put down on paper whatever we have to retain, thus allowing the imagination to devote itself freely to the ideas immediately before it" (*CSM*, 1:67). Or further: "If we can set it down on paper, we never need commit to memory anything that does not demand our constant attention" (*CSM*, 1:69).[6] These written symbolic lists will play another role, namely, the materialization of the site for methodological procedure Descartes names "enumeration." (*CSM*, 1:67).

In an April 1, 1640 letter to Marin Mersenne, Descartes distinguishes between a corporeal and intellectual conception of memory, arguing that the former may be distributed around the brain and even outside of the human body as such. Just as the lute player can be understood to have part of his memory located in his hands, "When we have read a book, not all the impressions which can remind us of its contents are in our brain. Many of them are on the paper of the copy which we have read" (*CSM*, 3:146).[7] Thus, not only methodologically constructed paper instruments serve the externalization of our memory but so too do the totality of books we have read, such that the material world begins, little by little, to resemble a mnemonic library of the mind or a vast memory palace whose architecture is congruent with the order of all physical things. Even the internal structures of the body all begin to be transformed into surfaces for memorial inscription. In letters to both Lazare Meyssonnier and Denis Mesland, Descartes proposes that insofar as it has not been dispersed in the world of books and symbolically constructed lists, our corporeal memory consist of impressions or traces in the brain. In an act of remembering, these traces "dispose" the body to motion or affect the soul such that they provoke a recapitulation of prior movements (literal for the body, metaphorical for the soul). As imprinted by motion and passion in this sense, the brain and its memories are figured as a sheet of paper and "folds which remain in the paper after it has once been folded" such that it is "easier to fold again in that way than it would be if it had never been so folded" (*CSM*, 3:143 and 233). Thus, despite what initially looked like a dematerialization of the site of corporeal inscription, the Cartesian brain—the site of corporeal memory, imagination, figuration, and sensation—becomes a sheet of paper.

THE CRITIQUE OF ALL BOOKS

Descartes' autobiographical account in the *Discourse on Method* of his turn away from books and libraries toward "the book of the world" is well known. He claims to have been a voracious reader of all the books he could get his hands on while a student at La Flèche and observes that reading good books "is like having a conversation with the most distinguished great men of past ages—indeed, a rehearsed conversation in which these authors reveal to us only the best of their thoughts" (*CSM*, 1:113). This conversation with the great dead authors through the medium of their books, however, was not enough for him. Just as after traveling too long in foreign lands one "becomes a stranger in his own country" despite having learned to appreciate the value of other cultures and to better judge one's own, so too does spending too much time in conversation with the books of the dead lead to an inability to formulate and judge reasoning related to the present (*CSM*, 1:113–14). The problem is not only that reading too much results in an alienation from the familiar home of one's own mind, but is also related to the precise nature of the books that Descartes was reading before embarking on his travels.

Specifically, Descartes' critique in the *Discourse* is that the Scholastic framework of these books remains dialectical, that is, they offer merely probable reasoning rather than certain demonstrations (*CSM*, 1:117). Even more precisely, these Scholastic textbooks (as these seem to be what Descartes is referring to) are philosophical compendia or miscellanies, whose science "is compounded and amassed little by little from the opinions of many different persons" instead of proceeding in the simple fashion that would be undertaken by any man of good sense (*CSM*, 1:117).[8] Rather than organic models of scientific and philosophical investigation, they are merely histories of dialectical utterances by recognized authorities.[9]

In early notebooks kept between 1619 and 1622, Descartes gave two accounts of his own practices of reading, or rather, of his attempt *not* to read.[10] "In my youth," wrote the still very young Descartes, "when I was shown an ingenious invention, I used to wonder whether I could work it out for myself before reading the inventor's account. This practice gradually led me to realize that I was making use of definite rules" (*CSM*, 1:2). This refusal to engage with books gives rise to Descartes' first intuitions regarding methodological thinking. Part of the reason this strategy is possible is that Descartes holds the contents of books in low esteem when it comes to evaluating their usefulness for the discovery of knowledge: "In the case of most books, once we have read a few lines and looked at a few of the diagrams, the entire message is perfectly obvious. The rest is only added to fill up paper" (*CSM*, 1:2). Descartes reformulates and specifies these criticisms of books several years later in the *Rules*. Having come upon a book whose title seemed to promise a new discovery or an advance in knowledge, Descartes relates, he would first mobilize his "innate discernment" to see whether he could achieve the same result without depriving himself "of this innocent pleasure through a hasty reading of the book" (*CSM*, 1:35).

Despite the problems involved with depending on knowledge contained in books, according to Descartes, we ought to read the writings of the ancients insofar as they have instrumental value, "for it is of great advantage to be able to make use of the labors of so many men" (*CSM*, 1:13). Put anachronistically, we should thus read the history of philosophy as rational reconstructionists, seeking to reconstitute textual arguments not only as they are, but also as they should be. Nevertheless, the texts of the ancients pose a great danger to any would-be rule-governed thinker. Their subtleties may intrigue us too intensely and their obscurities may lead us astray. In the standard translation, Descartes describes the problem physiologically: "Traces of their errors will infect us and cling to us against our will and despite our precautions" (*CSM*, 1:13), and this does indeed capture the spirit of what Descartes writes. To read is to open the mind to infection and the errors of the ancients are unfortunately extremely contagious. However, I would like to suggest that in the same passage, Descartes is self-consciously mobilizing a figure of the book—or more specifically, the ink-wet pages of a recently written or printed book—to explain the danger of the editions of ancient philosophy circulating with ever increasing speed under the seventeenth-century explosion of the production of printed objects and their distribution. There is considerable danger that when we take up the books of the ancients, to retranslate the passage just cited, "if we read them excessively, the stains [*maculae*] of their errors will adhere [*adhaereo*] to us against our will and despite our precautions" (*AT*, 10:366). In other words, Descartes' metaphor is physiological, but not necessarily only with respect to understanding the history of philosophy as a particularly virulent vector for intellectual disease. If we read the ancients excessively, the ink on the pages of their books—the material instantiation of their many errors and sophistic subtleties—will adhere to our fingers. The closer we read their works, the more the physical traces of their pages mark our bodies and transform us into ink-stained thinkers inscribed with the signs of ancient errors, no matter how carefully we attempt to reason.

Thus, Descartes' critique of reading the ancients is part of a generalized and metaphorically *materialized* critique of reading and writing as a legitimate part of the philosophical endeavor. First, figurally speaking, if we study the pages of the ancients too intensely, the ink of their errors will adhere to our fingers. Second, once *scriptores* have taken up a position on some question, they tend to employ needlessly subtle argumentation to persuade their readers. In other words, the construction of a certain kind of argument is a cover for a type of intellectual lethargy. These arguments are constructed not in order to investigate the certainty and clarity of a given proposition, but simply in order to defend that proposition as such, regardless of its truth. Descartes has in mind what he saw as the absurdities of the *disputatio* tradition, which was later mocked relentlessly by Bayle. Third, if these writers should, by happenstance, have stumbled upon something demonstrably certain and evident, they "present it enfolded [*involutum*] in various ambiguities"—wrapped together like the leaves of a book hidden behind a false and deceptive binding—"either because they fear that the simplicity of their argument may depreciate the importance of their findings, or because they begrudge us the plain truth" (*CSM*, 1:13). Fourth, even if all writers were actually "sincere and open" and wrote in "good faith," a reader would still not be able to determine whom to believe, for no writer says anything that escapes contradiction by another. Discerning who the real *auctores* are (i.e., the writers with *auctoritas*) through a comparison of texts is not directly possible, because for difficult questions it is more likely that the few are correct than the many. Finally, even if all our potential authors agreed, we would still be lost. The best we could do in this case would be to engage in the practice of the art of memory, thereby training ourselves to reproduce by rote the structure of their demonstrations. According to this procedure, we would be able to produce only a history of the search for truth, something that for Descartes is not, in itself a guarantee of intellectual aptitude.

Descartes extends his critique of pedagogical works based on techniques of collecting and commonplacing when, in an August 1638 letter to the Dutch physician Cornelius van Hogelande, he excoriates Johann Amos Comenius' *Conatuum comeniorum praeludia* (1637), which proposed an anthologized encyclopedia that would collect all the useful claims in all books hitherto published. The problem here is double. First, Comenius' encyclopedia lacks an efficacious disposition or arrangement, since the principles by which it organizes its claims are not derived systematically but are externally imposed on the collection of "particular truths." Second and more crucially, Descartes conceives the multitude of books as a disorderly and "scattered" realm in which true propositions are hidden beneath layers of obfuscation and disorder. "The particular truths which are scattered in books," he writes, "are so detached and so independent of one another that I think one would need more talent and more energy to assemble them into a well-proportioned and ordered collection . . . than to make up such a collection out of one's own discoveries" (*CSM*, 3:119).[11] These discoveries, in the Cartesian context, must depend on the exposition of the foundations of the sciences rather than being merely an assemblage of individual propositions, and one who possesses the necessary acumen to articulate these foundations "would be wrong to waste his life finding scraps of knowledge hidden in the corners of libraries" (*CSM*, 3:119). One only capable of this library scouring, Descartes furthermore claims, would lack the requisite intellectual power to distinguish good propositions from bad and to systematically order the commonplaced knowledge collected. In *The Search for Truth by Means of Natural Light*, Descartes makes similar claims that frame the problem even more starkly, in that the satisfactory collection of compendious knowledge is framed as completely impossible: "Even if all the knowledge that can be desired were contained in books, the good things in them would be mingled with so many useless things, scattered haphazardly through such a pile of massive tomes, that we should need more time for reading them than our present life allows, and more intelligence for picking out the useful material than would be required for discovering it on our own" (*CSM*, 2:401).

In his extremely polemical open letter to Voetius (Gilbert Voét, the Dutch theologian responsible for the condemnation of Cartesian philosophy by the faculty of the University of Utrecht), Descartes adds another dimension to his critique of textbook compendia: their entire argumentative force relies on fallacious appeals to authority and a tendency to address complex problems with abbreviated syllogisms that never engage the real issues. The problem with scholars, presumably including Voetius, who rely on "standard texts and indexes and concordances" is that though these print technologies allow them to "pack their memories with many things" they emerge neither wiser nor better for it (*CSM*, 3:222). To become "learned" (*eruditio*) by immersing oneself in encyclopedias, compendia, and textbooks is, on Descartes' account, to allow the natural light of one's mind to be dimmed, in that "those who seek learning from these sources become accustomed to placing equal trust in the authority of any writer . . . so little by little they lose the use of their natural reason and put in its place an artificial and sophistical reason" (*CSM*, 3:222). One who pursues this path has thereby forsaken "education" (*doctrina*), or the improvement of natural intelligence and character by frequent and repeated "discriminate" reading of only those books containing well-formed arguments concerning foundational notions (connected to discussion with the educated and with a practice of "continually contemplating the virtues and pursuing the truth") (*CSM*, 3:221–22).[12] Indeed, the letter to Voetius extends this attack on compendia, and the practices of erudition Descartes associates with them, to include syllogistic dialectic as such. In opposition to their easily "isolated syllogisms," Descartes insists on the careful inclusion of every step required for reasoning through a problem in order to arrive at truth, something he holds "can almost never be expressed in syllogisms" since they allow their readers to proceed as if the particular stages of an argument can be dealt with in isolation from its broader systematic unfolding and thus demand a piecemeal reading strategy that effectively fragments the good order of the mind.

Having mastered the existing textbooks and forsaken the practices of scholarly commonplacing, the *Discourse* relates, Descartes embarks on several years of travel, the value of which is greater than the reasoning of any scholar, since the judgments made therein have consequences far greater than those made in a study (the precise distinction is between "les raisonnements que chacun fait touchant les affaires qui lui important" and those made by "un homme de lettres dans son cabinet") (*AT*, 6:9–10; *CSM*, 1:115). Eventually, however, Descartes turns away from the book of the world once again: "I resolved one day to undertake studies within myself" (*CSM*, 1:116). Descartes' path leads, first, from the textbook compendia of the Jesuit classrooms and library at La Flèche, second, to the great book of the world consisting of exposure to a diversity of situations and a multitude of practical judgments regarding matters of personal concern, and finally, to himself, in order to begin to answer the question "What path in life should I follow?" The fruit of Cartesian textual selection, in other words, is not a turning away from the metaphorics of the book, but the progressive transformation of the reader into a textual object: the narrative voice of the *Discourse on Method*, conceived as "a history, or if you prefer, a fable," recounting the tale of Descartes' attempt to discover the proper way of directing his own reason (*CSM*, 1:112).

INSTRUCTIONS FOR READING

Less well known are the remarks Descartes offers about how the *Discourse*, the accompanying *Essays*, and his other writings ought to be approached by his readers. In the brief preface to the *Discourse*, Descartes mentions only that his readers are permitted to split their encounter with the book into six different sessions corresponding to its six parts (*CSM*, 1:111). A December 20, 1637 letter to the Dutch physician and philosopher Plempius (Vopiscus-Fortunatus Plemp) suggests not only that Descartes expects his readers to linger with his arguments, but also that he wants them to purchase their own copies of the book. "I do not expect a sufficiently ripe judgment on my book from anyone who only reads it hurriedly through a borrowed copy," he writes (*CSM*, 3:77). The reasons for this have to do with the systematic nature of Cartesian argumentation. Comprehension of the claims made in the later sections of the *Essays*, Descartes insists, require the reader to retain in her memory everything from the earlier ones. At the same time, the propositions presented at the beginning of the text gain the force of proof (i.e., rise from the status of axiomatic presuppositions to rationally demonstrated conclusions) only on the basis of the evidence presented in the later ones. But why must his readers purchase rather than borrow his book? One clue may be found in an October 1637 letter to an anonymous correspondent where Descartes insists that the *Geometry* must be read with pen in hand, so the reader is able to reproduce Descartes' calculations in its margins (*AT*, 1:457–58). Descartes himself originally perused the "customary lore" of mathematics in this fashion, he relates in the *Rules*, only accepting textbook claims as true after he had gone over the calculations himself (*CSM*, 1:17–18). Strangest of all, we might conjecture, the book must be purchased by its readers in order to avoid a borrowed copy being stained with experimental blood! In part 5 of the *Discourse*, Descartes claims that a necessary condition for understanding his arguments regarding the mechanical nature of the human body is the dissection of an animal heart. Since his demonstrations will be accomplished through a redescription of the function of the heart and the major arteries attaching to it, the reader of the *Discourse* is urged "to take the trouble, before reading this, to have the heart of some large animal with lungs dissected before him" (*CSM*, 1:134). What follows is a detailed account of exactly what the reader should be shown during this anatomical demonstration. These instructions are so specific, in fact, that it is impossible to imagine the dissection taking place properly without a copy of the *Discourse* itself close at hand.

The "Preface to the Reader" in the *Meditations* offers a different set of instructions. Given the performative nature of this text, it is unsurprising that Descartes demands readers who are willing to engage not just with the structure of his arguments but also with the meditative, reflexive framework of his rhetoric. "I would not urge anyone to read this book," he writes, "except those who are able and willing to meditate seriously with me, and to withdraw their minds from the senses and from all preconceived opinions" (*CSM*, 2:8). The force of the arguments in Mediations One and Two, after all, relies primarily on a radical skeptical suspension of the reader's opinions and beliefs, and absent a willingness to at least hypothetically engage in that reduction, they present only the narrative of a philosophical meditator. From within the purview of this suspension, however, they invite interrogation of both the logical efficacy and completeness of each move demanded by the text. In the second set of Replies, Descartes acknowledges the work this demands from his readers. Where those approaching the *Discourse* had been granted leave to read it in six separate sessions if they were unable to digest the whole at once, readers of the *Meditations* are urged "to devote several months, or at least weeks, to considering the topics dealt with" in Mediation One "before going on to the rest of the book" (*CSM*, 2:94).

There is a second aspect to Descartes' instructions for reading the *Meditations*. His readers, Descartes insists, must suspend the practices of textual engagement appropriate to the textbook compendia and commonplace books he rejects in his autobiographical narratives. "Those who do not bother to grasp the proper order of my arguments and the connection between them, but merely try to carp at individual sentences, as is the fashion, will not get much benefit from reading this book" (*CSM*, 2:8). From the perspective of contemporary practices of philosophical reading, this demand may sound so transparent as to be tautological. In the mid-seventeenth century, however, it had a very precise sense: the *Meditations on First Philosophy* is not to be read as a collection of independent syllogistic arguments or particular philosophical and scientific claims devoid of broader context. Rather, its structure must be understood to unfold systematically and to have been organized deliberately, without presupposing a set of categorical tables or generic divisions that would lend it an intellectual structure external to the order of its arguments. Furthermore, Descartes specifies in the second set of Replies that it has been constructed according to an analytic rather than synthetic method of demonstration, which is to say that it is structured as an art of *discovery* such that its reader will arrive at its axiomatic first principles (Descartes describes them as "primary notions") herself, rather than simply adopting them from the outset because they happen to accord with general sensory experience (*CSM*, 2:110–11).

When Descartes claims that the analytical method of demonstration at work in the *Meditations* compels belief only in the reader who is attentive to "even the smallest point," he does not mean that analysis consists primarily in the minutiae of syllogistic structure. To the contrary, the idea is that the *Meditations* is a text that demands that its readers immerse themselves directly in the development and order of the arguments, taking seriously its injunction to move *through* the philosophical problems its meditator encounters rather than simply evaluating them individually from a perspective external to the disposition of the text.

The *Principles of Philosophy* offers an even more elaborate theory of reading and even more specific instructions for the reader of the Cartesian text. This book is written precisely in the style of the *cursus* textbooks Descartes had previously condemned, though without their reliance on the collection of authoritative quotations.[13] Descartes had, in fact, twice proposed to Mersenne (in letters of November 11, 1640 and December 1640) that his text—which he describes as both a *cours* and an *abregé*—be bound in the same volume as a classical Scholastic compendium, mostly likely that of Eustache de Saint-Paul. In addition to the "series of theses which will constitute a complete textbook of my philosophy," the *quaestiones* in Eustache would be supplemented by Descartes' anthology of commentaries on these topics advanced by various philosophers. It would also include his own commentary on the issues and the history of the discourse regarding them (*CSM*, 3:156–57). The proposed text was also to contain a systematic, synthetic comparison of the *Principles* to Eustache's *Summa philosophica quadripartia*. The result was to be a textbook that would be more useful to students than even the instruction of their teachers, since as the students begin to understand Scholastic philosophy "they will learn to scorn it at the same time" (*CSM*, 3:161).[14]

When the *Principles* was published in 1644, it lacked the proposed presentation of and attack on Eustache, but in its place the 1647 French translation was accompanied by a "Preface to the Reader." This preface laid out elaborate instructions for making use of the volume. In it, Descartes identified five "levels of wisdom" (*degrés de sagesse*). The first consists of notions so self-evident that no profound meditation of any sort is required to apprehend them. The second involves all that we learn through sense experience. The third involves knowledge acquired through conversation with others. The fourth recapitulates Descartes' notion of reading as a conversation with the dead, initially raised in the *Discourse on Method*. This level, Descartes claims, involves "what is learned by reading books—not all books, but those which have been written by people who are capable of instructing us well; for in such cases we hold a kind of conversation with the authors" (*CSM*, 1:118). Just as in the *Discourse*, however, this conversation with the dead is superseded by another, more important, level of wisdom, namely, philosophy: "the search for first causes and the true principles which enable us to deduce the reasons for everything we are capable of knowing" (*CSM*, 1:181).

Presumably, the *Principles* is meant to be a guide to this fifth level. Reading it, then, must require a particular strategy that differentiates it from those books that are merely "written by people who are capable of instructing us well." How then, are we to read the *Principles*? Just as Descartes had earlier suggested that a few good works should be read many times over instead of the reader dispersing her attention in the multitude of books flooding early modern Europe, so too will the *Principles* require multiple passes by its readers. Descartes' initial suggestion here is surprising: the first time through, the *Principles* should be read like a work of fiction. "I should like the reader first of all to go quickly through the whole book like a novel, without straining his attention too much or stopping at the difficulties which may be encountered. The aim should be merely to ascertain in a general way which matters I have dealt with" (*CSM*, 1:185). A second reading will focus on the argumentative reasoning the text presents. In cases where the arguments or the meanings are initially unclear, Descartes suggests, the reader must "mark with a pen the places where he finds the difficulties and continue to read on without a break" (*CSM*, 1:185). Just as Descartes insisted that the *Geometry* (and presumably the other essays accompanying the *Discourse*) must be read with pen in hand, with the reader recapitulating problems and argumentative difficulties by writing in the margins of the book, so too does the *Principles* demand a physical, scriptive engagement with the surface of its pages. Turning a third time to the book after having marked its difficulties, Descartes claims, "I venture to think that he will now find the solutions to most of the difficulties he marked before" (*CSM*, 1:185). If not, the solution is yet one more reading, which Descartes guarantees will result in the discovery of the solution to any remaining obscurities. In short, Descartes' "Preface to the Reader" recommends a specific methodological procedure for its readers' interactions with the Cartesian text, namely written engagement with the pages of the physical book and a structure of repeated reading that, given a properly attentive reader, will render its seeming obscurities clear and its apparent confusions distinct.[15]

THE EXTRAVAGANT TEXTUALITY OF
RULES FOR THE DIRECTION OF MIND

Several of the previously cited passages from Descartes' early notebooks demonstrated his alliance of a particular mode of encounter with books and his earliest formulations of philosophical method. Earlier, I emphasized the sense in which Descartes' refusal to read books announcing new inventions in favor of seeking to work out for himself the promised discoveries gave us insight into the way he conceived philosophical reading as such. The remainder of this chapter will focus on the other implication of those passages: the refusal to read as he reconstitutes inventions by means of practical experimentation coupled with his own "innate discernment" gradually leads Descartes to realize that he is making use of a series of definite rules for thinking. These rules—formulated in a negative encounter with books—eventually become the earliest threads of Cartesian philosophical method. In roughly 1628, these insights are drawn together in Descartes' first truly rigorous philosophical treatise, an unfinished, fragmentary, and somewhat chaotic text composed, in part, of denunciations of the unfinished, fragmentary, and chaotic in favor of the total, systematic, and rule-governed. *Rules for the Direction of Mind* is a methodological treatise on the proper conduct of one's reason. The text proposes 36 distinct rules, but only manages to articulate the first 21 of these (and the final 3 lack the full discussion Descartes accords the rest).[16] The entire text is wracked with lacunae, missing words, repeated and rephrased arguments. A text that provides a set of rules to follow for the right conduct of one's thinking, the *Rules* in general (and Rule 8 in particular) have the peculiar characteristic of demanding that a form of textual reiteration occur at the heart of the very appearance of Cartesian method. Rather than simply offering a once-discovered and already-articulated path for the reader to follow, the *Rules* function, in a manner of speaking that Descartes would reject but by a metaphorics he explicitly proposes, as an experiential text, demanding that its readers not merely follow the method it prescribes, but use its rules to forge a method for themselves. These methods will, of course, finally coincide in the universal, each governed by the strict structure of *mathesis universalis,* their articulation nevertheless absolutely particular.

The reflexive structure of the *Rules* extends beyond any ordinary conception of Cartesian epistemology. Descartes illustrates Rule 8 with a strange example: the first task of methodological thinking must be the generation of the structure of method itself. A resolve to reflexive methodological ordering, this example is repeated no less than three times in the text of a rule that outlaws all superfluous and repetitive considerations from the body of method. This rule and its reiterative structure provide an important resource for understanding Descartes' neglected early methodology, entailing a number of surprising consequences: they imply a Cartesian theory of exemplarity, elevate repetition to methodological principle, and provide a derivation of reflexive subjectivity without recourse to the *cogito.* I begin by examining the content of Rule 8's explicit claims, which insist on the necessity of the principle of ordering while also defining the limits of method. Moving to a consideration of the rule's examples, I explore the problem of reflexive methodological self-constitution, whereby a single rule of method is to be understood with reference to the generation of the very methodological structure in which it appears. This investigation requires a philological analysis of the repetitive structure of that example, which has important philosophical consequences for the relationship among Cartesian method, example, and repetition. Finally, I demonstrate that this relationship entails the constitution of a specific form of Cartesian subjectivity by way of Rule 8 that prefigures the later positions of the *Discourse* and the *Meditations on First Philosophy* without relying on their mode of argumentation.

The *Rules* has often been interpreted as little more than a fragmentary prolegomena to a method not fully articulated until 10 years later. This is the position most often taken in the critical literature, which either unhappily dismisses the unfinished text as a fragmentary propaedeutic to a never-written Cartesian logic, or relegates the *Rules* to the status of an early (though perhaps fuller) elaboration of the rules presented in the second part of the *Discourse.* In recent decades, however, there has been an explosion of interest in the *Rules* along an entirely different line, seeking to understand the text as an autonomous and systematic work in the Cartesian corpus. On the one hand, this new approach has been fueled by the discovery of enough new textual evidence to produce three late-twentieth-century scholarly editions and one critical translation.[17] On the other hand, it has been driven by the extension of earlier historical research in the most classical vein of Descartes scholarship, such that Étienne Gilson's philosophical genealogy of Descartes' relation to medieval Scholasticism has yielded both Jean-Luc Marion's re-alliance of the early Descartes with Aristotelianism and André Robinet's interpretation of the *Rules* in terms of sixteenth-century Scholasticism and Ramism.[18] As this mode of research has demonstrated, the autonomy and systematicity of the *Rules* extend far beyond any ordinary description of Cartesian epistemology, or at least beyond an approach that simply overlays the early text with conceptions gleaned from the *Discourse*, the *Meditations*, or the *Principles of Philosophy*.

Any investigation concerning the rigorous structure of Descartes' fragmentary text must take into account the strange history of absence and textual loss that surround it. To begin with, no rigorously Cartesian version of the *Rules* exists. On February 14, 1650, three days after Descartes' death in Sweden, an inventory was made of the philosophical and scientific papers he had brought to Stockholm. This inventory, by all rights, ought to serve as the unshakable foundation on which to build an historical account of the *Rules,* standing as the earliest philological evidence for its existence. Yet after the fashion of all documents pertaining to the elusive *Rules,* the original of the inventory has been lost and only copies remain.[19] An issue as apparently minor as the status of an inventory that offers proof for authenticity of the fragmentary work could be easily dismissed were not the history of the *Rules* fraught with such textual multiplication and disappearance of original documents. As no original version of the *Rules* remains in existence, the major differences between the various copies considered to be authentic have been a driving force behind much contemporary scholarship dealing with this work.

In essence, the *Rules* as we know the text today has four sources. I will describe them in detail not in the name of affected pedantry, but because I hope that the reader will get a sense of the difficulties and even absurdities bound up with charting the history of a text like this. What they demonstrate, among other things, is the radical difficulty of pinning down exactly what a text is and where it comes from once we assume that it is somehow metaphysically divorced from a particular site of material instantiation, a theme I will return to later in the chapter.

First, the complete text remained unprinted (except in fragmentary translations and summaries) until the 1701 publication of Descartes' *Opuscula Posthuma*.[20] The *Opuscula* edition (referred to as the Amsterdam text) is most likely based on a now-lost copy of the original autograph made by the Dutch Cartesian Jean de Raey, though possibly on the basis of a different copy (also lost) made by Ehrenfried Walter von Tschirnhaus.[21] The earliest printed version of the *Rules* is therefore two steps away from the original, as it is a printing of a lost copy made from the lost autograph.

A second copied version (the Hanover text) was discovered among Leibniz's papers in the nineteenth century, but its status is very much in dispute. Either it was purchased by Leibniz from the Amsterdam doctor and Spinozist Georg Schuller sometime between 1670 and 1678 (the date is disputed) or it was sent to Leibniz by Tschirnhaus in 1683. The argument for the former position rests on a note in Leibniz's papers that declares he had purchased several folios from Schuller, a manuscript of the *Rules* among them (*A*, 6.3:60–61). More recently, several scholars have argued that this note is in fact a fabrication, forged by Leibniz to divert money intended for ducal library book purchases into alchemical experimentation. In this case, the Hanover text would be a copy sent to Leibniz by Tschirnhaus in 1683, made on the basis of the Tschirnhaus' lost copy of Clerselier's (subsequently lost) copy of the autograph.[22] Thus, there is little to definitively adjudicate whether the Hanover text is a copy of the same copy of the original that serves as the source of the Amsterdam text, a direct copy of the original autograph, or a copy from any other copies that may have been made.

Third, complicating matters further, Leibniz heavily amended the Hanover text, which contains many lacunae and errors, and the alterations effectively constitute yet another extant text, since they are assumed to be corrections made on the basis of Leibniz's viewing of the original manuscript.

Fourth and finally, de Raey's copy (the probable lost source of the Amsterdam text) was likely used as the basis for a 1656 Dutch translation by Jan Hendriksz Glazemaker, an artisan involved in many Dutch editions of Descartes and Spinoza and an associate of Tschirnhaus. While subject to the vagaries of translation, this printed version (the Netherlands text) has the sole advantage of being the only edition almost certain to have a source as close to Descartes' original manuscript as the Amsterdam text.[23] As should be unsurprising at this point, the pedigree of even this translation is in dispute, with one scholar claiming that Glazemaker had already died by the time the translation was made.[24]

Tremendous efforts have been made to certify the unity of the various texts, most turning on Giovanni Crapulli's speculation that all so-called extant texts are based on a single, mysterious, lost copy of the original (*CR*, x–xii). These efforts, however, remain speculative. Even if we were to grant that all these variations could be traced back to a single source (presumably Tschirnhaus' copy), the Amsterdam text would then be a printed copy of a manuscript copy of a manuscript copy of the autograph (*Opuscula Posthuma*-de Raey-Tschirnhaus-Descartes), the Hanover text would be a manuscript copy of a manuscript copy of the autograph (Leibniz-Tschirnhaus-Descartes), and the Netherlands text would be either a printed translation of a manuscript copy of the autograph (an unknown translator publishing in Glazemaker's name-Tschirnhaus-Descartes) or a printed translation of a manuscript copy of a manuscript copy of the autograph (Glazemaker-de Raey-Tschirnhaus-Descartes). Whether Crapulli is right or wrong, the extant texts of the *Rules* thus constitute a sorry lot.

One reason the fragmentary nature of the text and its early modern instantiations are important is that internal textual conflict and lack of a definitive edition have led to interesting developments in contemporary scholarship that reflect the structural metaphysics at work in Rule 8. A first example of this relates to the admirable audacity the *Rules* has called forth from its editors. While all editors of the *Rules* must make a decision about which text to rely on (Charles Adam and Paul Tannery choose the Amsterdam text, Heinrich Springmeyer strongly favors the Hanover text, Marion balances the two, etc.), Crapulli's edition takes this to a new level. While taking account of all extant texts, Crapulli privileges Glazemaker's Dutch translation (the Netherlands text) to the extent that much of what he presents as the definitive text of the *Rules* is a *de facto* retranslation into Latin from Glazemaker's seventeenth-century Dutch. His project then, is no less than the reconstitution of a nonexistent original text based on evidence obtained from what are, at best, a copy three degrees of separation from the original (Amsterdam), a copy of indeterminable distance from the original (Hanover), the emendations of that copy (Leibniz), and a translation of a copy of the original (Netherlands).

A second example of the scholarly extravagance the situation of the *Rules* provokes is the work of Jean-Paul Weber. Based on an intensely rigorous historical-philological analysis of the differences between all extant copies, Weber has attempted to trace the composition of Cartesian method via a genetic decomposition of the text. His rigorously detailed project seeks to identify the historical affinities of various sections of the work and thus to assign each a date of composition. In this manner, he claims to have discovered the genetic stages of early Cartesian method itself and to have reconstituted what amount to *fifth, sixth, and seventh* versions of Descartes' *Rules,* each corresponding to a particular historical phase of its production.[25] For my purposes, what is most interesting about these conflicting editorial precepts is that the wild proliferation of the *Rules* coupled with the impossibility of locating the material origin of an interminably repeated text reflect the conceptual structure of the *Rules* itself. The *Rules*, I will demonstrate, mobilize a very peculiar and powerful sense of textualized method, one that grips its readers in an inescapable compulsion to repeat. Its fragmentary status belies a structural totality that precludes the option of escape by closing off the very possibility of a realm exterior to the methodological principles it articulates.

ORDER, DISPOSITION, AND METHOD

Turning away from the complex textual situation of the *Rules*, we can begin to assess what it has to say regarding Cartesian method. Rule 5 rigorously defines method for the first time: "The whole method consists entirely in the ordering and arranging [*ordo et dispositio*] of the objects on which we must concentrate our mind's eye if we are to discover some truth" (*CSM*, 1:20). Even before delving into the differences among intuition, deduction, and enumeration (Descartes' three distinct methodological procedures), we can see that rigorous ordering of the objects of investigation lies at the heart of Descartes' method. This should be unsurprising, as such ordering is perhaps the most essential methodological rule found later in the *Discourse* (*CSM*, 1:20). This ordering and arrangement, in fact, stands at the very center of methodological thought, protecting us from the dangers of error and deception, and offering a path out of their maze into the clear light of certainty and truth. "This one rule," Rule 5 continues, "covers the most essential points in the whole of human endeavor. Anyone who sets out in quest of knowledge of things must follow this rule as closely as he would the thread of Theseus if he were to enter the Labyrinth" (*CSM*, 1:20). Rule 4 had described the necessity of this thread and our entrance into this labyrinth: "We need a method if we are to investigate the truth of things" (*CSM*, 1:15). There, Descartes defines method in terms of its pragmatic value rather than its form: "By 'a method' I mean reliable rules which are easy to apply, and such that if one follows them exactly one will never take what is false to be true or fruitlessly expend one's mental efforts, but will gradually and constantly increase one's knowledge until one arrives at a true understanding of everything within one's capacity" (*CSM*, 1:16). He goes on to identify this method with *mathesis universalis*—"a general science which explains all the points which can be raised concerning order and measure irrespective of subject matter" (*CSM*, 1:19)—and he resolves "to adhere unswervingly to a definite order, always starting with the simplest and easiest things and never going beyond them until there seems to be nothing further which is worth achieving where they are concerned" (*CSM*, 1:19).

In its broadest sense, Rule 8 is one that offers respite from the inexorable march of analysis, deduction, and enumeration demanded by the earlier rules. It reads: "If in the series of things to be examined we come across something which our intellect is unable to intuit sufficiently well, we must stop at that point, and refrain from the superfluous task of examining the remaining items" (*CSM*, 1:28). While this claim abrogates the rules for reading Cartesian philosophy Descartes would later articulate in the "Preface to the Reader" of the *Principles* (there, Descartes would have demanded that rather than stopping the investigation we run through it a second, third, and fourth time), it nevertheless provides an important aspect of Descartes' methodological thought. By circumscribing the positive limits of methodological, rule-governed thought, Rule 8 allows rigorous epistemological procedure to stop when it encounters an essentially unanswerable question. Yet in the course of explicating these limits the rule moves far beyond any simple explanation of a methodological step in a search for clear and distinct knowledge. A strange series of reiterations mark the structure of the text, developing a logic of repetition and reflexivity. As I will argue, these reiterations figure the *Rules* as a text that continually wraps around itself in an infinitely repeated self-positing movement, allowing nothing to escape the grasp of its necessity. The entire series of rules reinscribe themselves and their reader in a single point of their own structure, inexorably moving into the rule-governed fissure of return. Far from standing only as gesture or arbitrary movement, this repetition of rules within rules involves a decisive configuration of Cartesian methodological thought as such. Positing both its own necessity and that of ordered thinking in general, Rule 8 demands that rule-governed thought be interpreted as universally constitutive of thinking substance.

There are two major functions of Rule 8. First, it is meant to focus the intellect on those terms of an investigation that are absolutely necessary while allowing it to pass over those whose elucidation is inessential. In other words, methodological order is necessary when we examine "whatever constitutes an integral step" in the argument, but merely useful for other relations (*CSM*, 1:28). In this way, Rule 8 tells us that methodological investigation may breach the strict order of epistemological objects set up in the preceding rules in order to concentrate on those that advance the whole path of reasoning toward its goal. Thus, its first function seems to promise the thinker freedom from the burden of inexorable investigation, lightening the load of methodological thought. This freedom, however, is merely apparent. While Descartes' exposition emphasizes this meager liberty from the principles of order and enumeration, the corollary of his claim is that with regard to "integral steps," order and enumeration are inescapable. Indeed, despite a tone that seems to frame this rule as one that allows greater methodological freedom for those who accepts its stricture, Rule 8 demands that we abandon these superfluous temptations for thought. In other words, while we are free to dismiss the irrelevant as soon as we have established a chain of causation or logical priority, methodological thinking itself is limited to the necessary. Descartes surreptitiously uses this rule to jettison everything in excess of and supplemental to pure rational investigation, invoking the necessity of examining (to repeat) "whatever constitutes an integral step in the series" that leads from relative to absolute terms or vice versa.

The second general function of Rule 8 is to define the limits of method by granting the intellect leeway to cease investigation of a particular area upon recognizing its arrival at a fundamentally obscure term or unanswerable question. Descartes is quick to point out that this limitation of methodological knowledge is in fact an acceptable and positive outcome of the application of the rules as a whole. Because these rule-governed limits do not stem from any "defect of intelligence" but rather from "the obstacle which the nature of the problem itself or the human condition presents," grasping the limits of knowledge is itself a positive form of knowledge and a satisfactory outcome of rule-governed methodological thought (*CSM*, 1:28–29). In other words, this aspect of the rule simply explicates the conditions for methodological teleology and the satisfaction of reason's desire: "results so satisfactory that there is nothing further they will desire to achieve" (*CSM*, 1:28). But this *telos* brings knowledge of the limits of method itself under methodological jurisdiction, as through it we are able to understand the point at which the project of positive understanding becomes futile. In other words, Descartes' claim is not merely that we can be aware of our own ignorance, but that this ignorance is a decisive and definitive aspect of methodological thinking in general. As I shall suggest shortly, the subordination of limitation and finitude to method does more than this. It also instantiates the necessity by which methodological thinking turns back on itself; reflexively inventorying its own capacity for thought, method's first task soon becomes its self-articulation.

ONE EXAMPLE OR ANOTHER . . .

In order to examine this methodological reflexivity, I now turn to the examples Descartes offers in Rule 8, or rather to the three sets of examples offered in what some commentators have described as various textual layers. Descartes' first example details the manner in which one might apply the entire battery of rules, and Rule 8 in particular, to a problem he was to definitively solve 9 years later in the *Optics* (the derivation of an anaclastic). First one runs back through a series of relative terms to an absolute (the example used is the concept of a "natural power"). This absolute must then be intuited in itself, after which the investigator retraces her steps from this absolute to the question at hand. In other words, beginning with a fully enumerated series of particular truths about light and its refraction, the investigator reasons backward and more deeply until intuiting the concept of a "natural power" that grounds their connection. With the base of this certitude to stand on, she then reexamines all the previous steps until a solid chain of reasoning has been established and the anaclastic receives its definition (*CSM*, 1:28–29).

As Descartes is giving "one example or another" (*CSM*, 1:28, trans. mod.) to illustrate the rule, he quickly moves to a very different kind of example, one he describes as "the finest example of all" (*omnium noblissimum exemplum*) (*CSM*, 1:29).[26] This second example should be substitutable for that of the application of method in the derivation of the anaclastic. Yet from the moment it is announced, Descartes' second example is inextricably inscribed within a chain of valuation, set above and apart from all the rest of its possible kindred examples. So what, for Descartes, constitutes "the finest example of all?" It is nothing less than the procedure of methodological thinking. Thus, with one of the earliest examples of the rhetorical gesture that is most characteristic (and exemplary) of the Cartesian corpus, Rule 8 makes a reflexive move. Rule 8 proposes that a rule for methodological thinking is best explained via the example of the constitution of methodological thought itself.[27]

This "greatest example of all" is located at precisely the textual site where the fragmentary nature of the *Rules* makes it extremely difficult to interpret. It is articulated through a series of textual repetitions with a powerful structural function and subject to vehement editorial dispute. The problem is that rather than simply articulating the task required by this example and moving on to the next rule, Descartes repeats it no less than three times:

1. "Setting oneself the problem of investigating every truth for the knowledge of which human reason is adequate" is "something everyone who earnestly strives after good sense should do once in his life."
2. "It is necessary, once in our life, before we set out to go after things to be known in particular, carefully to have inquired as to what sort of knowledge human reason is capable of attaining."
3. "To ask: What is human knowledge and how far does it extend?" is "the first question of all to be examined by means of the rules . . . something which everyone with the slightest love of

truth ought to undertake at least once in his life."[28] (*CSM*, 1:30–31)

To different degrees of comprehensiveness and with emphases on different points, the longer explanations linked to each of these three epitomized repetitions determine this particular example to be the proper elaboration of the process of rule-governed methodological thought. The task at stake in "the problem of investigating every truth for the knowledge of which human reason is adequate" (*CSM*, 1:31) is not grasping the totality of possible objects of investigation, but rather reflecting on the proper method of thinking. Rule 8, that is, designates structured consideration of methodological thinking in general as the primary example of method itself, and identifies the example that best illustrates the application of a particular rule in the *Rules* as the generation of the entire set of rules that constitute the text.

The first iteration of the example begins by affirming the priority of the intellect, and distinguishing it from its subordinate faculties. It continues by declaring the necessity of ordering and enumerating "all the paths to truth which are open to men, so that [the investigator] may follow the one which is most certain." It concludes with an affirmation of the second consequence of Rule 8, the limitation of method to its proper questions (*CSM*, 1:30). Like the first, the second iteration proposes inquiry into the nature of human reasoning itself as a task prior to that of investigating "particular" problems. Descartes explicitly considers the problem of method's reflexive self-formation, arguing that it needs no external or prior ground in order to constitute itself. "Our method in fact resembles the procedures in the mechanical arts, which have no need of methods other than their own, and which supply their own instructions for making their own tools" (*CSM*, 1:31). Just as the blacksmith must forge an anvil, hammers, and tongs before attempting swords and helmets, methodological investigation first seeks to define and delimit its own structure before turning to "philosophical disputes or . . . mathematical problems" (*CSM*, 1:31).[29] The third iteration repeats its predecessors, proceeding in a similar manner and discussing each point with slightly more detail. It defines the first task of rule-governed thinking as that of investigating "human knowledge and how far it extends," claiming that to "define the limits of the mental powers we are capable of possessing" is neither "arduous" nor "difficult." Likewise, "to seek to encompass in thought all the things contained in the universe" is not "an immeasurable task" because "nothing is so multifaceted or diffuse that it cannot be circumscribed by certain limits or arranged under a certain number of headings by means of the method of enumeration" (*CSM*, 1:31).

So why the repetitions of the example? Do they constitute a methodological violation or are they necessary for the structure of the text? As Descartes is giving "one example or another" to illustrate the rule, this second example (the first is the anaclastic) can be nothing more than a repetition of the first. A particular case illustrating a general rule, its structure and meaning ought not vary in any essential sense from that of any other possible example. To do otherwise would be to violate Rule 8's exclusion of the unnecessary by way of the injunction "to refrain from superfluous labor" (*CSM*, 1:28). Thus, a Cartesian example must be a member of a set of mutually substitutable statements or discursive situations, all of which are reducible to the general characteristic that defines their set. In other words, as a repetition of the anaclastic example, "the finest example of all" ought to have been excluded from the text altogether. If the rules are themselves governed by the legal model they articulate, then Rule 8 requires that the investigation avoid every nonessential step. Consequentially, if the example of the anaclastic is an adequate one, then this second example—including all three of its iterations—ought not to appear in the text.

But is this description of Cartesian exemplarity correct? Certainly one can distinguish at least two different functions of examples. Either they stand as the paradigmatic element of a general concept, or they do the work of explanation by way of transposition into other contexts. Thus, on the one hand, we can conceive the example as a unique and superlative interpretation, while on the other it can be taken as an instantiation of a rule, an occasion for induction, or an aid to understanding. These distinctions roughly mirror the differences between the Platonic and Aristotelian senses of *paradeigma*, and can also be understood in terms of a difference between the denotative example (necessarily linked to what it exemplifies; figure taken as figured) and the connotative example (related arbitrarily to what it exemplifies; a metaphorical metaphor).[30] My analysis of this moment in Descartes' text begins with a simple axiom: the *Rules* cannot violate the methodological rules it prescribes. This axiom is authorized by Descartes' own posing of the generation of rules for methodological investigation as an example of methodological thinking. Therefore, a text that articulates the rule-governed nature of discursivity must, as a presumably valid discourse, subject itself to its own strictures. This is a necessary component of any text that lays claim to rigorous systematicity, and at the very least, Descartes' account of the origins of methodological thought (and thus of any methodological text) demands that we adhere unswervingly to this protocol. If method both supplies its own tools and demands a rational reckoning of itself, then there can be no moment prior or exterior to the juridical force of methodological reason.[31]

Perhaps both these sets of comparison are still too rough. Notice that the occasion for differentiating between these two conceptions of exemplarity is limited to the internal analysis of any particular example. As long as we isolate a single Cartesian example from its textual context, it is easy to claim that examples need not be equivalent. If we isolate, fragment, and textually scatter these examples on the model of the compendia and Scholastic commonplace books that Descartes rejected while composing the *Rules*, then the claim that some Cartesian examples are better than others (or even just nonsubstitutable) is not problematic. However, if we take seriously Descartes' claims regarding the integral conceptual structure of books worth reading, and if we assume that Descartes would have placed his own work in this textual category, then it becomes clear that Descartes' examples are never merely examples in themselves. The notion that they could be isolated in this fashion entails a general hermeneutic that dispenses with system, structure, and methodological derivation in favor of a mere aggregation of constituent elements (sentences, syllogisms, principles, tropes, words, rhythms, etc.). One may not even claim to examine various series of such elements, since the very arrangement of elements in a series presupposes the ordering systematicity that the move to isolated constituents disallows. Approaching the problem of exemplarity from this perspective and keeping in mind Descartes' exclusion of all that is unnecessary from methodological thought, it follows that in order to be constituted as Cartesian *exemplum*, any particular example must have already submitted to the principle of identity and substitutability that marks the example proper.

Or so it would seem. Recall that Descartes is asking us to "take the finest example of all." A formally unnecessary example—in principle methodologically excluded—is described as the best of all possible examples within a context where all examples should be systematically substitutable. This example, furthermore, calls for nothing less than the methodological discovery of the rules for methodological thinking itself.

EXEMPLARY INSCRIPTION, MATERIAL AND IMMATERIAL

Recall the radically fragmented and conflicting nature of the extant texts that are the basis for our contemporary reconstruction of the *Rules*. One of the most crucial points on which the various manuscripts diverge concerns the status of a large portion (almost 40%) of Rule 8, specifically the section that contains the three iterations of the "finest example of all."[32] While including all of them in his edition, Adam effectively dismisses their philosophical significance. Noting the series of semantic and syntactic similarities along with the discrepancies between the Amsterdam and Hanover texts, he speculates that the whole of what I have identified as the first iteration of "the greatest example of all" is a draft version that would have been discarded had Descartes ever finished preparing the text for publication (*AT*, 10:485–86).

If Adam is correct, the iterations' repetition may be reduced to the mere unedited redundancy of an unfinished text. His analysis turns on the absence of any reference to memory as an auxiliary faculty of the intellect in the first iteration, which names only imagination and sense perception (*phantasia* and *sensus*) (*CSM*, 1:30). By contrast, he emphasizes the third iteration where Descartes writes, "while it is the intellect alone that is capable of knowledge, it can be helped or hindered by three other faculties, namely imagination, sense perception, and memory" (*imaginatione, sensu, et memoria*) (*CSM*, 1:32). His basis for exclusion of the passage containing the first iteration therefore relies on a general reading of the *Rules* in which Descartes includes memory, positing four auxiliary faculties rather than three.

Adam ignores, however, Descartes' careful problematization of the status of memory in relation to imagination (both as *phantasia* and *imaginatione*) and sense perception in Rules 7, 11, and 12. In those contexts, Descartes writes, memory "is left with practically no role to play" as it is "weak and unstable" (*CSM*, 1:25), "no different than the imagination" (*CSM*, 1:38), and must be "constantly refreshed and strengthened" by the understanding (*CSM*, 1:43).[33] Indeed, the methodological strategy presented in the *Rules* generally turns on the minimization and externalization of memory through specifically textual and material means. Given the unreliability of human memory and because the activity of recollection distracts the intellect from the systematic pursuit of knowledge, Descartes encourages us to make use of "that happy invention—the practice of writing." We should "leave absolutely nothing to memory," but instead "put down on paper whatever we have to retain, thus allowing the imagination to devote itself freely to the ideas immediately before it" (*CSM*, 1:67). Or again, "if we can set it down on paper, we never need commit to memory anything that does not demand our constant attention" (*CSM*, 1:69). Likewise, the methodological procedure of enumeration allows us to engage in "a continuous and wholly uninterrupted sweep of thought" by which the imagination runs back and forth along complex chains of deductive propositions (*CSM*, 1:25). Moving ever more quickly through the web of written or mental symbols denoting their argumentative connections, this procedure eventually enables the intellect to grasp the whole system of deductive connections in a single mental glance, reforming the mobile temporality of deduction so that it resembles or imitates as far as possible the motionless simultaneity of intuition: "I shall run through them several times in a continuous movement of the imagination, simultaneously intuiting one relation and passing on to the next, until I have learnt to pass from the first to the last so swiftly that memory is left with practically no role to play, and I seem to intuit the whole thing at once [*rem totam simul videar intueri*]" (*CSM*, 1:25).

Furthermore, both *Studium bonae mentis* (a short treatise written approximately 7 years before the *Rules*) and *The Search for Truth by Means of Natural Light* (a fragmentary dialogue probably from the same period as the *Rules*) follow the three-faculty model and exclude memory.[34] Finally, this position on the status of memory is also reflected in an untitled fragment from the early notebooks where Descartes rejects Lullist *ars memoria*. Memory, in this early text, cannot be distinguished from the intellect or the imagination, and "the true art of memory" is an operation of the intellect performed without the help of some fourth faculty (*AT*, 10:230). While the temptation to dismiss such early writings as expressing philosophical positions soon to be abandoned may be strong, this fragment from the notebooks is *also* the site of the first articulation of what would become Rules 5 and 10, as well as the third (and most important) methodological rule of the *Discourse*.³⁵ In the notebooks, Descartes first proposes the principle of methodological ordering, its centrality to rule-governed thinking, and the procedure of imposing an arbitrary order where none is readily apparent. As even Adam eventually admits, the philological reduction of Descartes' triple articulation "is probably only a conjecture" (*AT*, 10:486).

Much of the persuasive force of Adam's position relies on the Hanover text's transposition of portions of the text to the end of the rule. Though he does not explicitly claim that the first iteration is expendable *because* it is displaced, he nevertheless begins by relying on this transposition as the basis for philological skepticism and only later turns to the problem of memory. Because the location of the section is textually disputable, the argument goes, it is easy to claim that its contents are intrinsically expendable.³⁶ This is in fact the position taken by Weber in his genetic analysis of the *Rules*. While Weber's careful analytical work deserves the greatest respect, he, like Adam, eventually relies on the first iteration's exclusion of memory in order to make his historical claims. He argues that though this absence coincides with the *Studium*, at the same time it contradicts "all the other texts of the *Rules*."³⁷ As I have just demonstrated, this is simply not the case. Furthermore, despite the vehemence of his rhetoric and the tortuously exquisite character of his genetic recomposition, Weber's argument suffers from a number of other glaring problems. He—like Springmeyer—simply assumes that the Hanover text is a more genuine copy of the lost original, denying the radical undecidability that marks the fragmentary and conflicting nature of the surviving versions of the work.³⁸ Thus, first, he accuses Adam of an illegitimate editorial conservatism rather than merely pointing out that the latter has chosen to rely on the Amsterdam text. Second, Weber mischaracterizes the state of the Hanover text itself, claiming that the transferred fragment of Rule 8, like its counterpart in Rule 4, has been "transposed into an appendix in the original manuscript." While the text from Rule 4 is indeed found at the end of the entire Hanover text, the passage from Rule 8 is in fact merely shifted to the end of its own rule, not to an appendix. Finally, in his most problematic, fascinating, and compelling move, Weber claims to have reconstituted "a treatise finally conforming to Descartes' explicit intentions, unrecognized for three centuries."³⁹ Whereas Crapulli's edition merely had the audacity to claim that it had comparatively reconstituted a nonexistent original text, Weber asserts that he has

(1) demonstrated the diachronic genesis of the text, based on the state of one of three manuscripts, itself a copy of indeterminate distance from the original; (2) produced a reordered and reedited original text, modified according to the results of this genetic analysis; and (3) clearly discerned "the explicit intentions of Descartes" as the principle of this reordering and reediting, such that his reconstituted text is not only more original than the copies, but also more authentic than the lost document written in Descartes' own hand. His claims imply, in other words, that he has discovered the *Rules for the Direction of Mind* that even Descartes never wrote, one that nevertheless guided and defined the philosopher's methodological procedure for his early investigation and writing.

From a perspective that takes seriously the textual repetition that governs the *Rules*, the audacious conclusion of Weber's project must be held in the highest esteem. From the same position, however, one is forced to notice that Weber has betrayed the very possibility of such a repetition in his zeal for the extratextual and immaterial origins of philosophical inscription. Despite his fidelity to "explicit intentions," Weber ignores the essential move by which the *Rules* marks method as reflexive, reiterative, and self-forging and thus turns a deaf ear to the metaphysics of self-constitution that govern the texts' own account of rule-governed thinking. If "our method in fact resembles the procedures of the mechanical crafts, which have no need of methods other than their own, and which supply their own instructions for making their own tools" (*CSM*, 1:31), then the only viable path to the origin of Cartesian method is the exposition of its own methodological structure. Searching behind and below the text for an originary position supposedly prior and thus external to it, Weber's project lands in contradiction.

Weber's exclusion of the entire disputed passage might have allowed him and Adam to defend their positions on somewhat more legitimate grounds. The singular philosophical advantage of this move would be that it relieves Rule 8 of its tension with regard to exemplarity, dispensing not only with "the finest example of all" but also with the example of the derivation of the anaclastic. In other words, the content of the rule itself ought to disallow *either* the anaclastic example *or* the rule-governed thought example on the same grounds by which it ought to exclude the repetition of the iterations within the latter. Thus, a strategy of dispensing with the entire disputed passage has the advantage not only of restricting the text to a single case (the rule-governed thought example, insofar as it is limited to the second and third iterations and defined as a single development), but also of removing any overt identification of that case with exemplarity. In fact, the passage that would be excluded this way is the only part of the rule that directly marks the discussion of both examples as examples *per se*. If Weber and Adam are allowed to exclude both the anaclastic example and what I have called the first iteration of the rule-governed thought example, *exemplum* would occur in the rule only twice, and then merely in passing as Descartes explains the analogy to craftsmanship. The second and third iterations of method's self-constitution would remain, but they would now serve to further unfold the rule's primary claims regarding the positive limits of methodological thinking. Thus, the remaining text would be nothing more than a further elaboration of the rule itself, included only for reasons of certainty in the service of pragmatic value: "Now to prevent our being in a state of permanent uncertainty about the powers of the mind, and to prevent our mental labors from being misguided and haphazard . . ." (*CSM*, 1:30); or later, "But the most *useful* inquiry we can make at this stage is to ask . . ." (*CSM*, 1:31, my emphasis). The necessity of exemplarity and its link to repetition would be abolished, as none of the remaining text would thus be marked as exemplifying Rule 8.

The question is whether or not the full excision of the passage in dispute (including both the example of the anaclastic and "the finest example of all") does in fact dispense with the centrality of exemplarity and repetition for Rule 8. Focused as it is on the structure of rule-bound investigation and its necessary starting point, the surviving text continues to move well beyond either of the immediate implications of the rule itself: to restrict methodological consideration to the necessary and recognize the limits of method and their positive epistemological value. Notice, however, that even the proposed exclusion cannot avoid another doubling of the discourse, each repetition now beginning with the second and third iterations. As mentioned earlier, Adam's focus on the disappearance of memory as the term at issue allows him to conflate these repetitions into a single "development" following the excludable "simple sketch" (the first iteration) and Weber follows his lead. While Rule 8 itself disallows all repetition other than that of a necessary example, Adam and Weber cannot shear the force of *that* repetition from the text by way of their proposed exclusion. In the absence of the passage in question, my analysis merely shifts one level closer to the interplay of iterations.

Until now it may have seemed that the structure of repetition at work in Cartesian discourse necessitated a certain reliance on exemplarity. Now, however, it should be clear that this cannot be the case. Cartesian textual repetition gives rise to exemplarity, or rather, repetition gives the example its textual necessity. Only *because* they stand as multiple iterations of a rule demanding singularity are these examples *exempla* in the specifically Cartesian sense. If we accept Adam and Weber's position that the passage must be ignored, then we can no longer claim that the text has been illustrated "with one example or another," as long as those examples are taken to refer to (1) the derivation of the anaclastic, and (2) the *omnium noblissimum exemplum*. But even if the initial avenue of approach is thus rendered unavailable, the remaining series of repetitions stands in no less tension with the force of the rule itself. Shorn of its exemplary status, however, the presence of the text in question must, once again, follow directly from Rule 8. If the text is not to violate its own principles, then the remaining paragraphs must be intimately involved with both these considerations, regardless of their explicit status in terms of exemplarity. Double or triple, investigation of the rule-bound nature of rational discourse and the multiple textual repetitions thereof is a necessary consequence of the legal framework of Cartesian methodological reason, regardless of the status of the disputed passages. In other words, even if we exercise the greatest possible editorial and philological violence in order to exclude exemplarity from the *Rules*, Rule 8 itself still requires that its articulation be nothing other than example, an impossible and repeated example of the necessity of exemplarity. Neither philological-historical critique nor attempts to limit exemplarity succeed in derailing this structural relation. A text that explicitly excludes the possibility of textual redundancy, Rule 8 functions philosophically in the space delimited by these repetitions.

INSCRIBING SUBJECTIVITY

The repetition at work in Rule 8 demands the constitution of a written, authorial subject position defined by what is, for Descartes, a universalized and necessary rationality. While this is ultimately unsurprising given Descartes' later philosophical commitments, in the *Rules* this form of subjectivity is generated via the force of methodological repetition alone, that is, without reliance on anything resembling the more familiar *cogito* argument. The key is this: despite its presentation as something that "we" or "everyone" "should" or "ought" to do, the task assigned by Rule 8 (the repetition of methodological rules by way of rule-governed investigation of rules for the direction of mind) is constitutive for Cartesian thought as such.

Notice that the second iteration does not explicitly qualify its subject as one with a particular aim in the same way as the first and third. To the question "Who should investigate knowledge and its extent by means of the *Rules*?" the first iteration answers "*everyone* who earnestly strives after good sense" and the third responds "*everyone* with the slightest love of truth" (*CSM*, 1:30 and 31, my emphasis). But the second iteration moves to an inclusive "we" unmarked by any particular qualifying characteristic: "It is necessary . . . before *we* set out to go after things to be known in particular, carefully to have inquired as to what sort of knowledge human reason is capable of attaining" (*CSM*, 1:30, my emphasis).[40] If the triple articulation is in fact a repetition, this move to the plural must generalize the qualifications of the first and third iterations, transforming "earnestly striving after good sense" and "having the slightest love of truth" into characteristics of Cartesian subjectivity shared by everyone, and not just qualities belonging to the rare, qualified philosopher.

However, the project elaborated by the first and third iterations is not directed at "everyone" in general, nor does it appear to be a constitutive task. It is rather the force of inclusion in a specific community, genus, or set, and the demand can still be construed as an option contingently dependent on an act of will, a function of a particular mode of thought, or an imperative present in certain minds and absent in others. Notice once again that the "finest example of all," and thus the first iteration, begins by marking the task as "something everyone who earnestly strives after good sense [*bonam mentem*] should do once in a life." Like the *bon sens* of the *Discourse* the *bona mens* of the *Rules* must be within the grasp of anyone and everyone, shared equally by all.[41] Unless he universalizes this capacity, Descartes runs the risk of allowing for the possibility of true methodological failure: thinking that is forced to cease neither because its object is clearly and distinctly known nor clearly and distinctly unknowable, but rather because its subject is unable to properly apply method. As discussed earlier, however, in the *Rules* Descartes categorically rejects the possibility of this type of failure, and thus *bona mens* must be a universal capacity.

Yet "capacity" is not sufficient here. If rule-governed thinking is to be understood as a necessity for Cartesian subjectivity, then it must be a constitutive element of that subjectivity as such.[42] Gilson has convincingly argued that while the *bon sens* of the *Discourse* translates the *bona mens* of the *Rules*, the two are not strictly identical. Whereas *bon sens* signifies a natural aptitude or faculty for distinguishing truth from falsity (*CSM*, 1:111) and is thus an instrumental human capacity that need not be brought into play in any given instance (i.e., we are all capable of acting contrary to good or common sense), *bona mens* indicates "universal wisdom" (*sapientia universalis*), an inescapable condition of the Cartesian subject.[43] Descartes is quite clear on this identification in Rule 1: "Indeed, it seems strange to me that so many people should investigate with such diligence the virtues of plants, the motion of the stars . . . and the objects of similar disciplines, while hardly anyone gives a thought to good thinking [*bonam mentem*]—to universal wisdom [*sapientia universalis*]" (*CSM*, 1:9). Thus, unlike *bon sens*, which allows itself to be split or parceled out, the *bona mens* of the *Rules* is neither faculty nor tool. It is not merely instrumentally possible for each and every thinker, but necessary for any and all acts of discursive thought, its possibility entailing its necessity. Thus, those capable of striving after good thinking (*bona mens*)—and this includes everyone, according to Descartes—are already locked within an ordered and rule-governed structure of thought.

Further, the *Rules* are not merely directive and prescriptive, but also descriptive: the rule-governed thinker "*will* discover that nothing can be known prior to the intellect" (*CSM*, 1:29, my emphasis). This form of investigation appears to preserve a distinction between the investigative subject and the object of investigation. Were this disjunction general, operative good thinking would be impossible to universalize, as the speculative object in Rule 8 would fail to recoil on the mind intuiting it. Nevertheless, at least one possibility for methodological application exceeds this failure: the reflexive description of method. If the rules are mere instrumental guides for scientific investigation with no bearing on their own validity—if, for Descartes, structures of thinking are not essentially ordered but merely orderable—then thought could never perform the reflexive doubling wherein it takes itself as its own object. If the object of this description were not already ordered and rule-governed, then the description itself would be *a priori* impossible. In this case, the process of description would be unable to proceed in a methodological fashion, because it (the *bona mens* of methodological investigation) would itself not be orderly and regulated. Correlatively, if method examines itself, and does so methodologically, then the object of its description (*bona mens*) must already be ordered and rule-bound. In other words, the very possibility of thought doubling itself to take itself as its own object *requires* that it always and already be regulated and ordered by rules. If the operation is ever to be possible, then all thinking (as a potential object of rule-governed description) must be good thinking (*bona mens*). As discussed earlier, however, this potential special case is demanded by the very structure of rule-governed thought itself, or at least by its eighth rule. This possibility that all thinking is already good thinking is actualized in the first instantiation of rule-governed thought. Thus, if method examines itself, and does so methodologically, then the object of its description must already be ordered and rule-bound; all thinking (as potential object of rule-governed description) must already be good thinking (*bona mens*).

Returning to the initial problem and surveying the results of this investigation, we can see that "everyone who earnestly strives after good sense" and "everyone who has the slightest love of truth" in the first and third iterations should be universalized to include every possible configuration of Cartesian subjectivity. The structure of repetition must therefore extend to the "we" of the second iteration who "ought once in our life carefully to inquire as to what sort of knowledge human reason is capable of attaining" as well as to every thinking thing. For the early Descartes, all thinking is equivalent to *bona mens* and the "task" of "striving after good sense" is a necessarily constitutive structure of thinking beings.

READING AND SCRIPTIVE INVENTION

This analysis of Descartes' practices of reading, inscription, and methodological reflection has investigated problems revolving around the significance of exemplarity and its repetition for Cartesian methodological thought. After exploring Descartes' critique of books and reading, I turned to his explicit and implicit instructions to his readers. The second half of this chapter radicalized the claims he makes about how the Cartesian text must be read by presenting a reading of the *Rules* that insisted that we must understand its conceptual development to be governed by the methodological structure its content articulates. A particularly rich example of a seemingly dematerialized text that is in fact simply dispersed over a complex set of material instantiations, the *Rules* simultaneously exemplifies the Cartesian critique of the materiality of the book and the ineluctably material and historically-embedded nature of philosophical textuality itself. After indicating the structural necessity and totality of this fragmentary work, the chapter explored the corollaries entailed by Descartes' seemingly innocuous repeated claims in the body of Rule 8. Rather than merely freeing the intellect from bondage to the ordered and ordering process of methodological thinking when it encounters an unsolvable problem, Rule 8 further subordinates it to the principle of regularity by restricting understanding to the necessary and prohibiting the inessential. Arguing that the rule-governed text must subject itself to its own strictures, I pointed out that Rule 8 marks the first task of rule-governed thinking as the articulation of the structure of methodological thought. Exploration of this reflexive self-constitution through an analysis of the stratified layers of textual and philosophical reiteration that figure Rule 8, I reflected on the status of exemplarity and its function in the *Rules*. Even as the text barred methodological thought from any nonessential step, and thus seemingly from all repetition, its examples not only (1) repeated one another, and (2) were themselves reiterated several times, but also (3) violated the necessary equivalence and substitutability governing Cartesian exemplarity *per se*, as method became its own best example. A defense of the textual reiteration of the passage containing this example allowed further reflection on the relation between exemplarity and repetition, such that repetition gained the status of a Cartesian methodological precept. Finally, I turned to the implications of such reiterative rule-governed thinking for subjectivity, demonstrating that Descartes is able to sustain a universalized, rule-governed subjectivity even in the absence of a *cogito* argument. Since in the Cartesian context *all* thinking is *bona mens* and takes the regularity of method as its constitutive task, the order and repetition of method is a necessary and integral structure of the Cartesian self.

To read the *Rules* according to Descartes' own prescription for philosophical reading is thus at once to encounter an entirely unexpected philosophical event and at the same time be condemned to a limitless repetition of the Cartesian text. Demanding its own iteration, and locating that iteration as an unnecessary example of a method limiting itself and its practitioners to the necessary, the *Rules* collapses every reading of it into an instance of its own textual reproduction. The problem that this chapter has attempted to address is that of the status of this condemnation and collapse, and the structure of this repetition. Just as attempts to analyze the *Rules* by Adam, Weber, Crapulli, Marion, and others have each resulted in a reiteration of the structure and force of the text, this chapter has been an attempt to expose the framework by which Cartesian discourse structures and is structured by its method. Interminably turning in on itself, rule-governed discursivity reinscribes itself in the very event of reading.

Lacking that radically external origin that Leibniz posited for his infinitely recopied geometrical manuscripts in "On the Ultimate Origination of Things," this reiteration of the *Rules* does not repeat itself like a virulent strain of signifiers, an original transposing itself and producing a copy each time the text is read. The logic here is not that of following an already hewn but difficult path to the summit of Mont Ventoux, nor of the lonely copyist monk enclosed in a monastery scriptorium reproducing words and manuscripts, embellishing them occasionally with gold and mercury rubrications or marginal commentary. Placing ourselves as readers under the jurisdiction of Cartesian rule-governed thinking, we write the *Rules for the Direction of Mind* rather than copy it. Regularity and lawfulness—standing as a universal, constitutive, instantaneous, and singular methodological event—thus cannot belong to a field of mimetic reinscription. The *Rules* continue to articulate themselves, leaving their reader only another instant (and instantiation) of their repetition.

CHAPTER 5

THE BODY AND THE BOOK

The body is the inscribed surface of events (traced by language and dissolved by ideas), the locus of a dissociated self (adopting the illusion of a substantial unity), and a volume in perpetual disintegration. Genealogy, as an analysis of descent, is thus situated within the articulation of the body and history. Its task is to expose a body totally imprinted by history and the process of history's destruction of the body.

Michel Foucault, "Nietzsche, Genealogy, History"

ANXIETIES OF TEXTUAL MULTIPLICATION

At 31 years of age, 7 years after his expulsion from the Jewish community of Amsterdam, Baruch Spinoza published the first of two books to appear in print during his lifetime. *Principles of Cartesian Philosophy* (1663) recasts Descartes' *Principles of Philosophy* according to the synthetic, geometrical method of demonstration suggested and exemplified by Descartes in his response to the second set of objections to his *Meditations* (*CSM*, 2:110–20). According to the preface to Spinoza's text written by his friend Lodewijk Meyer, this method is "the best and surest way to discover and teach truth" in "the unanimous opinion of all who seek wisdom beyond the common lot" (*SW*, 116; *PPC*, Pref). Ostensibly a direct presentation and redescription of the propositions and arguments of parts 1 and 2 of Descartes' text (along with a fragment on part 3 and Spinoza's own short but crucial *Metaphysical Thoughts*), *Principles of Cartesian Philosophy* subtly conveys the first stages of Spinoza's radicalization of several postulates of Cartesian thought in the development of his own monistic, immanentist metaphysics. For his part, Meyer insists that Spinoza "has simply given Descartes' opinions and their demonstrations just as they are found in his writings" (*SW*, 119; *PPC*, Pref), but he also notes that Spinoza's own metaphysical positions differ from Descartes' in several crucial ways, particularly insofar as he rejects the Cartesian attribution of freedom to the will and differs with respect to the conception of particular minds and bodies in relation to thought and extension as such. In other words, while Meyer is quite clear that he takes Spinoza to present Descartes' views, he is also adamant that Spinoza is no orthodox Cartesian.

In the midst of his presentation of the ten axioms from Descartes' replies to the second set of objections, Spinoza pauses to consider a notion crucial to Descartes' "objective perfection" *a posteriori* proof for the existence of God: "The objective reality of our ideas requires a cause in which that same reality is contained not only objectively but also formally or eminently" (*SW*, 131; *PPC*, 1Ax9).[1] His explication of this axiom makes use of a curious figure referring to the materiality of the book that, at first glance at least, bears little relationship to the axiom itself:

> If anyone sees some books (imagine one to be that of a distinguished philosopher and the other to be that of some trifler) written in one and the same hand, and if he pays no attention to the meaning of the words (i.e., insofar as they are symbols) but only to the shape of the writing and to the order of the letters, he will find no distinction between them such as to compel him to seek different causes for them. They will appear to him to have proceeded from the same cause and in the same manner. But if he pays attention to the meaning of the words and of the language, he will find a considerable distinction between them. He will therefore conclude that the first cause of the one book was very different from the first cause of the other, and that the one cause was in fact more perfect than the other to the extent that the meaning of the language of the two books, or their words considered as symbols, are found to differ from one another. (*SW*, 132; *PPC*, 1Ax9)

We have already seen several senses in which the early modern philosophers treated here worried about the establishment of a position of authorship external to the material sequence by which one book could be copied from another. Descartes' critique of collecting and commonplacing techniques for the construction of books charged that their results lacked the organic, methodologically determined systematicity necessary for the pursuit of clear and distinct truths. Meanwhile, his *Rules for the Direction of Mind* functioned like an epistemological virus, insinuating the mechanism of its own infinite textual reproduction into the structure of methodological thinking that it presented to its readers.

Bayle, while introducing a vast array of parts of texts from other books into the complex citational structure of his *Dictionary*, subjected them all to the critical gaze of an encyclopedic commentary, such that they provided the medium for philosophical reflection rather than its content. The *Dictionary*, in other words, reproduced a seemingly infinite number of texts, but did so in such a way that they became the topological features of a landscape structured by a typographical *mise en page* inseparable from the critical articulation of the concepts it presented.

Leibniz's anxieties and excitements with respect to the multiplication of books were evident in a wide variety of contexts. The allegory at the end of the *Theodicy* is already immersed in a tradition of textual repetition, restaging, extending, and critically transforming an allegorical dialogue from Valla that was itself a restaging, extension, and critical transformation of Boethius' allegorical dialogue. The vast pyramidal library of possible worlds thereby produced not only contained every possible book, but every possible library, that is, every internally consistent and non-self-contradictory collection or arrangement of possible books. The structure of *all* these libraries is then recapitulated twice, despite the failure of all but one to become actual. First, they are repeated negatively, with respect to their relationship to the library at the apex of the pyramid (the possible library containing the greatest diversity or expressing the most intense existential exigency, that is, the actual world). Second, they are repeated positively, as Jupiter browses the stacks of this possible library of libraries in order to reaffirm his choice (which was, in a certain sense, no choice at all) and—perhaps more crucially—as Pallas Athena escorts the author-metonym Theodore on his tour of unactualized possible worlds.

In Leibniz's considerations of the problems surrounding the proper structure for the encyclopedic organization of knowledge, the problematics of textual repetition were generalized to any structure oriented toward classification by conceptual content. Put somewhat metaphorically, Leibniz's proposals evacuate books of the "expressed meaning" Spinoza's figure separates from their material formation, replacing it with an infinitely referential, internal structure of formal organization. The result is that each book (if we may extrapolate in this way from the objects of Leibniz's encyclopedic organization) now consists entirely of a structural recapitulation of the whole of the total library on whose shelves it sits. This repetition of all books in every book (a site identical to Spinoza's metaphysical anxiety about relying on the material structure of the page) nevertheless allows for their radical singularity, as each of these books becomes what they are by way of their particular, individuating, perspectival recapitulation of the totality of knowledge or the whole of the library.

Several times in previous chapters, reference has been made to Leibniz's "On the Ultimate Origination of Things," the text in which he most clearly articulates the position that the actualization of the best of all possible worlds is simply a matter of the perfection of its own internal structure (its *exigentia existentiae*, that is, its urge or straining for existence). Its actuality is, of course, a function of divine "choice," but that choice is framed on the model of God's calculative activity rather than as the exercise of an indeterminate will. Though he recoils from this implication, this is the version of Leibniz's cosmogony that comes closest to Spinoza's position that God could not have done otherwise, that is, the principles of logical necessity overshadow freedom conceived as the model of the will rather than the effective production of free subjects. Leibniz insists that God could have chosen the worse should he have so willed, but that by virtue of our knowledge that he possesses the attribute of perfection, we can be certain that he would not.

"On the Ultimate Origination of Things" also presents an image reflecting early modern philosophical anxiety in the face of material textual reproduction and, like Spinoza's figure of the two books, its function is to present a proof for the existence of God. This position of extratextual authority is necessary, according to Leibniz, to satisfy the demands of the principle of sufficient reason. No examination of the collection or total series of individual things, Leibniz argues, can discover a sufficient reason for their existence.

> Let us suppose that a book on the elements of geometry has always existed, one copy always made from another. It is obvious that although we can explain a present copy of the book from the previous book from which it is copied, this will never lead us to a

complete explanation, no matter how many books back we go, since we can always wonder why there have been such books, why these books were written, and why they were written the way they were. What is true of these books is also true of the different states of the world, for the state which follows is, in a sense, copied from the preceding state, though in accordance with certain laws of change. (*AG*, 149)

In order to satisfy the demand for explanations of why the world is and why it is the way it is, we must have recourse to an extramundane (and thus extratextual) author who stands outside the series of particular states of the world or particular states of the text. God is understood as a primary and teleological explanation for the sufficient reason of things, that is, he must be exterior to that sequence insofar as he constitutes its extramundane "ultimate origin."

Spinoza's reading of Descartes' *Principles of Philosophy* is one possible direct source for Leibniz's figure of the world as a set of books infinitely copied one from the other. This is somewhat ironic, of course, since Spinoza's mature metaphysics will reject entirely the notion that God, as the sufficient reason for the existence of the world, can be radically separated from it. Instead, he advances an immanent monism that identifies God, substance, and nature, distinguishing them only with respect to whether they are grasped in terms of their productive power (*natura naturans*) or in terms of their expression in the dispersed totality defined by the infinite modes that follow in infinite ways from God (*natura naturata*) (*SW*, 227; *E*, 1P16).

We have now located Spinoza's engagement with the figure of the book within the general framework of the early modern anxieties regarding textual multiplication with respect to Leibniz, Bayle, and Descartes. The first locus of analysis in what follows will be Spinoza's recapitulation, exemplification, and transformation in the *Principles of Cartesian Philosophy* of a key principle in the Cartesian proof for the existence of God. In order to treat the Spinozan figures of the book and their inscription more fully, the next section will briefly turn away from the problematic of the book in order to explicate a properly Spinozan conception of materiality, arguing that in the physical, metaphysical, and political registers materiality must be understood as a dynamic, dispositional theory of constitutive motion rather than as a straightforward thesis of the reducibility of sensible entities to their micro-level physical constituents. The third and final section simultaneously brings together the results of the second section's analysis with Spinoza's engagement with the Cartesian claims regarding the formal and objective reality of ideas (treated in the first section), his engagement with the materiality of writing, and his elaboration of a dynamic, materialist theory of meaning in the *Theological-Political Treatise.*

FORMAL AND OBJECTIVE INSCRIPTION

In order to tackle the relationship between Spinoza's figure of the two books and his account of Descartes' axiom and the argument in which it is embedded, it will first be useful to recall the role that the axiom plays for Descartes. To the consternation of many non-specialist contemporary readers, in Meditation Three Descartes introduces a modification of Francisco Suarez's distinction between the formal, objective, and eminent reality of ideas. Briefly stated, formal reality refers to the ontological status ("degree of perfection") of any existent thing, and being eminently real means possessing all formal reality. With respect to ideas *qua* ideas, then, all must possess the same formal reality. Because ideas are merely modes of my thought and thus "borrow" their reality from it, whether I am thinking of the number 8, the Empire State Building, or Bayle's *Dictionary*, my ideas all have the same ontological status. Objective reality, by contrast, refers to the representational content of an idea, that is, the sense in which the reality of the idea is determined by the reality of its object (its *ideatum*). Thus, ideas are not all equal with respect to their objective reality, since some ideas represent entities with a high level of formal reality (a perfect being, for example) and some represent imperfect things that barely exist at all. Descartes' crucial axiomatic claim is that whatever objective reality a given idea has (i.e., whatever representational power it possesses) "it must surely derive it from some cause which contains at least as much formal reality as there is objective reality in the idea" (*CSM*, 2:28–29). Thus, the object of any idea (the *ideatum*) must be at least as real as the idea's representational content. This claim rests on the further axiom that there must be at least as much reality in a cause as there is in its effect. Thus, since *ideata* are the causes of ideas *qua* representations, there must be at least as much formal reality in the object of the idea as there is in that idea considered as a representation. My idea of

God considered as a representation, Descartes argues, contains an ideational predicate (infinitude) with an objective reality that exceeds my own formal reality (for I am finite). Therefore, if my idea of the infinite is not a false one, I cannot be the cause of this idea.[2] Instead, its cause must be something at least as formally real as this predicate is objectively real, that is, it must be caused by something infinite. Thus, God—an infinite substance—exists.[3]

As Spinoza does, we must notice that this argument, if it is efficacious, has extremely minimal implications for traditional theology and almost none for religious dogma. It proves only that an infinite substance exists and not that this substance carries any of the weight or additional characteristics imputed to the concept of God by theologians. Indeed, even the other predicates Descartes claims are contained in our idea of God (eternity, immutability, independence, omniscience, and omnipotence) require what Descartes frames as a separate argument: a cosmological proof based on the indubitable givenness of my own existence, as established in Meditation Two. Thus, with the first proof in Meditation Three Descartes is able to claim that this infinite being is God only with reference to the idea of God he claims we all have, whether or not we hold that there actually is an existing being corresponding to that idea. Even to deny the existence of God, in other words, involves accepting the definition ("God is an infinite substance . . .") while claiming that no actually existing thing corresponds to this definition (". . . but there is no infinite substance"). However, if we accept the definition and we also accept Descartes' axioms regarding formal and objective reality, then, if Descartes' reasoning is correct, it would be absurd to deny that there is in fact such an actually existent infinite entity, and that this entity is God. Philosophically, too, the immediate implications are less stunning than one might suspect. The real point of the argument is simply to establish that I know with certainty that there is something that actually exists outside of me. That God is the first thing beside myself that I am able to know exists with certainty is, if we take the order of Descartes' reasons seriously, merely a happy accident for the tradition of onto-theology and for the arguments that follow in the *Meditations*.

In any case, this is certainly a Cartesian argument that demanded restatement in synthetic form, and perhaps even the restatement of the restatement that Spinoza's *Principles of Cartesian Philosophy* supplies with respect to Descartes' own geometrical version. When

Descartes explicated the axiom in question, he emphasized that it was necessary for all our knowledge of things, sensible or otherwise. Spinoza's explication takes it in a very different direction and leads us back to the question of the materiality of the book. Recall Spinoza's thought experiment. If we pay no attention to the meaning of the words written in two books physically indistinguishable but differing in quality, and concentrate only on "the shape of the writing and the order of the letters," they will seem "to have proceeded from the same cause and in the same manner." But if we focus on the meaning of the words we will conclude that they have different causes and that one of these causes is more perfect than the other (*SW*, 132; *PPC*, 1Ax9).

One particularly strange thing about Spinoza's comparative book image is exactly what it exemplifies. It does not directly illustrate the Cartesian notion that the causes of representations must be at least as real as the representational content of their effects, that is, that the formal reality of the cause of an idea (its *ideatum*) must be as great as the objective reality of the idea itself. Instead, Spinoza's figure of the two books primarily shows that ideas taken merely as ideas are indiscernible from one another. To consider an idea merely as an idea is equivalent to considering a book as a book: a bound set of pages covered in written symbols disposed according to a particular order. From this perspective, Spinoza suggests, all books bearing identical material characteristics (written in the same hand or printed in the same font, presumably bound in the same style) are interchangeable, or at least, all such books "will appear to have proceeded from the same cause and in the same manner." Notice that in a stunning reversal of the usual metaphorics, "ideas *qua* ideas" have become ideas taken in terms of their material articulation, where "ideas *qua* representations" have become mere images—Spinoza's "symbols" (*imagines*). Thus, meaningful differences between ideas are differences in representational, "symbolic," ideational content. In the two-books figure, this means that differences in the relative "perfection" (*realitas*) of meanings of words or discourse indicate differences in the perfection of their author-causes. Attention to the meaning of words is opposed to attention to their shape and order, such that only differences in the former register can indicate differences in causal origin.[4]

Spinoza's two-book figure—the image of two materially indiscernible books expressing qualitatively different causal genealogies—does *not* take the further step of demonstrating that the materiality of the book indicates nothing regarding its cause. In one sense, it leaves open a material condition for differentiating between the two books (and thus by extension, for differentiating among the ideas they allegorize). The condition for the figurative example is "two books written in the same hand." Perhaps we can frame a distinction that is not reducible to differences between the letters of the alphabet or the order in which they are inscribed on the page. In the case of two different transcribing hands or two discernible printed fonts, for example, no one would mistake the two books for products of the same cause (unfortunately, this would also mean that a single manuscript transcribed by two different copyists could not be referred to the same author or meaning). If there is a register in which we may distinguish between "idea-types," then, the Cartesian assertion of the identity of all ideas with respect to formal reality is overcome. One way to advance this thesis would be to introduce an ontologically or causally differentiated typology of sensations and intellectual affections that could serve as a comprehensive catalog of our various ways of knowing (something like a Baconian epistemological encyclopedia that would offer a complete catalog of natural histories of methods for intellectual apprehension). Another would be to frame a differentiated epistemological hierarchy that would distinguish between levels of ideational power, conceptual efficacy, or kinds of knowledge. Such a hierarchy could, for example, differentiate adequate and inadequate ideas, or again, sensible linguistic knowledge, common notions regarding shared qualities or predicates, and intuition of singular essences. These last possibilities, of course, are precisely the ones that Spinoza proposed in his *Ethics* (*SW*, 267–68; *E*, 2P40S2).[5]

There is a second sense in which Spinoza's figure of the two books fails to show that considering the materiality of books (or the formal being of ideas) bars us from connection to their causes, based on Spinoza's explicit restriction (via Descartes) of causal analysis to primary causes. Specifically with respect to apprehension of these primary causes, Spinoza proposes that attention to the materiality of books is insufficient (so too with attention to the idea *qua* idea). For the apprehension of material or efficient causes, by contrast, the books *qua* books are enough, and these efficient and mechanical causes are what fundamentally concern Spinoza in his own metaphysical work. They are also what occupy Descartes when he moves beyond the methodological establishment of an epistemological ground and toward the explication of the natural world and its mechanisms. While in the *Ethics* Spinoza will constantly insist that having an adequate idea of a thing means grasping it in terms of its production by an adequate cause and therefore that an adequate idea of God must precede adequate knowledge of the world, he will also radically identify God with nature and insist that their causal relationship be explicated in terms of the immanence of the former to the latter. God, like any immanent cause in Spinoza's ontology, exists *in* his effects rather than externally or prior to them (even while the effect depends on or is contained within its cause).

Indeed, at the close of his discussion of the two-books figure, Spinoza acknowledges this specification or limitation of his image with respect to causal reference. He adds, "I am speaking of the first cause of books, and there must necessarily be one although I admit—indeed, I take for granted—that one book can be transcribed from another, as is self-evident" (*SW*, 132; *PPC*, 1Ax9). That this caveat regarding the problem of the propagated book may be an actual worry for Spinoza is evident in his recasting of the two-books figure in a March 25, 1667 letter to his friend Jarig Jelles. There, Spinoza draws a distinction between determining the efficient causes of a given motion (which may properly involve an infinite regress) and determining the causes of the expression of meaning (which may involve no such regress). If I am asked what it is that sets a determinate body in motion, I may answer, "It is determined to such motion by another body, and this again by another, and so on to infinity" (*SW*, 865; Ep40). On the other hand,

> If I see a book containing excellent thoughts and beautifully written in the hands of a common man and I ask him whence he has such a book, and he replies that he had copied it from another book belonging to another common man who could also write beautifully, and so on to infinity, he does not satisfy me. For I am asking him not only about the form and arrangement of the letters, with which alone his answer is concerned, but also about the thoughts and meaning expressed in their arrangement, and this he does not answer by his progression to infinity. (*SW*, 865–66; Ep40)

Explicitly referring Jelles to the section of *Principles of Cartesian Philosophy* where the two-books figure first occurs, Spinoza nevertheless transforms the example such that, in the letter, it focuses on the issue the *Principles* relegates to the status of caveat. In the letter, the central problem is not that of distinguishing between two books written in the same hand but of adequately determining the cause of the content of the books. Where the two-books figure in the *Principles* demonstrates that the difference between two ideas considered only in terms of their formal reality is indiscernible, the figure in the letter shows that reference to the representational content of an idea, that is, objective reality, is necessary in order to determine the idea's cause. In 1667, already well on the way to an ontology holding "the order and connection of ideas is the same as the order and connection of things" and erecting a causal barrier between the realm of ideas and the realm of bodies through asserting the ontological identity of idea and *ideatum*, it is unlikely Spinoza means that representational content bears no relationship to the material disposition of ideas (*SW*, 247 and 279–82; *E*, 2P7 and 3P2).[6] While the missive to Jelles continues to distinguish the form and order of letters from the meaning of discourse, its emphasis is on warning that the infinite regress of efficient and material causal explanation is not appropriate to explanations in terms of primary and final causes. However, this latter set of causes is precisely what Spinoza's own metaphysics was to attempt to purge from the explanatory vocabulary of philosophy. This was also the focus of Spinoza's second figure for the Cartesian axiom in the *Principles*. In parallel with the two books, Spinoza asks us to consider a set of portraits, among them one of a prince. Attention to the material out of which the portrait of the prince is constructed will get us nowhere, he asserts. Not only will we be unable to distinguish it from other portraits (ideas *qua* ideas have the same formal reality), we will be satisfied with understanding its origin as a chain of copying and mechanical repetition. The alternative is "to attend to the image as an image" (*SW*, 133; *PPC*, 1Ax9) (which ironically means *not* to consider the idea as an idea) and thereby to seek a cause for the portrait that contains formally or eminently what is in the image objectively.

When Spinoza insists that attention to the materiality of the book is a barrier to the apprehension of its cause and content, he is engaged in precisely the type of textual repetition that seems to underwrite his anxiety regarding the multiplication of texts. *Principles of Cartesian Philosophy*, after all, is framed as nothing more than a recapitulation of Descartes' *Principles of Philosophy*, with the difference that the two books are presented according to a different methodological art of demonstration. What differentiates them, in other words, is "the shape of the writing and the order of the letters" rather than "the meaning of the words," when these words are taken as images with representational content. It seems, then, that Spinoza's apparent reluctance to admit the possibility of any significant form of causal knowledge on the basis of the material apprehension of texts should not be separated from the strange textual situation in which it is articulated. In denying that texts supposedly identical in meaning can generate knowledge of causal difference and authorial distinction, there is a sense in which Spinoza is disavowing his own authorship of *Principles of Cartesian Philosophy*, ironically, the only published text to bear his name during his lifetime (the *Theological-Political Treatise* appeared anonymously). From this perspective, Descartes is the one who has written these principles while Spinoza has only recast the order of the letters to make the meanings they express more directly manifest. Nevertheless, as was indicated earlier, there are several clear premonitions of Spinoza's metaphysical break from Cartesianism here, not the least of which is the pronouncement by Meyer in the preface that Spinoza is no Cartesian.[7]

MATTER IN MOTION

Louis Althusser's posthumously published essay, "The Underground Current of the Materialism of the Encounter" advances a theoretical position he calls "aleatory materialism." Dealing with Lucretius, Spinoza, and Machiavelli while touching on Epicurus, Hobbes, Rousseau, Marx, Heidegger, Derrida, and Deleuze, Althusser develops a nonreductivist, nonexclusively physicalist, and nondialectical materialism. Reversing the typical reading of classical materialism that posits atomic bodies as irreducible and ontologically given constituents of an aggregational world formed by virtue of their extrinsic operation, Althusser proposes a materialism that derives from the irreducibility of the *clinamen* and the material encounters it causes. In Althusser's aleatory thesis, then, it is not so much *bodies* that constitute the "matter" of materiality as it is determinate, yet hardly predictable, *motions* (riven by relations of force) and the corporeal encounters that result from them which constitute an ontological ground—motions and encounters that the tradition frames as mere modes or accidents belonging to already given bodies. This means conceiving materiality in terms of an aleatory provocation of being, such that the encounter "creates nothing of the reality of the *world*, which is nothing but agglomerated atoms, but . . . confers their reality upon the atoms themselves, which, without swerve and encounter, would be nothing but abstract elements, lacking all consistency and existence." One immediate consequence of this is that the relationship between contingency and necessity is refigured as differential: "Instead of thinking contingency as a modality of necessity, or an exception to it, we must think necessity as the becoming-necessary of the encounter of contingencies."[8] At the same time, this necessity is to be conceived strictly nonteleologically, that is, as a consequence of the aleatory. Althusser thus posits a necessary determination of corporeality which is contingent on a material encounter that may or may not take place, and which may or may not "take hold."[9] Another consequence—and the one that orients the engagement with Spinoza's textual materialism in this chapter—is that Althusser's late theoretical framework forces a reconsideration of what we mean when we say or write "matter," and does so with explicit reference to the very series of early modern natural philosophical and metaphysical debates that set the ground for the development of the concept of corporeality in modernity proper.

Spinozan textual materialism involves reconfiguring matter itself as power and the notions of "idea" and "body" in terms of movement and its capacity to produce effects. The connection between this position and Spinoza's engagement of the figure of the book in the *Theological-Political Treatise* will be explored at length in the next section. In order to get there, however, we need to pause to consider the status of materiality in the Spinozan project writ large. Spinoza's mobilization of the figure of the two books in *Principles of Cartesian Philosophy* and the letter to Jelles have brought us to the brink of questions that have haunted twentieth-century Spinoza scholarship: What is a body and what can it do? Reframed in terms of the issues at stake in this chapter, these questions become: What is Spinozan materialism?[10] Thus, this section will be devoted to a proleptic explication of the concept of materialism in relation to Spinoza's work, which will allow us to return to his figure of the two books and extend its implications to his treatment of paper, ink, and letters in the *Theological-Political Treatise*.

Spinoza is obviously no straightforward Gassendian atomist or Boylean corpuscularist, but the importance of his account of physical individuation and his proximity to Hobbes are clear.[11] Spinoza's account of materiality, I will argue, is instead best understood as a dynamic one. In what follows, by dynamic materialism, I mean the position that nature may be explicated by reference to bodies conceived as complex patterns of movement as well as equally complex and constantly mutating articulations of a power or force to act and to exist. Dynamic materialism need not be eliminative nor even properly physicalist, and Spinoza's version is certainly not. It does not dispense with immaterial objects such as ideas and minds, but it does involve the claim that nature (or being) is fully explicable from the perspective of matter conceived as productive power. We can contrast this dynamic conception to the mechanistic notion of matter prominent among the varying schools of the "new philosophy" that resisted the Scholastic relegation of matter to formless and unarticulated passivity. Mechanical materialism, a stance found among the Cartesians as well as the neo-Epicureans and their corpuscularist allies, understands bodies to be physical elements that behave according to the set of kinematic principles that constitute the laws of physics. For the Cartesians, bodies were infinitely divisible substantive spatial abstractions: measureable regions of dimensionality that submitted to mathematical analysis.[12] For the neo-Epicureans (such as Gassendi) and the corpuscularists (such as Galileo and Boyle), they were the irreducible micro-level physical objects that were constitutive of macro-level phenomenal objects. Descartes and his followers, as discussed in Chapters 3 and 4, would deny being materialists in any reductive or eliminative sense. They certainly held (as did several of the corpuscularists) that nonmaterial entities existed and were even, in some cases, more perfect (and certainly more perfectly known) than bodies. At the same time, when it came to giving an account of nature, the Cartesians generally abandoned the idealist tendencies that remain most prominent in the way we read them today.

One key difference between the dynamic and mechanical conceptions rests on their fundamental intuition regarding the object of material analysis. For the mechanists beginning with Galileo, this object was matter in motion. Spinoza's dynamic materialism rests on the claim that matter *is* its motion, that is, bodies can only be understood as the articulations of complex patterns of motion and expressions of motive force. This stance actually derives from several Cartesian propositions regarding the relation between the essence of material substance and its modes (discussed in terms of Bayle's reading of them in Chapter 3 and again elaborated here), radicalized to such an extent that they become unrecognizable from the Cartesian perspective.

Spinoza's proto-physics following the scholium to proposition 13 in the *Ethics* introduces a way of conceiving bodies as determinations or ratios of motion and rest, speed and slowness.[13] Since bodies are not substantially but only modally distinct, they differ from one another with respect to how they are bodies, that is, in terms of their motion, rest, and speed. Since Descartes took the divisibility of extension to be more than just a conceptual fiction, his physics required the possibility of the division of any given body into its infinity of parts (*CSM*, 1:91, 231, and 239). The divisibility of bodies, however, implies a "consequent mobility in respect of its parts, and its resulting capacity to be affected in all the ways in which we perceive as being derivable from the movement of the parts." Thus, "any variation in matter or diversity in its many forms depends on motion" (*CSM*, 1:232). That is to say, motion, for Descartes, is a mode of extended substance from which all other modifications of it are, in principle, derivable.

Spinoza's insight is that if this Cartesian position is pushed to its limit, a body should be understood to be *constituted* by the relations of motion and rest that it expresses, that is, by the extent to which it remains in contact with some bodies and changes its contact with others. Here, it no longer makes sense to speak of motion and rest as modes of bodies. If, as Spinoza's ontology tells us, particular bodies are modes of substance expressed under the attribute of extension (*SW*, 244; *E*, 2Def1), and if, as Cartesian physics tells us, motion is a mode of corporeal substance, then bodies must be patterns of motion. Since modal corporeality can no longer be understood as directly substantial, finite modes of substance expressed under the attribute of thought must actually be more or less complex systems that express ratios of motion and rest. Bodies, that is, are dynamic functional patterns of movement, rather than either passive substantial *hypokeimena* or static regions of mathematically specifiable extension.

This allows Spinoza to develop a typology of bodies, distinguishing among (1) simple bodies, (2) composite bodies, and (3) extremely complex bodies. Simple bodies are those distinguished from one another solely with respect to motion and rest, considered as a positive magnitude. With the introduction of these simple bodies, however, Spinoza is by no means positing atom-like irreducible constituents of the world of corporeal motion and rest. Since he espouses a plenist physics that rejects the void and finds divisible bodies everywhere, either Spinoza's simple bodies are merely conceptual fictions, or they can be understood to be only relatively simple. That is, these bodies are simple only with respect to whatever other bodies they encounter, or to use the corresponding Cartesian terminology, to those bodies that constitute their corporeal "vicinity" (*SW*, 252; *E*, 2Ax1'-L1).[14] A composite body results when different bodies are forced into close contact by the pressure of surrounding bodies, or, more importantly, when such packing together results in a condition under which "they move, with the same or different degrees of speed" so that "they communicate their motions to each other according to a certain fixed manner [*ratio*]" (*SW*, 252–54; *E*, 2L2–L7). In other words, when a series of relatively simple bodies maintain an unvarying relation of movement and rest with respect to one another they constitute a composite body, something that can also be understood to be an individual. It is important to note that in Spinoza's other discussions of individuation, "being an individual" means being the direction of several causal powers toward the production of a singular effect (*SW*, 244; *E*, 2D7).[15] As for the third type of body, Spinoza writes, "So far we have conceived an individual which is composed only of bodies which are distinguished from one another only by motion and rest, speed and slowness, that is, which is composed of the simplest bodies. But if we should now conceive of another, composed of a number of individuals of a different nature, we shall find that it can be affected in a great many other ways, and still preserve its nature" (*SW*, 254; *E*, 2L7). Such is the human body: an extremely complex composite individual composed of still other composite individuals of various natures, all of which dynamically express a single complex pattern or *ratio* of motion and rest, speed, and slowness that persists over time (*SW*, 254–55; *E*, 2L7S–Post6).

Neither composite nor extremely complex bodies consist merely of parts that passively "communicate" their motion to one another; they are also causally efficacious, united in a single individual to the extent that together they produce an effect. Composite individual bodies (extremely complex or not) are things whose very materiality derives both from this causal efficacy (an aptitude to act or be acted upon) and, what is really the same thing for Spinoza, from their continuous overall motive pattern. Thus, the identity, size, number, position, direction, and motion of the parts of a complex body can vary as long as the whole body expresses an unvarying *ratio* of motion and rest. Individuality, then, is a dynamic system of corporeal variation. This means that a body is neither a collection of simple and atomic corpuscles nor even an infinitely divisible region of extension. A body is a complex and systematic function of motion and rest, speed and slowness that maintains its individual identity as *one* body even as the material out of which it is composed continually alters its magnitude, direction, and motion, and even as that material is exchanged for other material capable of the same type of dynamic function. Better: materiality itself is dynamic rather than atomistic or straightforwardly mechanistic. Matter *is* its motion, and natural laws regulate the internal dynamism of bodies as such, not simply their interactions.

Connected to this account is a conundrum. As it is presented in the late chapters of the *Theological-Political Treatise*, the key concept of Spinozan materialism (matter as effective power) is framed primarily in terms of its usefulness for political control, that is, the affective production or inculcation of obedience (with the production of devotion as its affective means) in the minds and bodies of subjects. Thus, Spinoza's dynamic conception of materiality has explicitly political implications. In the *Ethics*, framing the nearly impossible community involving only human beings living the life of reason, Spinoza insists, "If two individuals of completely the same nature were joined to one another, they would compose an individual twice as powerful as each one singly" and that "Men . . . can wish for nothing more helpful for the preservation of their own being than that they should all agree in all things, that their minds and bodies should compose, as it were [*quasi*], one mind and one body, and that all together should endeavor as best they can to preserve their own being, and that all together they should seek for themselves the common advantage of all" (*SW*, 331; *E*, 4P18S). But, as Steve Barbone points out, since the condition for this meta-unification is that the natures of the individuals must be qualitatively identical ("completely the same nature") the proposed composition of one meta-level mind and body will not in fact occur.[16] While human beings ought to *desire* that their natures completely agree and *strive* for the constitution of this community by living the life of reason, similarity in nature is not enough to establish numerical identity of essence. For Etienne Balibar, this constitutes the paradox of Spinozan democracy: "The less sovereignty is physically identified with one fraction of society (in the limiting case, with one individual), the more it will tend to coincide with the people as a whole, and the stronger and more stable it will be. But at the same time, the more difficult it will be to imagine its unity (its *unanimity*) and its *indivisibility* (its capacity for *decision*), and the more complicated it will be to organize them in practice" (*SP*, 57–58). The democratic distribution of political power within the politically unified multitude is the strongest ground for the constitution of sovereignty, but such distribution also renders the constitution of a unified body-politic unlikely.

Hobbes—who begins his masterwork by intentionally mistranslating a Latinized Socrates' *nosce teipsum* as "read thy self"—had in fact offered a complex political theory that culminates not only with the production of an absolute sovereign power but also with the unification of the multitude into one singular body-politic.[17] *Leviathan* offers an ontology of representation wherein the sovereign stands as an artificial person who "personates" or represents the multitude and who thereby quite literally acts in their name.[18] This action (and this is the technical sense of Hobbes' definition of an "actor") is "owned" and "authored" by the represented multitude, the authors of the actions of the artificial person who holds authority in the commonwealth. Indeed, it is only in this moment of collective authorship of the actions undertaken by the sovereign power that "personates" the multitude that the multitude actually comes into being, for, Hobbes insists, "it is the *unity* of the representer, not the *unity* of the represented, that makes the person *one*" (*Lev.*, 104). Prior to the transfer of natural right to sovereign power, the multitude is, strictly speaking, not one but many. The Hobbesian multitude, in other words, constitutes a singular and unified body-politic at the very instant that it renounces and transfers its political power. At this moment, it ceases to act, instead authoring the actions of an artificial actor in the person of sovereign power. While this body-politic is indeed motivated by a single, complex conative drive (fear of violence) its *unification* is key. Hobbes has described the genesis of a united political body that is incapable (by virtue of the first, most general, and fundamental formulation of natural law) of going to war with itself and thus of degenerating back into a mere mass of men.

Spinoza's unfinished *Political Treatise* develops a naturalized political theory that regards "affects such as love, hatred, anger, envy, pride, pity, and other agitations of the mind not as vices of human nature but as properties pertaining to it in the same way as heat, cold, storm, thunder, and such pertain to the atmosphere" (*SW*, 681; *TP*, 1.4).[19] A state should be organized in such a way as to realistically confront the meteorological fact that human beings are motivated mostly by their passions and that the force of this affective drive increases the more we look at collectivities rather than scanning the crowded political field for the exceptional enlightened few. The *Political Treatise*, then, theorizes the relationship between the development of the passions and desires of individuals and the formation of the multitude as, to use Antonio Negri's fortunate term of art, a "constituent" political power.[20] One of the accompanying theoretical changes this demands is a rethinking of the relationship between sovereign power and natural right. Whether in the late chapters of the *Theological-Political Treatise* where Spinoza adapts the language of the social contract or in the *Political Treatise* where he rejects that contract entirely, his basic political slogan is *jus sive potentia*—right or power; right, that is to say, power—and his basic political strategy, as Alexandre Matheron, Negri, Barbone, and Lee Rice have pointed out, depends on the differentiation of *potentia* (natural power or ability to act, identified with the conative essence of individuals) from *potestas* (sovereign authority, the power of command).[21] Natural right is coextensive with natural *potentia*, and any constitution of sovereign authority (*summa potestas*) rests with the *potentia* of those who will be its subjects. Hobbes reserved a modicum of natural right for the subject—I retain the right to flee or fight the jailers who come to drag me in chains to my execution, for otherwise I would violate the fundamental law of nature—while also subjecting this retention to the condition that its exercise remain politically powerless (*Lev.*, 141–42). My condemnation to death by the sovereign is necessarily just since that epithet belongs to any action undertaken by the *summa potestas*. Spinoza insists that very little, if any, natural right is actually transferred. In fact, his equation of right with power extends to sovereignty itself—it is not simply *my* right that is coextensive with *my* power; *sovereign* right is coextensive with *sovereign* power, and thus never absolute in the Hobbesian sense (except in the limit case of a radically democratic polity).

Sovereignty is invested with an authoritative right to tyranny—to "govern in the most oppressive way and execute citizens on the most trivial pretexts" (*SW*, 566–67; *TTP*, 20)—but in doing so it reflexively destroys its own authority (its *potestas*) together with its very power of existence (its *potentia*). Strictly speaking, since tyrannical oppression is self-undermining, sovereigns "do not have the absolute power [*potentia*] to do these and other such things, and consequently they do not have the absolute right to do so" (*SW*, 567; *TTP*, 20).

Thus, *summa potestas* does not imply *summa potentia*. While the authority of the state may be absolute in principle, that authority (*potestas*) rests on a sovereign right coextensive with sovereign *potentia*. Since no such *potentia* can ever be absolute (at the very least because our force of existence is always subject to the infinite power of external causes), sovereign right and the authority it guarantees are always circumscribed within definite limits. These limits are determined by that for the sake of which individuals ceded their private authority in the first place: "to free every man from fear so that he may live in security as far as is possible, that is, so that he may best preserve his natural right to exist and to act, without harm to himself and others" (*SW*, 567; *TTP*, 20).

In the *Political Treatise* this account is extended into an ontology of the multitude radically different from that of Hobbes and connected to Spinoza's dynamic conception of materialism. Because in the natural state human beings are vulnerable to an infinity of external causes that militate for their destruction, strictly speaking the very notion of individual natural right is merely conceptual, insofar as it cannot actually be exercised: "As long as human natural right is determined by the power of each individual and is possessed by each alone, it is of no account and is notional rather than factual, since there is no assurance that it can be made good" (*SW*, 687; *TP*, 2.15). Collective *potentia* and collective *jus* are the true origins of that individual right which is coextensive with individual power: the power of the multitude ontologically precedes the power of the individual, as *jus communis* is identified with *potentia multitudinis*. Put another way, our individual power (and thus our individual right) is meaningful only insofar as we are embedded not just in a social context, but within a properly political framework: one in which juridical authority and economic contract no longer serve as the retrospective foundation with respect to which the power of any given existing political state is legitimated. Instead, the *potentia* of the multitude is always engaged in practices of legitimation and delimitation of existing relations of force and articulations of authority in the form of *summa potestas*.[22] In other words, except in the extremely rare or even impossible case of the community of rational beings (the community proposed in the *Ethics* as the end for which rational human beings strive), Spinoza's multitudinous body-politic is only metaphorically "one"—it is quite literally a multitude of individuals driven by their passions, thus not agreeing entirely in nature, and therefore failing to constitute a single, meta-level individual. Nevertheless, its collective power is the real origin of the natural right (and thus the natural power) of the actually individual body.

This means that Spinoza is claiming more than that for my very existence I depend on the reality of a politically unified multitude with no essence of its own, and more than that the individual is a politically relational entity. The conative striving (*potentia*) of individuals is meaningful for Spinoza not merely as a theoretical abstraction from the corporeal (a transcendental representation of any object whatever, *conatus* = x). Rather, power is real only in its material exercise, and this exercise is always in relation to other actually existing individuals: other minds and other bodies arrayed in the complex situation of sociality and conflict that Spinoza names the multitude. Think of the multitude, then, as the material and dynamic medium of social power, one without which individual power is simply an abstraction. It follows that every political formation (Spinoza considers several forms of monarchy, aristocracy, and democracy, but in principle his analysis should extend to any type of political formation we can imagine) derives its legitimacy from the power of the multitude, an imperfect and quasi-individuated body-politic. The construction of sovereignty, for Spinoza, should not be understood as the erection of a vast artificial entity which, at the moment it comes into being, actualizes a merely potential body-politic (this was the Hobbesian model). Rather, sovereign authority is *always being produced* by the power of the fluctuating, disunified multitude, is *always under revision* as the figure of the multitude alters, and only finds its legitimation in a fundamentally democratic impulse that precedes, subtends, and legitimates any given strategy for structuring political authority.

"LIKENESSES AND IMAGES, THAT IS, PAPER AND INK"

The preceding analysis of how materiality may be conceived in the Spinozan context and the exploration of its broadly political ramifications now allows us to return to the narrower problem of specifically *textual* materialism in his work.[23] As detailed in the first section of this chapter, Spinoza has used the two-books figure to argue that attention to the meaning of words and discourse (as opposed to the shape and order of the letters with which they are inscribed) allows us access to an interpretive level whereby we are able to posit primary causes and, in his extension of the Cartesian project within which the axiom was articulated, to evaluate their relative perfections and imperfections. Spinoza begins to put this method to work for the interpretation of scripture in the only other of his works printed during his lifetime, the *Theological-Political Treatise*. The results he presents there, however, do not involve the generation of a concept of an extramundane authorial God whose meaning is expressly present in the written text of scripture. Instead, by first mobilizing and then explicating the principles for a radically materialist interpretation of texts, Spinoza argues that scripture is degenerate, that is, it has been ineluctably corrupted by the passage of time, the vagaries of copying, the loss of nonconjectural access to the grammar and idiom of ancient Hebrew, and the disappearance of the contextual horizon necessary to understand what words written by particular prophets actually mean (not to mention what Spinoza holds to be the essential incommunicability of whatever truth there may be in prophetic revelation itself).[24] Even more crucial for Spinoza than these extrinsic forms of historical damage to the text is the sense in which attention to the literal meanings of its words plainly shows that scripture contains passages that contradict one another, both within what a single figure is reported to have said and among the various narratives presented in the text. These narratives, Spinoza insists we realize, were written by different people, in different situations, at different times, and with different ends in view (*SW*, 465–66; *TTP*, 7). In the face of such passages, he argues, we should not attempt to wring consistent meanings from the text by proposing reconciliations of sense where none are explicitly discovered in the words themselves but should instead suspend judgment with regard to their signification altogether (*SW*, 459; *TTP*, 7).

Resting on the assertion of the inseparability of the text in its materiality from divine meaning, any philological dogmatisms or mystical Cabbalisms are forced into what Spinoza thinks is the absurd position of maintaining "that God by some singular act of providence has preserved all the Sacred Books uncorrupted" and that therefore "the variant readings signal mysteries most profound" (*SW*, 485; *TTP*, 9). Instead, Spinoza suggests that the presence of lacunae and variants in a historically embedded text with a complex history signals nothing but its ineluctable materiality. We may attempt to engage in the historical and philological reconstruction of scriptural sense, Spinoza argues, but only insofar as we refrain from imposing allegorical meanings on literal claims, stitching together discontinuous and contradictory narratives with the thread of contemporary dogma and superstition, or assuming that all its writers present the plain truths of historical events. Attention to the words of scripture taken as "symbols," in other words, must be limited by and framed within attention to the material situation of the scriptural text, one which an honest historical assessment shows to be deeply flawed.[25] At the same time, even if the text is damaged or the language partly inapprehensible, the presence of such faults do not render its meaning fully irretrievable at least insofar as there are cases where "a book is clearly expressed and the author's meaning is unmistakable" (*SW*, 497; *TTP*, 10). Spinoza insists that even while his historical-philological analysis of the material text of scripture reveals that it has, for the most part, been corrupted beyond retrieval, this does not mean that nothing of its "divine" or "sacred" meaning has survived. Instead, he argues that the core meaning of scripture has reached modernity uncorrupted. The meaning of this "word of God" as actually retrievable from the scriptural page, however, amounts to an extremely minimal ethico-moral injunction that constitutes a single uncorrupted, universal teaching: "to love God above all, and one's neighbor as oneself" (*SW*, 508; *TTP*, 12). Elsewhere, the injunction is "to obey God with all one's heart by practicing justice and charity" (*SW*, 392; *TTP*, Pref). In chapter 14, Spinoza argues that a set of "dogmas of universal faith" can be formulated on the basis of this single, textually retrievable "divine word": God exists, is numerically one, is omniscient, possesses supreme right and dominion; worship consists solely in the practice of justice and charity and to be "saved" means merely to practice them; and finally, God forgives repentant sinners. Soon to articulate a conception of an impersonal God radically immanent to and identified with nature, Spinoza is quite clear even in the *Theological-Political Treatise* that these dogmas are justified pragmatically rather than scripturally or logically. They are "salutary" and "necessary in the state if men are to live in peace and harmony," but they involve "piety rather than truth" (*SW*, 517–19; *TTP*, 14).

The significance of Spinoza's claims is much broader than the minimization of the ability of readers of scripture to refer to it in support of religious practices and belief systems, forms of political legitimation, natural philosophical dogmas, and supposedly historical accounts of nations, cultures, and peoples. Instead, his materialist philology is both destructive, in that it reduces truth claims that rely on tortured, allegorical, ahistorical, or fanciful readings to the status of superstition, and constructive, in that it provides the tools for the retrieval of what literality remains even under conditions of textual dismemberment. Thus, the sphere of sense inhabited by "the word of God" has been radically restricted and reduced, while the fundamental and literal sense of that "word" has been rescued from its historical dispersal and rendered visible once more to the minds of the readers of scripture.

It should also be noted that Spinoza's literalism with respect to scripture, of course, is a far cry from a perspective that would insist that anything written on its pages is true simply by virtue of appearing there. Rather, conformity with reason becomes the standard by which the corrupt status of the text may be judged. With respect to natural philosophy, for example, Spinoza holds that while it must be the case that "everything related in scripture as having truly happened came to pass necessarily according to the laws of Nature," this means that any passages contravening known physical law must be historically corrupt (Spinoza suggests that these passages must have been "inserted into Holy Scripture by sacrilegious men") and are thereby uninterpretable. "For whatever is contrary to Nature is contrary to reason, and whatever is contrary to reason is absurd, and therefore should be rejected" (*SW*, 452; *TTP*, 6).

Two views of textual materiality follow from Spinoza's interpretive practice, and they initially seem to stand in contradiction. In its first aspect, scripture is understood to be a set number of material books constituted by certain letters written or printed in ink in a particular order on paper or parchment. This aspect of scripture is effectively destroyed through its subjection to Spinoza's historicist critique. The books of scripture simply constitute one more set of objects among the multitude of books, stripped entirely of the sacred character attributed to them by interpretive, theological, and religious traditions. Meanwhile, the *meaning* of scripture—what Spinoza identifies as "the word of God"—is retrieved from whatever still remains interpretable within these now-secularized pages. That meaning remains constant (the word of God is linked to "eternity itself") while its material instantiations in ink and paper are subject to becoming, transmutation, corruption, and erasure (the books of scripture are connected to "the legacy of time") (*SW*, 392; *TTP*, Pref). Therefore, "the revealed Word of God" is not reducible to the shattered framework of its material articulation. Those who insist on the inviolability and sacredness of scripture as it is historically given practice a form of idolatry in that they "worship the books of Scripture rather than the Word of God," the latter being something that "is not to be identified with a certain number of books" (*SW*, 392; *TTP*, Pref).[26] Or again, those who object that scripture as historically given is identical to the word of God "are carrying their piety too far, and are turning religion into superstition; indeed, instead of God's Word they are beginning to worship likenesses and images [*simulacra et imagines*], that is, paper and ink" (*SW*, 504; *TTP*, 12). While the paper and ink of scripture are what give us access to the ethico-political divine word when they are subjected to the literalizing strictures of historical criticism, this same paper and ink would become a graven image were we to assume that they bear a hermeneutic purity immune to the ravages of history. By insisting on the irreducibly material character of the scriptural text, meaning is therefore divorced from matter. Thus, Spinoza initially appears to have embraced an antimaterialist semiotic dualism in which the universal meaning of a text is exterior to its particular material instantiation. From this perspective, the materiality of the book is nothing but a hollow shell or a textual graveyard where the corpses of dead letters rot in neat columns and rows.

This first aspect of Spinozan interpretive practice must appear to make him an implacable enemy of the forms of textual materialism explored in earlier chapters of this book. Spinoza holds that with respect to their formal reality, letters and their shapes indicate nothing but the indiscernibility of textual objects from one another. They render their authorial causal origins accessible to us only insofar as we allow their materiality to recede from view and concentrate on the immaterial meaning bound up with their expression. Thus, he denies the efficacy of ink, paper, and the book for the metaphysical and natural philosophical projects of uncovering primary causes. Furthermore, the infinite reproducibility of textual objects (whether through hand copying in scribal practice or the standardization and dissemination bound up with the rise of print technologies) renders books objects of causal anxiety insofar as their ineluctably material nature seems to locate them in the infinite regress of efficient causal explanation associated with the motion of matter. He condemns as textual idolaters those who collapse sense into material instantiation and who thereby deny the impact of the violence and oblivion of history on the book. Instead, he insists, the formal reality of texts is an unavoidable site for their historical dispersal, disincorporation, and destruction. Finally, he claims that after their subjection to a destructive historical analysis, even the most corrupted texts may be found to articulate a meaning that transcends their corporeal vicissitudes, even if the condition for the apprehension of that meaning is a restriction of interpretation to the absolute literality of linguistic expression.

The antimaterialist aspect of Spinoza's interpretive practice is, however, accompanied by a second aspect that appears to stand in direct contradiction to the first. The second view rests on Spinoza's position that the retrieval of the meaning of the text—the rediscovery of "the word of God"—is axiomatically restricted within the limits of the materiality of the letter. We cannot simply dogmatically posit "love God above all, and one's neighbor as oneself"; we can only find this meaning within the bounds of what remains written in ink on the scriptural page subject to historical critique. In other words, whatever meaning there is that *can* be retrieved from a historically embedded, fragmented, and corrupted text—even a sacred one—is indelibly connected to its material surface. The meaning of scripture therefore cannot transcend the material conditions of its articulation and is in fact inseparable from them. As Warren Montag puts it, the meaning of the word of God is not a "residue beyond the surface" of the scriptural text but an effect produced by it (*MB*, 20). From this perspective, the primary methodological injunction of the *Theological-Political Treatise* is to radically respect the materiality of the text. Framed negatively, this means that even central religious and theological commitments (especially in an early modern Calvinist context) must be abandoned whenever we are unable to legitimately move from the shape and order of the letters to the meaning of the discourse (i.e., from the first book of ideas grasped in terms of their formal reality to the second book of ideas grasped in terms of their representational content). Put positively, "the word of God" is radically immanent with respect to its materialization in the book. At a fundamental level, *both* books must be grasped in terms of their formal reality, as unless it exists, a representative idea can represent nothing at all. Thus, in direct contradiction with the first effect of Spinoza's interpretive system, the significance of a text is fully immanent to the disposition of letters and words in ink on paper. The meaning of scripture is therefore ineluctably bound to the materiality of the letter.

THE BOOK OF POWER

Are these two aspects of Spinoza's ontology of the page reconcilable? I would like to suggest that the apparent contradiction between them stems from an ambiguity in the way that the articulation of both views frames "matter" and "material conditions" themselves. If Spinoza is able to embrace both aspects of this theory at once, then the material conditions under which the retrieval of scriptural meaning becomes possible—the textual site for its articulation—must not refer to the sheer facticity of a book containing nothing more than dead letters. The *Theological-Political Treatise*, in fact, injects a third and crucial concept between meaning and the letter: movement. Consider a celebrated set of passages where Spinoza again identifies the paper and ink of the book with the evacuation of meaning:

> Words acquire a fixed meaning solely from their use; if in accordance with this usage they are so arranged that readers are moved to devotion [*legentes ad devotionem moveant*], then these words will be sacred, and likewise the book containing this arrangement of words. But if these words at a later time fall into disuse so as to become meaningless, or if the book falls into utter neglect, whether from malice or because men no longer feel the need of it, then both words and book will be without value and without sanctity. Lastly, if these words are arranged differently, or if by custom they acquire a meaning contrary to their original meaning, then both words and book will become impure and profane instead of sacred . . . So Scripture is likewise sacred, and its words divine, only as long as it moves men to devotion to God; but if it is utterly disregarded by them, as it once was by the Jews, it is nothing more than paper and ink, and their neglect renders it completely profane, leaving it exposed to corruption. (*SW*, 505; *TTP*, 12)

Here, the disposition of words in a book may move readers to devotion to God (i.e., to nature or substance), to its opposite, or (if they are meaningless) to nothing at all. The thing that should be noticed here is that the meaning of words—what endows them with an objective reality whereby they refer beyond their own articulation—is a function of the way their disposition moves their readers toward or away from devotion. Devotion, in turn, is understood affectively, that is to say, as an effect of an encounter simultaneously cognitive and corporeal.

Spinoza formally defines affect in the following way: "By *affectus* I understand the affections of the body by which the body's power of activity is increased or diminished, assisted or checked, together with the ideas of these affections" (*SW*, 278; *E*, 3Def3). To understand what is at stake here, we need to be very careful not to confuse affect (*affectus*) with affection (*affectio*), a term Spinoza introduces in the first book of the *Ethics* as a synonym of "modification" to denote the relationship between modes and substance, and metonymically transfers to the relations among finite modes in the second book as a way of describing the changes caused in an extended mode by the impact of external bodies. In this second register, I perceive external bodies through the affections my body undergoes when it interacts with them, and I grasp my own body as a site of corporeal affection. *Affection* thus refers to the composition or decomposition of my body by another body and the sense in which the current state of my body retains a trace of an encounter. *Affect*, by contrast, is an affection together with the idea of that affection. It denotes a transition to a greater or lesser state of perfection, which means a modulation of the power of a singular thing to act and to exist. Affect is thus an expression of power, while "affection" only refers to what has happened to my body, that is, affection is the effect of my encounter with another body. Strictly speaking, then, an affect involves a unification (across attributes) of corporeal affections with the ideas of those affections to which they ontologically correspond under the identity of the order of ideas with the order of things. Thus, affect can never be a mere psychological state or existential mood. "Disposition" is the appropriate way of thinking about it, if we understand this to refer not to the passively given receptive character of a subject, but to an activity of *dispositio* or to a *dispositif* taken in its classical dialectical, rhetorical, and military senses: the methodological activity by which the essential parts of an argument are organized; the arrangement of arguments and tropes in a discourse to produce effects in the minds and bodies of listeners or readers; and a distribution of forces in the conduct of war. Affect is thus a concept describing the regular distribution, arrangement, or configuration of a dynamic system.

To see the implications of this for our question more clearly, we need to understand what Spinoza means specifically when he refers to the affect of devotion, as it bears little relation to the usual signification of that term. In the *Theological-Political Treatise* devotion receives a minimal definition provided in the context of Spinoza's claim that the injunction to celebrate and rejoice associated with the high holidays and the Sabbath in the post-Mosaic Hebrew state was an element of an ideological strategy for the inculcation of political obedience. "No more effective means can be devised to influence men's minds," Spinoza writes, "for nothing can so captivate the mind as joy springing from devotion, that is, love mingled with awe" (*SW*, 548; *TTP*, 17). We also learn that such devotion can be known only through its external manifestations: through the works of the one so affected, that is, her charitable acts (*SW*, 569; *TTP*, 20). Devotion, then, should not be mistaken for mere religious sentiment or a spiritual orientation toward the divine. Rather, as framed in the *Theological-Political Treatise*, it functions more properly as a secular mechanism of affective and ideological political control.

A more detailed sense of the meaning and function of devotion can be gleaned from the *Ethics*, where devotion is explicitly defined as "love toward one at whom we wonder" (*SW*, 313; *E*, 3AD10). Unpacked in terms of Spinoza's nested set of definitions of the affects, this means that devotion is love, that is, pleasure accompanied by the idea of an external cause (*SW*, 312; *E*, 3AD6), where that external cause is a thing on which the mind stays fixed because the idea of that thing has no connection with any other, that is, that affects us with wonder (*SW*, 312; *E*, 3AD4). The pleasure so produced, furthermore, is a transition of the one affected to a state of greater perfection, that is, an intensification of her power and desire (*SW*, 311; *E*, 3AD2). My experience of devotion, then, *means* an increase in my power to act and to exist, which I undergo specifically by virtue of my fascination by the idea of a unique thing, in this case, my absorption with the idea of God. What is crucial to understand here is that to be *moved* to devotion by the *disposition* of the words in scripture means to be *affected* by them in a simultaneously cognitive and corporeal way. In a confrontation with the affective text, the complex of ideas that constitutes my mind is reconfigured, at the same time and in the same manner that the complex of corporeal things constituting the affective surface of my body is reconfigured. Thus, under a Spinozan regime of textual materialism the framework of merely cognitive ideational representation gives way to a discourse of simultaneously ideational and corporeal power. That a concatenation of letters on the page is capable of generating in me devotion to God (or its opposite: a decrease in my power to act and to exist—pain—accompanied by my wonder before God as its external cause) means the disposition of these letters *produces effects in my mind and in my body*, and that those effects are transitions in my power to produce effects (i.e., to act and to exist).[27] This is what constitutes the meaning of the words in question: the meaning of words is nothing but the effects they produce.

Thus, when Spinoza insists that we avoid the trap of becoming idolaters who worship dead letters in ink on paper (or the merely formal being of ideas) and that we instead attend to a meaning irreducible to the site of its articulation in words, his apparent antimaterialist dualism is in fact a red herring. A Spinozan textual materialism does not rely on the valorization of the page merely insofar as it is the page, but upon understanding it as a site for the production of real effects and real modulations of power in both the cognitive and corporeal registers. Spinoza's critique of the book of formal ideas (the first book, that is, the volume that we attempted to understand with reference to nothing but its characters, letters, and their order) was not that it mistook mute textual matter for the site of the production of meaning, but that it misunderstood the meaning of meaning itself. The problem was not so much that the first book bracketed the representational objective reality of the words contained within it, but that it failed to understand its own materiality. Partisans of the first book take the materiality of its paper and ink to lack a referential function and therefore refuse to attend to the meaningfulness of its words. Their mistake, however, is not that they miss the opportunity to posit a form of signification that transcends the characters of the book, but rather that they fail to see that the true materiality of the book is its power to produce real effects in the minds and bodies of its readers, that is, to set them in motion both cognitively and corporeally. These effects (whether they be framed in terms of devotion or any other affect) *are* the meaning of the ordered characters and words, and this effective power—not the ink and paper or words and characters alone—is what constitutes the materiality of the book. Rather than standing in opposition to meaning, materiality is the locus of dynamic causal power. The materiality of the book, in other words, is its capacity to produce effects.

In sum, Spinoza's articulation of a radically materialist form of textual criticism rests on three core principles. First, textual meaning can be legitimately derived only from dispositions of words and letters through a grammar, a semantic content, and a historical context that give readers access to the bare literality of the words as they are present on the surface of the page. Allegorical, allusive, and mystical interpretations that attempt to salvage the wrecks of historically corrupted texts are ruled inadmissible because they mistake the accidents of characterological or typographical disposition for the essences of literal meanings. Second, insofar as these literal meanings can be apprehended (even in the remainder of a corrupted text subject to a dogmatic interpretive tradition), they are not reducible to the formal being of scriptural characters (i.e., the textual surface as sedimented by history). Third, meaning and the disposition of characters come together when we realize that meaning is located neither in the words on the page taken only as inked marks on paper, nor in a mystical realm of pure signification that transcends them, but in the causal efficaciousness mobilized by the disposition of the marks themselves. Thus, meaning is itself the materiality of the book, that is, the *power* of paper and ink to produce cognitive and corporeal effects and generate desires. Attention to this productive and affective power of the book is what renders Spinoza a partisan of textual materialism and a philosopher of the ontology of the page.

CONCLUSION: THE END OF THE BOOK

A book has neither object nor subject; it is made of variously formed matters, and very different dates and speeds. To attribute the book to a subject is to overlook this working of matters, and the exteriority of their relations. It is to fabricate a beneficent God to explain geological movements. In a book, as in all things, there are lines of articulation or segmentarity, strata and territories; but also lines of flight, movements of deterritorialization and destratification. Comparative rates of flow on these lines produce phenomena of relative slowness and viscosity, or, on the contrary, of acceleration and rupture. All this, lines and measureable speeds, constitutes an assemblage. A book is an assemblage *of this kind, and as such is unattributable. It is a multiplicity . . .*

Deleuze and Guattari, A Thousand Plateaus

Figures of material inscription in the history of philosophy cannot be limited to those associated, in early modernity, with the physical codex and its elements (ink, paper, binding), with the activities connected to their production and use (setting type, locking formes, typographical *mise en page*, writing in margins, reordering copied fragments), or with the apparatuses by which they are disposed and organized (printing houses, booksellers, libraries, encyclopedias). For one thing, my account has not included an exhaustive treatment of the figure of the book in philosophical discourse in general let alone in its full seventeenth-century framework. For another, this project has not fully explored all the connections between these figures of material inscription and the complex history of the articulation of matter in early modernity. At the same time, I have

CONCLUSION

demonstrated that a rhetorical reliance on the set of figures organized by the image of the book is tightly bound to the history of the philosophical consideration of materiality. Thus, this project has more than merely antiquarian relevance for contemporary theoretical and cultural debates regarding both the history and the future of the book as well as its associated metaphors.

Since at least the middle of the twentieth century, most of those writing seriously about the book have thought it necessary to treat the problem of its ineluctably vanishing future and its artifactual supersession by newly emerging technologies of textual production, circulation, reading, and writing. Many contemporary scholars find themselves productively and creatively struggling to invent a new language when they attempt to describe exactly what book-objects are in the face of their seemingly infinite and dematerialized proliferation as electronic editions, scanned portable document format facsimiles of specific and locatable copies, and the resultant accessibility of entire libraries (or in some cases, libraries of libraries) via any connection to global information networks. One prominent example is Roger Chartier's argument that technologies of material inscription are now in the process of undergoing a shift more radical than anything seen since the emergence of the codex form of the book. The proper historical analog for our current shift in medium away from the page and toward the screen (a single object on and through which any text whatever may be displayed and read), he argues, is not the shift from the "scribal culture" of the manuscript era to the "print culture" of the mechanical (and eventually industrial) era, but the turn from the material form of the scroll to that of bound pages. The latter shift is more fundamental, he holds, because the true site of the materiality of the book is, on the one hand, whatever delimits the possibilities for the manipulation, use, and engagement that occurs when the book encounters the reader and, on the other hand, the formal conditions for the organization of the written word and the textual apparatuses constructed for its negotiation (tables of contents, indexes, margins available for note-taking, etc.).[1]

While Chartier may underestimate the real diversity of the technologically specifiable and even practically incommensurable forms that the screen can take—the differences between reading or writing on a laptop computer and a cell phone, for example, may be in some respects greater than those between using a scroll and a codex—he is certainly correct to insist that a fundamental shift is taking place and that the materiality of inscription is one plane on which it is occurring. At the same time, the theoretical and terminological problems associated with the struggles of contemporary media theorists and historians to delineate what exactly is happening to the book are often surprisingly isomorphic with those consuming their early to mid-twentieth-century counterparts when they considered the challenges posed by the ubiquity of photomechanical reproduction technologies, whether in the form of photographic facsimiles of individual pages, microfilm and microfiche miniaturization technologies, or the cheap photostatic and xerographic reproduction of entire works.[2] These issues, in turn, are in several significant senses congruent with the early modern debates surrounding the explosion of hand-presses and the fundamental changes they wrought on the dissemination, formalization, production, and use of books and other printed materials.[3] In each case, fundamental technological shifts surrounding books and their dissemination have been accompanied by solemn pronouncements regarding the imminent closure of the era of the book: the end of the book and its replacement by the printed codex, the abstract or review in the intellectual journal, the soulless object of industrial mass production, the photograph or the photostat, the hypertextual website, the electronically produced or reproduced document, and so forth.

Doubtless, each of these technological shifts (as well as many others this abbreviated list does not include) has accompanied a set of profound transformations in practices and postures of reading, economies of textual circulation, production of legal and conceptual regimes of authorial sovereignty and subjectivity, institutions and social structures for the organization and management of the ever-increasing flood of written matter, as well as practices of legitimation or normative judgment regarding which material is to be credited and which discredited. With reference to a series of philosophers in the early modern continental rationalist tradition, I have argued that in fundamental ways these transformations do not remain extrinsic to the discursive and philosophical positions and arguments to which they are historically connected. Rather, the historical and physiological sites, technologies, strategies, and apparatuses for philosophical reading, writing, and knowledge organization make their way *intrinsically* into the concepts and rhetoric of the philosophical text whose production they govern (though without playing a technologically deterministic role). They do so specifically under the form of what

CONCLUSION

I have called figures of material inscription, that is, the concatenation of philosophical metaphors whereby the corporeal, technological, and conceptual elements associated with the structure of the printed book, the written page, pen and ink, the letter, the library, the dictionary, and the encyclopedia are embedded in philosophical writing. These figures, I have argued, are material in a double sense. First, their metaphorical power is connected directly with their corporeality in such a way that the very physical paraphernalia, bodily practices and postures, and institutional apparatuses connected with the production and circulation of philosophical discourse consistently find a crucial place *within* their enunciations. Second, a particularly prominent conceptual location for the exercise of that metaphorical power is the philosophical confrontation with or conceptual development of accounts of materiality itself.

In the end, one fundamental philosophical question posed by the problems associated with the latest proclamations of the end of the book may be whether the codex and all its associated technologies are merely a material support for a set of concepts, narratives, tropes, arguments, and so-called information that fundamentally transcends them. If the objects and practices that constitute (or constituted for the early moderns) a crucial series of metaphors *for* materiality itself are to be superseded, then are we on the verge of leaving the concept of matter behind? Is it all over (yet again) for the book, and if so, does the discourse of materiality itself stand in need of revision? From a philosophical perspective, I think the stakes of this question are not truly congruent with those of a technical-empirical query regarding "the future of the book." Instead, it may be more productive to ask what we can still *do* with the figures of material inscription associated with the book. In that vein, one of the most powerful philosophical and strategic models for a revision of the figure of the book mobilized (albeit anachronistically) in the face of the contemporary ubiquity of electronic and seemingly immaterial inscription technologies may be the enigmatic "rhizome-book" offered by Gilles Deleuze and Félix Guattari in *A Thousand Plateaus* (1980).[4] It therefore seems appropriate to end this engagement with the relationship between philosophical discourse and figures of material inscription with a brief consideration of the nature of Deleuze and Guattari's figure. What follows will be specifically oriented toward the elucidation of the connection that figure posits between a reconceptualization of the structure of the book and a recasting of the materiality with which it has so long been linked.

The introduction to Deleuze and Guattari's volume distinguishes between three specific book types, each articulated through a different botanical model: the root, the radicle, and the rhizome (*ATP*, 5–7).[5] The first two are "arborescent" images of thought essentially deriving, as Umberto Eco has extensively demonstrated, from the Porphyrian logical tree and the connected Aristotelian system of definition by proximate genus and specific difference.[6] The root-book (the most classical and metaphysically conservative form) is organized simultaneously and isomorphically along the spine of the trunk and the taproot, both aspects of a single and simple conceptual and ontological unity (Being) which is then developed through a system of progressive division or branching. The root-book is therefore governed by the binary logic of the derivation of multiplicity and difference from a more essential unity and identity. Deleuze and Guattari's second figure of the book is organized by the linked figures of the radicle (an embryonic root emerging directly from a seed and the preeminent site for grafting) and the fascicle (an inseparable cluster of intertwining root systems of various plants, but also, of course, the name for each installment in the serial publication of a single book). This radicular figure of the book encompasses the kinds of textual, syntactical, narratological, and typographical experimentation with the book-form that came to prominence with the rise of high modernism and that had prompted Derrida, in *Of Grammatology*, to announce the end of the book and the beginning of writing. This form of the book challenged the hierarchical linearity of the root-book through a mobilization of chance, carefully constructed incongruous juxtaposition, and strategies of cut-up and reassembly of fragments from other books (as in Mallarmé, Joyce, and Burroughs). Unlike Derrida, Deleuze and Guattari minimize the radicalism of the radicle-book in that they insist that its rejection of the ordered totality of the Aristotelian root-framework conceals a demand for an even more comprehensive conception of unity. This demand is still governed by a binary logic, now structured by the oppositions of order and chaos, necessity and chance. A totalizing philosophical and aesthetic image of the fundamental fragmentation of human reality and its world, in other words, is precisely what is reflected in the structure of the modernist radicle-book. In this sense its renunciation of the closed model of a hierarchically ordered ontology expresses all the more intensely the project for the construction of a book that representationally

CONCLUSION

corresponds to a reality outside of its pages (a world), now understood on the model of fragmentation. The problem, as Deleuze and Guattari see it, is that these arborescent models constitute two aspects of the dream that the book could become the mimetic image of the world: a representationalist recapitulation of a reality external to it. Both involve the elevation of unity—and thus being—to a position of ontological and epistemological primordiality under which is subsumed multiplicity and difference. The root-book accomplishes this elevation through a simple reflective affirmation of unity. The radicle-book realizes the same thing through a howl of protest that dialectically reflects an irrevocable loss of the "one." In some cases, it even points toward the possibility of the recapture of unity in a messianic time yet to come through a restructuring of chaos and a promised reduction of multiplicity.

To these arborescent images of thought and being, Deleuze and Guattari oppose the rhizome-book. For those readers unfamiliar with their work, this metaphor may appear absurd (one might wonder: do they mean a ginger book, a potato book, a fern book?). Botanically speaking (though just as with the other models, its metaphorical resonances are not limited to plant life), the rhizome figure refers to a nodal organization in which a plant sends out roots and shoots both horizontally and vertically in an opportunistic manner such that growth occurs wherever, whenever, and in whatever direction conditions are opportune. Rather than the directly expressed hierarchical structure of the root-book (which recapitulates an identical system of conceptual and ontological division: as above so below; as the world, so the book of the world) or the chaotic and fragmented graft-structure of a lost or aborted hierarchy in the radicle-book, the rhizome-book is a production of multiplicity as multiplicity and not as a binary derivation from unity or a fragmentary substitution for it. Unlike the arborescent images of the book, any point of the rhizome-book can be connected to any other without reliance on a pivotal point where a more primordial unity is bifurcated. Crucially, this does not mean that the rhizome-book lacks structure, but rather that its segmentary form is a constantly mutating explosion of productive force that responds to the pressures of whatever environments or entities it encounters (the rhizome-book operates, in Deleuze and Guattari's new terminology, along paths of rupture and lines of flight). The rhizome-book, then, does not depend on the expression of a deep, functional structure for the purpose of the realization or actualization of some end (as would an Aristotelian biological model of teleology). Instead, its structure is a complex map of the history of its production, its encounters, and its disruptions (*ATP*, 7–13). With respect to their critique of the arborescent models of the book, what is most important for Deleuze and Guattari is that the rhizome-book is not an image of the world. Rather, it is a way of conceiving the book that dispenses with the representational and mimetic dichotomy between the world and the book. In other words, the rhizome-book insists that *the book is a thing of the world and the world is a thing of the book*. To understand the figure of book in this sense, then, is to claim not that the book is like the world, repeats the world, or expresses the world, but instead that the book "forms a rhizome *with* the world" (*ATP*, 11; my emphasis).[7]

In what sense do these three curious botanical models for the book provide a means of concluding the discussion of the issues that have been treated here under the rubric of figures of material inscription? First, consider that while this section of *A Thousand Plateaus* presents these three book metaphors as if they correspond to three types of books or three eras in the history of the book (with *A Thousand Plateaus* itself standing as the primary exemplar of the rhizome-book it champions), it makes just as much sense to see them as three models for conceiving any book whatever. If, as Deleuze and Guattari suggest, we frame the book as an object that essentially expresses a metaphysical figuration of unity and multiplicity rather than as a static bearer of a transcendent signifying text produced by an authorial exteriority, then there are no obvious barriers to taking the arborescent and rhizomatic models to describe strategies for the figuration of whatever set of objects counts as a set of books. Second, consider the repercussions of the rhizomatic model for any description of the materiality of the book and the figural elements and activities attaching to it. To claim that the book forms a rhizome with the world and to insist that the rhizome-book be understood through the image of a cartography of encounters and lines of flight rather than a genealogy tracing origin and descent is to hold that *the book-as-rhizome is the effects it produces*. Such a conception—one directly congruent with the notions of early modern materiality treated in the preceding chapters—involves a shift away from a perspective that understands the book and its pages as a mere container for a text that transcends it (the Platonic model). It also dispenses with the position that takes the book to be a contingent

CONCLUSION

support or underlying site of articulation for a formal activity of writing that renders it actual (the Aristotelian model). Instead, it demands a perspective that understands the book as a locus of causal power. The rhizome, in other words, is the figure for a book that is what it is insofar as it produces a regime of singular effects. The rhizome-book is a dynamic individual that, on the one hand, maintains a consistent, complex pattern of motive action while simultaneously undergoing profound transformations with respect to its elements or parts (up to and including the limit-point of its own destruction when it can no longer maintain the integrity of its nature). This notion, I maintain, stands at the core of what Deleuze and Guattari mean when they describe the book as an assemblage (*agencement*). This concept of the dynamic unity of an individual whose parts undergo constant flux is also, as readers of the last chapter will recall, precisely the key to Spinoza's account of the body. In a very direct sense, then, I am suggesting that to understand the book on the rhizomatic model (potentially a figure for any and all books) is to insist on its fundamental and ineluctable materiality, where materiality itself is conceived dynamically.

It should by now be clear that such a dynamic conception of the materiality of the book—and subsequently of the broader field of figures of inscription that have been treated throughout this work—does not rely on a theoretical or ideological decision to favor a physical inscriptive framework over intellectual or meaningful content, let alone to engage in a direct polemic in favor of a conception of material capacity to the detriment of form. In the preceding discussions of Descartes, Spinoza, Leibniz, and Bayle, my emphasis has been on the sense in which these philosophers wrestle with the inescapable materiality of the apparatus, site, activity, and organization of figures of reading, writing, printing, and related concepts. Even as several of these philosophers stand on the precipice of articulating ontological dualisms or epistemological idealisms, a profound confrontation with this materiality and its possible configurations always fundamentally animates their philosophical projects. One reason for ending the final chapter of this book with Spinoza is that, in his engagement with the body and the book, this investigation of the mobilization of material figures of inscription in early modern thought leads to the development of two theses. First, early modern materiality itself can be conceived on a dynamic model directly connected with figures of material inscription. Second, given the character of this model of materiality, conceptualization and embodiment can be understood to be one and the same thing differently expressed. What a Spinozist conception of materiality and its identity with conceptuality will never allow, however, is the rhetorical and figural subsumption of the material under the immaterially conceptual. The crucial and inescapable figural language for the expression of a dynamic conception of materiality and the non-reductive identification of book and text belongs to the body, and in the early modern period at least, specifically to that discourse of the matter governed by the renewal of Epicurean and Lucretian images, arguments, concepts, and metaphors. Whether in the end this materialist discourse retains its power as our practices, vocabularies, technologies, and tropes continue to undergo the radical variations to which they have everywhere and always been subject depends entirely on the effects that this discourse produces in our bodies and in the world.

NOTES

INTRODUCTION

1. Pierre Gassendi, *The Selected Works of Pierre Gassendi*, ed. and trans. Craig B. Brush (New York: Johnson Reprint Corporation, 1972), 427–28. Hereafter cited as *GW*. For the Lucretius passages, see Titus Carus Lucretius, *De rerum natura*, trans. W.H.D. Rouse and Martin Ferguson Smith, rev. edn., Loeb Classical Library 181 (Cambridge, MA: Harvard University Press, 1975), 1.195–98, 1.823–29, 1.907–14, 2.688–99, and 2.1013–22 Hereafter cited as *DRN*.
2. On the early modern impact of Lucretius, see Howard Jones, *The Epicurean Tradition* (London: Routledge 1989) and Philip Ford, "Lucretius in Early Modern France," in *The Cambridge Companion to Lucretius*, ed. Stuart Gillespie and Philip Hardie (Cambridge: Cambridge University Press), 227–41.
3. On Gassendi's reconstruction of a prehistory for early modern atomism, see Lynn Sumida Joy, *Gassendi the Atomist: Advocate of History in an Age of Science* (Cambridge: Cambridge University Press, 1987); Antonia Lolordo, *Pierre Gassendi and the Birth of Early Modern Philosophy* (Cambridge: Cambridge University Press, 2007); and Saul Fisher, *Pierre Gassendi's Philosophy and Science: Atomism for Empiricists* (Leiden: Brill, 2005).
4. Petrarch to Neri Morando of Forlì (XXI.10), in Francesco Petrarca, *Letters on Familiar Matters: Rerum familiarium libri XVII–XXIV*, trans. Aldo S. Bernardo (Baltimore, MD: Johns Hopkins University Press, 1985), 186–87.
5. Jacques Derrida, "White Mythology: Metaphor of the Text in Philosophy," in *Margins of Philosophy*, trans. Alan Bass (Chicago, IL: University of Chicago Press, 1982), 207–29; Paul de Man, *Allegories of Reading: Figural Language in Rousseau, Nietzsche, Rilke, and Proust* (New Haven, CT: Yale University Press, 1979); and Michèle Le Doeuff, *The Philosophical Imaginary*, trans. Colin Gordon (London: Continuum, 2002).
6. Michel Foucault, *The Order of Things: An Archaeology of the Human Sciences*, trans. Alan Sheridan (New York: Vintage, 1970). Hereafter cited as *OT*.
7. Jacques Derrida, *Of Grammatology*, trans. Gayatri Chakravorty Spivak (Baltimore, MD: The Johns Hopkins University Press, 1974), 286. Hereafter cited as *OG*.

8. Ernst Robert Curtius, "The Book as Symbol," in *European Literature and the Latin Middle Ages*, trans. Willard R. Trask (Princeton, NJ: Princeton University Press, 1991), 302–47. Hans Blumenberg, *Die Lesbarkeit der Welt* (Frankfurt am Main: Suhrkamp, 1981). Though not histories *per se* but collections of elements for such histories, see the essays in *The Book of Nature in Antiquity and the Middle Ages*, ed. Arjo Vanderjagt and Klaas van Berkel (Leuven: Peeters, 2005) and *The Book of Nature in Early Modern and Modern History*, ed. Klaas van Berkel and Arjo Vanderjagt (Leuven: Peeters, 2006).
9. For his later and much more nuanced account of paper and the page, see Jacques Derrida, "Paper or Me, You Know . . . (New Speculations on a Luxury of the Poor)," in *Paper Machine*, trans. Rachel Bowlby (Stanford, CA: Stanford University Press, 2005). Here Derrida entirely renounces his *Of Grammatology* position that paper functions merely as a material support animated or instantiated by the text. He further proposes an intriguing investigation into the history of paper's figuration *as* "support" or "base."
10. Quires are gatherings, sections, or signatures composed of one or several leaves of paper folded together several times and then collated in order to be stitched together. Several quires sewn together constitute the text block, or the pages of a book. Boards are the hard, flat material used as the foundation for stiff book covers. They are cut to size, attached to the text block, and often covered in leather, cloth, paper, or other material.
11. Hans Blumenberg's *Die Lesbarkeit der Welt* is a good example.
12. Francis Bacon, *The Advancement of Learning*, in *Collected Works*, 3:301.
13. Robert Boyle, *The Usefulness of Natural Philosophy* in *The Works of Robert Boyle*, ed. Michael Hunter and Edward B. Davis, 14 vols. (London: Pickering & Chatto, 1999–2000), 3:279.
14. Galileo Galilei, *The Assayer* in *The Controversy of the Comets of 1618*, ed. and trans. Stillman Drake and C.D. O'Malley (Philadelphia, PA: Pennsylvania University Press, 1960), 183–84. Hereafter cited as *GA*.
15. George Johnson, "Vatican's Celestial Eye, Seeking Not Angels but Data," *New York Times*, June 23, 2009, D2.
16. Elizabeth L. Eisenstein, *The Printing Press as an Agent of Change: Communications and Cultural Transformations in Early-Modern Europe*, 1 vol. edn. (Cambridge: Cambridge University Press, 1979), esp. 575–635. There is a long tradition of scholarship on the history of the book though prior to the 1970s it tended to focus on the kind of large-scale documentary surveys undertaken by the Annales School of historiography. The masterwork of this tradition is (from 1958) Lucien Paul Victor Febvre and Henri-Jean Martin, *The Coming of the Book: The Impact of Printing 1450–1800*, trans. David Gerard (London: Verso, 1976). Also see (from 1988) Henri-Jean Martin, *The History and Power of Writing*, trans. Lydia G. Cochrane (Chicago, IL: University of Chicago Press, 1994).
17. See, in particular, Eisenstein's discussion of "typographical fixity" and its implications. Elizabeth Eisenstein, *Printing Press*, 113–26.
18. David McKitterick, *Print, Manuscript, and the Search for Order 1450–1830* (Cambridge: Cambridge University Press, 2003); Anthony Grafton,

"The Importance of Being Printed," review of Elizabeth L. Eisenstein, *The Printing Press as an Agent of Change, Journal of Interdisciplinary History* 11, no. 2 (Autumn, 1980), 265–86; Anthony Grafton, "The Humanist as Reader," in *A History of Reading in the West*, ed. Guglielmo Cavallo and Roger Chartier, trans. Lydia G. Cochrane (Amherst, MA: University of Massachusetts Press, 1999), 179–212; and Stillman Drake, "Early Science and the Printed Book: The Spread of Science beyond the Universities," *Renaissance and Reformation* 6 (1970), 43–52.
19. Roger Chartier, *The Cultural Uses of Print in Early Modern France*, trans. Lydia G. Cochrane (Princeton, NJ: Princeton University Press, 1987) and Adrian Johns, *The Nature of the Book: Print and Knowledge in the Making* (Chicago, IL: University of Chicago Press, 1998).
20. See Steven Shapin and Simon Schaffer, *Leviathan and the Air-Pump: Hobbes, Boyle, and the Experimental Life* (Princeton, NJ: Princeton University Press, 1986); Steven Shapin, *A Social History of Truth: Civility and Science in Seventeenth-Century England* (Chicago, IL: University of Chicago Press, 1994); and Bruno Latour, *We Have Never Been Modern*, trans. Catherine Porter (Cambridge, MA: Harvard University Press, 1993).
21. Douglas McKenzie, "Printers of the Mind: Some Notes on Bibliographical Theories and Printing-House Practices," *Studies in Bibliography* 22 (1969), 1–75.
22. The first thesis, frequently cited by Chartier, is articulated by Roger Stoddard, "Morphology and the Book from an American Perspective," *Printing History* 17 (1987), 9. The second is from McKenzie, "Printers of the Mind," 20.
23. Adrian Johns, *Nature of the Book*, 19–20 and 628–38. Also see the remarkable exchange between Eisenstein and Johns mediated by Grafton. Anthony Grafton, "Introduction," *The American Historical Review* 107, no. 1 (2002), 84–86; Elizabeth Eisenstein, "An Unacknowledged Revolution Revisited," *The American Historical Review* 107, no. 1 (2002), 87–105; Adrian Johns, "How to Acknowledge a Revolution," *The American Historical Review* 107, no. 1 (2002), 106–25; and Elizabeth Eisenstein, "Reply," *The American Historical Review* 107, no. 1 (2002), 126–28.

1 INFINITE MECHANISM AND THE ALLEGORICAL LIBRARY

1. G.W. Leibniz, *Theodicy: Essays on the Goodness of God, the Freedom of Man, and the Origin of Evil*, ed. Austin Marsden Farrer, trans. E.M. Huggard (La Salle, IL: Open Court, 1985), 53. Hereafter cited as *Theo.*
2. The principle and the story behind its formulation are recounted many times throughout Leibniz's corpus. Perhaps most famously, in his fourth letter to Samuel Clarke, Leibniz writes, "There is no such thing as two individuals indiscernible from each other. An ingenious gentleman of my acquaintance, discoursing with me in the presence of Her Electoral Highness, the Princess Sophia, in the garden of Herrenhausen, thought he could find two leaves perfectly alike. The princess defied him to do it,

and he ran all over the garden a long time to look for some; but it was to no purpose. Two drops of water or milk, viewed with a microscope, will appear distinguishable from each other. This is an argument against atoms, which are confuted, as well as the void, by the principles of true metaphysics." G.W. Leibniz, *Philosophical Essays*, ed. and trans. Roger Ariew and Daniel Garber (Indianapolis, IN: Hackett, 1989), 327–28. Hereafter cited as *AG*.

3. An excellent overview of the premodern history of the figure of the labyrinth is Penelope Reed Doob, *The Idea of the Labyrinth from Classical Antiquity through the Middle Ages* (Ithaca, NY: Cornell University Press, 1990). See also Hermann Kern, *Labyrinthe: Erscheinungsformen und Deutungen 5000 Jahre Gegenwart eines Urbilds* (Munich: Prestel Verlag, 1982). A partial history of the labyrinth as a medieval philosophical figure in the context of theodicy debates can be found in Richard Schenk, "Daedalus medii aevi? Die Labyrinthe der Theodizee im Mittelalter," *Jahrbuch für Philosophie des Forschungsinstituts für Philosophie, Hannover* 9 (1998), 15–35.

4. Libert Froidmont, *Labyrinthus, sive, De compositione continui liber unus: philosophis, mathematicis, theologis utilis ac iucundus* (Antwerp: Ex officina Plantiniana Balthasaris Moreti, 1631).

5. René Descartes, *Oeuvres de Descartes*, ed. Charles Adam and Paul Tannery, rev. edn., 11 vols. (Paris: Vrin, 1996), 10:354. Hereafter cited as *AT*.

6. René Descartes, *The Philosophical Writings of Descartes*, ed. and trans. John Cottingham, Robert Stoothoff, and Dugald Murdoch, 3 vols. (Cambridge: Cambridge University Press, 1984–1991), 1:20. Hereafter cited as *CSM*.

7. Francis Bacon, *Great Instauration* in *Collected Works of Francis Bacon*, ed. James Spedding, Robert Leslie Ellis, and Douglas Denon Heath, 12 vols. (1876; reprint, London: Routledge, 1996), 4:18.

8. For a discussion of Leibniz's sources for the labyrinth metaphor, see Catherine Wilson, *Leibniz's Metaphysics: A Historical and Comparative Study* (Manchester: Manchester University Press, 1989), 7–8 and 71–72.

9. On Leibniz and the continuum problem, amongst the enormous literature available see especially: Samuel Levy, "Leibniz on Mathematics and the Actually Infinite Division of Matter," *The Philosophical Review* 107, no. 1 (1998), 49–96; Samuel Levy, "Matter and Two Concepts of Continuity in Leibniz," *Philosophical Studies* 94, no. 1–2 (1999), 81–118; Pauline Phemister, *Leibniz and the Natural World: Activity, Passivity and Corporeal Substances in Leibniz's Philosophy* (Dordrecht: Springer, 2005), 81–132; and Donald Rutherford, *Leibniz and the Rational Order of Nature* (Cambridge: Cambridge University Press, 1995), 212–36.

10. Cf. "The Principles of Philosophy, or, the Monadology," §64, where "Each organized body of a living being is a kind of divine machine or natural automaton which infinitely surpasses all artificial automata" (*AG*, 221).

11. Leibniz begins to propose a fascinating alternative to this dichotomy in his 1709–1716 correspondence with Bartholomew des Bosses, taking up the Scholastic concept of the *vinculum substantiale* and proposing a level

NOTES

of substantiality of composites somewhere between simples and aggregates. G.W. Leibniz, *Die Philosophischen Schriften*, ed. Carl I. Gerhardt, 7 vols. (1875–1890; reprint, Hildesheim: Olms, 1996), 2:291–521. Hereafter cited as *GP*. The status of his reflections on these *vincula* remains very much in question, and while some interpreters reject their metaphysical relevance entirely, others have proposed that they constitute a second, subterranean monadology of substantialized relations. See Maurice Blondel, *Une énigme historique: Le 'Vinculum substantiale' d'après Leibniz et l'ébauche d'un réalisme supérieur* (Paris: Gabriel Beauchesne, 1930); Alfred Boehm, *Le 'Vinculum substantiale' chez Leibniz: Ses origines historiques* (Paris: Vrin, 1938); and Christiane Frémont, *L'Être et la relation* (Paris: Vrin, 1981). For the most up-to-date, extensive, and ultimately negative assessment of the capacity of Leibniz's *vinculum* theory to play a role in the development of a coherent concept of monadic corporeal substances, see Brandon Look, *Leibniz and the 'Vinculum Substantiale,'* Studia Leibnitiana Sonderheft 30 (Stuttgart: Franz Steiner, 1999).

12. G.W. Leibniz, *Sämtliche Schriften und Briefe*, ed. Berlin-Brandenburgerischen [form. Preussische] Akademie der Wissenschaften and Akademie der Wissenschaften in Göttingen, 48 vols. in 8 series (Berlin: Akademie Verlag, 1923–present), 6.4-c:2267. Hereafter cited as *A*.
13. R.S. Woolhouse and Richard Francks, eds. and trans., *Leibniz's 'New System' and Associated Contemporary Texts* (Oxford: Clarendon Press, 1997), 41.
14. Cf. Leibniz's later distinction in "Initia rerum mathematicarum metaphysica" among space (the order of coexistence among simultaneous things), extension (the magnitude of space), point (a spatial magnitude of zero), and position (a mode of coexistence, involving both magnitude and quality). G.W. Leibniz, *Mathematische Schriften*, ed. Carl I. Gerhardt, 7 vols. (1849–1863; reprint, Hildesheim: Olms, 1971), 7:18–20.
15. Peter Remnant and Jonathan Bennett's otherwise excellent translation of the *New Essays* conflates or semantically reduces several Leibnizian terms crucial to my argument (including, as noted earlier, the term "encyclopedia" itself), so while I have relied on their version of Leibniz's *Nouveaux essais sur l'entendement humain*, the translations presented here are my own (from *A*, 6.6). This will pose no problem for the interested reader, as their translation is paginated to the Akademie edition. G.W. Leibniz, *New Essays on Human Understanding*, ed. and trans. Peter Remnant and Jonathan Bennett (Cambridge: Cambridge University Press, 1993).
16. The most fascinating works on Leibniz as librarian and philosopher of the library are found in Louis Couturat, *La Logique de Leibniz d'après des documents inédits* (1901; reprint, Hildesheim: Olms, 1961); Margherita Palumbo, *Leibniz e la 'res bibliothecaria': Bibliografie, 'historiae literariae' e cataloghi nella biblioteca privata leibniziana* (Rome: Bulzoni Editore, 1993); and Ulrike Steierwald, *Wissen und System: zu Gottfried Wilhelm Leibniz' Theorie einer Universalbibliothek* (Köln: Greven Verlag, 1995).

NOTES

17. Lorenzo Valla, *Dialogue on Free Will*, trans. Charles Trinkhaus, in *The Renaissance Philosophy of Man*, ed. Ernst Cassirer, Paul Oskar Kristeller, and John Herman Randall, Jr. (Chicago, IL: University of Chicago Press, 1948), 155–82. Hereafter cited as *DF*. Anicius Manlius Severinus Boethius, *The Theological Tractates and The Consolation of Philosophy*, ed. and trans. H.F. Stewart, E.K. Rand and S.J. Tester, Loeb Classical Library 74 (Cambridge, MA: Harvard University Press, 1973). Hereafter cited as *Cons*. While I have benefited from Tester's facing translation, the translations of the *Consolation* used here are my own.
18. Paul de Man, "The Rhetoric of Temporality," in *Blindness and Insight: Essays in the Rhetoric of Contemporary Criticism*. 2nd rev. edn. (Minneapolis, MN: University of Minnesota Press, 1983), 207–9, 222–26. The touchstone for de Man's interpretation is, of course, Walter Benjamin, *The Origin of German Tragic Drama*, trans. John Osborne (London: Verso, 1998).
19. On the relationship between philosophy and rhetoric in Valla's work, see Salvatore Camporeale, "Lorenzo Valla: The Transcending of Philosophy through Rhetoric," *Romance Notes* 30, no. 3 (1990), 269–84; Hanna Gerl-Falkovitz, *Rhetorik als Philosophie: Lorenzo Valla* (München: Fink, 1974); Ernesto Grassi, *Einführung in philosophische Probleme des Humanismus* (Darmstadt: Wissenschaftliche Buchgesellschaft, 1986), 65–86; and Lisa Jardine, "Lorenzo Valla: Academic Skepticism and the New Humanist Dialectic," in *The Skeptical Tradition*, ed. Myles Burnyeat (Berkeley, CA: University of California Press, 1983), 253–86.
20. For a general introduction to Valla's work, see Lodi Nauta, "Lorenzo Valla and the Rise of Humanist Dialectic," in *The Cambridge Companion to Renaissance Philosophy*, ed. James Hankins (Cambridge: Cambridge University Press, 2007), 193–210; John Monfasani, "Humanism and Rhetoric," in *Renaissance Humanism: Foundations, Forms, and Legacy*, ed. Albert Rabil, Jr., 3 vols. (Philadelphia, PA: University of Pennsylvania Press, 1988), 3:171–235; Lisa Jardine, "Lorenzo Valla and the Intellectual Origins of Humanist Dialectic," *Journal of the History of Philosophy* 15, no. 2 (1977), 143–64; and Paul Oskar Kristeller, *Eight Philosophers of the Italian Renaissance* (Stanford, CA: Stanford University Press, 1964), 45–61.
21. For a set of vigorous debates regarding the status of Valla's linguistic realism, see the articles collected in two special issues of the *Journal of the History of Ideas* 50, no. 2 (1989) and 66, no. 4 (2005).
22. Thomas Aquinas, *Knowledge in God (1a. 14-18)*, vol. 4 of *Summa Theologicae*, trans. Thomas Gornall (New York: McGraw-Hill, 1964); John Duns Scotus, *Contingency and Freedom*, trans. A. Vos (Dordrecht: Kluwer, 1994); and William of Ockham, *Predestination, God's Foreknowledge, and Future Contingents*, trans. Marilyn McCord Adams and Norman Kretzmann (Indianapolis, IN: Hackett, 1983).
23. For a reading claiming that the *Dialogue on Free Will* is more fundamentally about the conflict between faith and reason than philosophy and rhetoric, see Christopher S. Celenza, "Lorenzo Valla, 'Paganism,' and Orthodoxy," *MLN* 119, Supplement (2004), s66–87. A very different

perspective, emphasizing the affective power of Valla's rhetorical strategies to determine belief rather than merely to support it is presented by Victoria Kahn, "The Rhetoric of Faith and the Use of Usage in Lorenzo Valla's *De libero arbitrio*," *Journal of Medieval and Renaissance Studies* 13 (1983), 91–109.
24. Friedrich Nietzsche, *Twilight of the Idols*, "The Problem of Socrates" §7, in *Twilight of the Idols/The Anti-Christ*, trans. R.J. Hollingdale (New York: Penguin, 1990), 42.
25. Leibniz paraphrases Valla's entire mythological dialogue and part of the preceding dialogical discussion at *Theo.*, 366–69.
26. The most definitive works on Renaissance interpretations and glosses of the *Consolation* are a series of essays by Lodi Nauta. See especially Lodi Nauta, "Some Aspects of Boethius' *Consolatio Philosophiae* in the Renaissance," in *Boèce, ou la chaîne des savoirs*, ed. Alain Galonnier (Louvain-Paris: Peeters, 2003), 767–78 and Lodi Nauta, "'Magis sit Platonicus quam Aristotelicus': Interpretations of Boethius's Platonism in the *Consolatio philosophiae* from the Twelfth to the Seventeenth Century," in *The Platonic Tradition in the Middle Ages: A Doxographic Approach*, ed. Stephen Gersh and Maarten J.F.M. Hoenen (Berlin: Walter de Gruyter, 2002), 165–204. An invaluable account of the circulation of Boethius' texts in the Renaissance is Robert Black and Gabriella Pomaro, *Boethius' Consolation of Philosophy in Italian Medieval and Renaissance Education* (Florence: Galluzzo, 2000). Both Nauta and Black/Pomaro argue explicitly against Anthony Grafton's claim (following Pierre Courcelle) that the importance of the *Consolation* had waned by the late Renaissance as it was transformed into a "classic" and thereby shorn of relevance for contemporary philosophical debate. Anthony Grafton, "Epilogue: Boethius in the Renaissance," in *Boethius: His Life, Thought, and Influence*, ed. Margaret Gibson (Oxford: Blackwell, 1981), 410–13.
27. Seth Lerer's *Boethius and Dialogue: Literary Method in the Consolation of Philosophy* (Princeton, NJ: Princeton University Press, 1985) presents an important reading of Boethius' text in relation to his theories of rhetoric and dialectic. Hereafter cited as *LB*.
28. This is actually the second of two "biting" stories Diogenes Laertius presents in relation to Zeno. In the earlier one, after his arrest Zeno asks to whisper something privately to Nearchus and, once allowed to approach, bites the king so violently that Zeno does not let go until he is stabbed (another variant has him biting off Nearchus' nose). Philosophia does not actually mention Zeno by name (though he is invoked elsewhere in the *Consolation*) and some suggest that the reference is actually to Anaxarchus' torture by Nicocreon, as Diogenes tells similar stories regarding both men (including both the biting of a king and execution by mortar pounding). Diogenes Laertius, *Lives of Eminent Philosophers*, trans. R.D. Hicks, Loeb Classical Library 184 and 185 (Cambridge, MA: Harvard University Press, 1925), 7.5 for Zeno and 9.2 for Anaxarchus.
29. See especially Pierre Courcelle, *La 'Consolation de Philosophie' dans la tradition littéraire: Antécédents et postérité de Boèce* (Paris, Études

NOTES

Augustiniennes, 1969), 90–99; Joachim Gruber, *Kommentar zu Boethius, De consolatione philosophiae* (Berlin: de Gruyter, 1978), 74–92; Joachim Gruber, "Die Erscheinung der Philosophie in der *Consolatio Philosophiae* des Boethius," *Rheinisches Museum für Philologie* 121 (1969), 166–86; and *LB*, 24–38.

30. Martianus Capella, *The Marriage of Philology and Mercury*, vol. 2 of William Stahl, Richard Johnson, and E.L. Burge, *Martianus Capella and the Seven Liberal Arts* (New York: Columbia University Press, 1977). Lerer also identifies Cicero's *Tusculan Disputations* as the source of Boethius' strategy (*LB*, 33). Marcus Tullius Cicero, *Tusculan Disputations*, trans. J.E. King, Loeb Classical Library 141 (Cambridge, MA: Harvard University Press, 1927), 2.6.16.

31. See Homer, *Iliad*, trans. A.T. Murray, rev. William F. Wyatt, Loeb Classical Library 170 and 171 (Cambridge, MA: Harvard University Press, 1999), 1.200 and 1.206. These connections are made by Gruber at *Kommentar*, 87–88.

32. Gruber connects this to Athena's self-woven *peplos* in the *Iliad* (1:5.743f) and Proculus' allegorical reading of it (*Kommentar*, 90). Henry Chadwick points out that the *peplos* was a major locus of allegorical interpretation for Neoplatonists and that Boethius was certainly familiar with such readings. Henry Chadwick, *Boethius: The Consolations of Music, Logic, Theology, and Philosophy* (Oxford: Clarendon, 1981), 264.

33. Boethius himself lays out the particular form of this hierarchy in *De Trinitate*. Cf. Aristotle's *Metaphysics* on the twofold division and Plato's *Symposium* for the ladder. Chadwick (*Boethius*, 226) expands interpretation of the letters in another direction, citing Prudentius of Troisyes' exposition of his practice of affixing a *theta* next to passages he wished to censure in the work of John Scot Eriugena. There, *theta* abbreviated *thanatos* and recapitulated the practice of marking the clothing of Roman prisoners condemned to death. Aristotle, *Metaphysics*, trans. Hugh Tredennick, Loeb Classical Library 270 and 271 (Cambridge, MA: Harvard University Press, 1975), 993b20, 1025b25, and 1178b21f. Plato, *Symposium*, in *Lysis, Symposium, Gorgias*, trans. W.R.M. Lamb, Loeb Classical Library 166 (Cambridge, MA: Harvard University Press, 1925), 211c.

34. For an extensive account of the general history of this imagery, see Lucien Braun, *Iconographie et philosophie: Essai de définition d'un champ de recherche* (Strasbourg: Presses Universitaires de Strasbourg, 1994), 199–214 and 305–32. For a historically-specific engagement, see Rudolf Wittkower's "Transformations of Minerva in Renaissance Imagery," in *Allegory and the Migration of Symbols* (Boulder, CO: Westview Press, 1977), 129–42. For a set of even more particular engagements with the iconographic history of the *Consolation* in Medieval commentaries and illuminations, see Courcelle, *Consolation dans la tradition*, passim and Pierre Courcelle, *Histoire littéraire des grandes invasions germaniques* (Paris: Études Augustiniennes, 1964), 223–302. Both these latter texts contain extensive collections of plates depicting scenes from the *Consolation*.

35. Jon Whitman, *Allegory: The Dynamics of an Ancient and Medieval Technique* (Cambridge, MA: Harvard University Press, 1987), 116. On

this point, see also Courcelle, *Consolation dans la tradition*, 105–6 and 115 and Myra L. Uhlfelder, "The Role of the Liberal Arts in Boethius' *Consolatio*," in *Boethius and the Liberal Arts*, ed. Michael Masi (Berne: Peter Lang, 1981), 17–18.

36. As an example of this new language of mimesis and resemblance, consider the following passage from the *Consolation*: "The infinite motion of things in time imitates this eternal state of the immobile presence of life. But since this infinite motion of things is not able to fashion and equal eternal immobility, it falls from immobility into motion and diminishes from the simplicity of presence into the infinite quantity of the future and the past. It cannot possess the fullness of its life all at once. Thus, in the sense that it never ceases to be, it seems to some extent to emulate that which it cannot fulfill or express. It does this by attaching itself to a sort of presence within this paltry and fleeting moment. This presence, because it bears the likeness of immobile presence, allows whatever comes into contact with it to seem to be" (*Cons.*, 5, pr. 6.40–53).

37. Most commentators on the *Theodicy* dismiss the allegory as nothing more than an instrumentalized and ornamental flourish Leibniz uses to conclude his book. Several alternative perspectives have been advanced, however, including those of André Robinet, "Leibniz: La Renaissance et l'Âge Classique," in *Leibniz et la Renaissance*, ed. Albert Heinekamp, Studia Leibnitiana Supplementa 23 (Wiesbaden: Steiner, 1983), 12–36; Gilles Deleuze, *The Fold: Leibniz and the Baroque*, trans. Tom Conley (Minneapolis, MN: University of Minnesota Press, 1993), 60–70; Peter Fenves, "Continuing the Fiction: From Leibniz's 'petit fable' to Kafka's *In der Strafkolonie*," *MLN* 116 (2001), 502–20; Peter Fenves, *Arresting Language: From Leibniz to Benjamin* (Stanford, CA: Stanford University Press, 2001), 61–73; Giorgio Agamben, *Potentialities: Collected Essays in Philosophy*, ed. and trans. Daniel Heller-Roazen (Stanford, CA: Stanford University Press, 1999), 265–74, hereafter cited as *AP*; and Christiane Frémont, *Singularités: individus et relations dans le système de Leibniz* (Paris: Vrin, 2003), 80–112, hereafter cited as *FS*.

38. It is worth recalling that Leibniz "first gained a tolerable understanding of Latin writings" after he taught the language to himself at age 11!

39. Few commentators have discussed the connection to Valla other than to mention that it exists. One exception is Nancy S. Struever, *Theory as Practice: Ethical Inquiry in the Renaissance* (Chicago, IL: University of Chicago Press, 1992), 130–35.

40. On Leibniz's specific negotiation of rhetorical tropes including allegory, see Fenves, *Arresting Language*, 13–79; Francesco Piro, "Are the 'Canals of Tropes' Navigable? Rhetorical Concepts in Leibniz' Philosophy of Language," in *Im Spiegel des Verstandes: Studien zu Leibniz*, ed. Klaus D. Dutz and Stefano Gensini (Munster: Nodus, 1996), 137–60; and Karen S. Feldman, "*Per canales Troporum*: On Tropes and Performativity in Leibniz's Preface to Nizolius," *Journal of the History of Ideas* 65, no. 1 (2004), 39–51.

41. For an overview of the history of the interpretation of this enigmatic fragment (scribbled in the margin of a 1677 dialogue), see Gino Roncaglia,

"*Cum Deus calculat*: God's Evaluation of Possible Worlds and Logical Calculus," *Topoi* 9, no. 1 (1990), 83–90.
42. Frémont also makes the connection to "The Ultimate Origination of Things," but in a way amenable to Agamben's critique. "The optimum is identical to the existent, and vice versa; it is therefore proper to say that there must be the sacrifice of the singular not so that the *optimal* whole exists, but simply: *so that a whole exists.*" Like Agamben, Frémont reads Leibniz's ontogenesis of the optimum as tragic and even tyrannical, in that it founds the empire of the real on a necessary sacrificial violence (the rape of Lucretia by Sextus and the "murder" of a possibly nonviolent Sextus by a God who refuses to grant him existence). Where Agamben sees the problem as the condemnation of the potentiality of unactualized worlds, Frémont insists that it devolves on the devastation of the singularities that constitute those worlds (*FS*, 86–87).
43. Both Robinet and Fenves insist on the impossibility of the task that Pallas Athena set Theodore here, pointing to the fundamental illegibility of the numbers inscribed on the foreheads of all the figures that appear on the stages and in the pages of each possible world. Since the totality of predicates that constitute the singularity of any given substance is analyzable to infinity, their specificity exceeds the grasp of human reason.
44. The manuscript is Harley Ms. 4335–4339 at the British Library. On the manuscript and its illuminations, see Fritz Saxl and Hans Meier, *Catalogue of Astrological and Mythological Illuminated Manuscripts of the Latin Middle Ages*, vol. 3, Manuscripts in English Libraries (London: The Warburg Institute, 1953), 165–68; Thomas Kern and Janet Backhouse, ed. *Renaissance Painting in Manuscripts: Treasures from the British Library* (New York: Hudson Hills Press, 1983), 157–61; and Claude Schaefer, "Les débuts de l'altier de Jean Colombe. Jean Colombe et André Rousseau, prêtre, librarire et escrivain," *Gazette des Beaux-Arts* 40 (1977), 137–50.
45. G.W. Leibniz, "Apokatastasis panton" and "Apokatastasis," in *De l'horizon de la doctrine humaine (1693); Apocatastase panton (La Restitution universelle, 1715)*, ed. and trans. Michel Fichant (Paris: Vrin, 1991), 60 and 66. Hereafter cited as *H*. Fichant's essay "Plus Ultra," appended to these texts, provides a fascinating and thorough overview of the context of permutation, calculation, and the theoretical exhaustion of possibilities in the sixteenth and seventeenth centuries (*H*, 125–210). One of the earliest evocations of this text is in Wolfgang Hübener, "Die notwendige Grenze des Erkenntnisfortschritts als Konsequenz der Aussagenkombinatorik nach Leibniz' unveröffentlichten Traktat 'De l'Horizon de la doctrine humaine'," *Akten des II. Internationaler Leibniz Kongress (1972), Band 4*, Studia Leibnitiana Supplementa 15 (Wiesbaden: Steiner, 1975), 55–71. Hans Blumenberg touches on it in his "Weltchronik oder Weltformel" chapter (*Lesbarkeit*, 121–49). Jürgen Knoppik, "Leibniz' Fortschrittskriterium: Das Übergehen zu Neuem," *Studia Leibnitiana* 14, no. 1 (1997), 45–62 deals with these texts primarily in terms of Leibniz's rejection of the possibility of historical repetition in favor of a conception of infinite progress, as does Michel Fichant, "Ewige Wiederkehr oder

unendlicher Fortschritt: Die Apokatastasisfrage bei Leibniz," *Studia Leibnitiana* 23, no. 2 (1991), 133–50.
46. Here we can clearly evoke Lasswitz's universal library, as well as Borges' adaptation and historicization of it. Kurd Lasswitz, "The Universal Library," trans. Willy Ley, in *Fantasia Mathematica*, ed. Clifton Fadiman (New York: Simon and Schuster, 1958), 237–43; Jorge Luis Borges, "The Library of Babel," in *Collected Fictions*, trans. Andrew Hurley (New York: Penguin Books, 1998), 112–18; and Jorge Luis Borges, "The Total Library," in *Selected Non-Fictions*, ed. Eliot Weinberger, trans. Esther Allen, Suzanne Jill Levine, and Eliot Weinberger (New York: Penguin Books, 1999), 214–16.
47. In later criticism of Origen, the limit case of such salvation was invoked in order to denounce the doctrine, as his opponents claimed that it meant salvation for the devil. "Apokatastasis," in *The Oxford Dictionary of World Religions*, ed. John Bowker (Oxford: Oxford University Press, 1997), 80.
48. Borges suggests this in "The Library of Babel," (Jorge Luis Borges, *Fictions*, 118n4). Leibniz prefigures this image as well, with the eternally repeated edition of Euclid's *Elements of Geometry* that he imagines in "On the Ultimate Origination of Things" (*AG*, 149–50), to be discussed in Chapters 3 and 5. Derrida, however, insists that this bibliographical involution expresses the essentially theological character of Leibniz's thought, in that it is reducible to the logic of the dominance of the transcendental referent of scripture over the inscription of the particular books that populate actual libraries. Jacques Derrida, "Force and Signification," in *Writing and Difference*, trans. Alan Bass (Chicago, IL: University of Chicago Press, 1978), 9.

2 ENCYCLOPEDIC METHOD AND THE UNINTERRUPTED OCEAN

1. *Encyclopaedia Da Costa* (1947), ed. Robert Lebel and Isabelle Waldberg [with the assistance of Marcel Duchamp], trans. Iain White in *Encyclopaedia Acephalica*, ed. Alastair Brotchie (London: Atlas Press, 1995), 122. It is unknown which of the contributors penned the "Encyclopedia" article. Fascicle 7, volume 2 of *Le Da Costa Encyclopédique* begins midword in an entry on a mysterious topic whose identity can only be guessed, but whose first letters are certainly "ec." It ends midparagraph in the entry "Extasiée." This section was the only part of the work ever to appear, though fascicles 1 and 2 of the non-encyclopedic *Le Memento universel Da Costa* were published in 1948, albeit in inverted order. For an account of these texts' history, see Brotchie, *Encyclopaedia Acephalica*, 17–19.
2. Leibniz's dissertation is partially translated in G.W. Leibniz, *Philosophical Papers and Letters*, ed. and trans. Leroy E. Loemker, 2nd edn. (Dordrecht: Kluwer, 1989), 73–84. The full text can be found at *A*, 6.1:16–30.
3. The literature on Leibniz's characteristic is extensive. Prominent exemplars are Hans Aarsleff, *From Locke to Saussure: Essays on the Study of*

NOTES

Language and Intellectual History (Minneapolis, MN: University of Minnesota Press, 1982); Marcelo Dascal, *Leibniz: Language, Signs, and Thought* (Amsterdam: J. Benjamins, 1987); Albert Heinekamp, "Sprache und Wirklichkeit nach Leibniz," in *History of Linguistic Thought and Contemporary Linguistics*, ed. Herman Parret (Berlin: De Gruyter, 1976), 518–70; Hidé Ishiguro, *Leibniz's Philosophy of Logic and Language* (Cambridge: Cambridge University Press, 1990); Paolo Rossi, "The Twisted Roots of Leibniz's Characteristic," in *The Leibniz Renaissance*, ed. Centro Fiorentino di Storia e Filosofia della Scienza (Florence: L.S. Olschki, 1989), 271–89; and Donald Rutherford, "Philosophy and Language in Leibniz," in *The Cambridge Companion to Leibniz*, ed. Nicholas Jolley (Cambridge: Cambridge University Press, 1995), 224–69. Derrida is an implacable enemy of Leibniz's characteristic, perhaps because it is the negative of arche-writing, an onto-theological recuperation of meaning in a pure formality that precedes it. Thus, "Leibniz's universal characteristic is the very death of enjoyment. It leads the representer to the limit of its excess" (*OG*, 313).
4. For an index of many of Leibniz's extensive writings on the encyclopedia, see Louis Couturat, *Logique*, 670.
5. For Plato on the great year (the recurring temporal period defined by the full revolution of the equinoxes), see Plato, *Timaeus*, 39c in *Timaeus, Critias, Cleitophon, Menexenus, Epistles*, trans. R.G. Bury, Loeb Classical Library 234 (Cambridge, MA: Harvard University Press, 1929). For Origen on *apokatastasis* as a notion of a final redemption of all things understood as a complete restoration of their primary state at the end of time, see, for example, Origen of Alexandria, *De Principiis*, I.6.1–3 in *The Writings of Origen*, trans. Frederick Crombie, vol. 10 of the Ante-Nicene Christian Library: Translations of the Writings of the Fathers Down to A.D. 325, ed. Alexander Roberts and James Donaldson (Edinburgh: T. & T. Clark, 1869), 53–58. For Hume on the role of repetition in the formation of custom via habit, see David Hume, *An Enquiry Concerning Human Understanding*, ed. Eric Steinberg, 2nd edn. (Indianapolis, IN: Hackett, 1993), 28 and 50. Repetition in various forms plays an extremely important role throughout the whole of Hegel's philosophy. Perhaps most famously, see §802 of the *Phenomenology of Spirit* where the transformation (*Verwandlung*) of the in-itself (substance) into the for-itself (subject) is a circular movement of cognition that has returned into itself (an *in sich zurückgehende Kreis*)—that presupposed its beginning (immediacy) but arrived there only at its end (absolute mediation). G.W.F. Hegel, *Phenomenology of Spirit*, trans. A.V. Miller (Oxford: Oxford University Press, 1977), 488. Various forms of methodological repetition (where the progressive movement of method though the determination of the concept is in fact a movement in reverse) are equally if not more important in the *Science of Logic*, where Hegel famously claims that "advance is retreat [*Rückgang*] into ground," explores various forms of methodological "infinite return" (*unendliche Rückkehr*) and "bending back" (*züruckbiegen*), and describes philosophical method as simultaneously a "progressive further deter-

mining" (*vorwärtsgehendes Weiterbestimmen*) and a "regressive grounding" (*rückwartsgehendes Begründen*). G.W.F. Hegel, *Science of Logic*, trans. A.V. Miller (Atlantic Highlands, NJ: Humanities Press International, 1989), 71, 158–59, and 390. For Schelling's version of methodological repetition, see his discussion of "the free recapitulation of the original series of acts into which the one act of self-consciousness evolves." F.W.J. Schelling, *System of Transcendental Idealism (1800)*, trans. Peter Heath (Charlottesville, VA: University of Virginia Press, 1993), 49 and surrounding discussion. For Kierkegaard on repetition as radicalized and despairing recollection, see most obviously *Repetition: A Venture in Experimenting Psychology* in Søren Kierkegaard, *Fear and Trembling. Repetition*, ed. and trans. Howard V. Hong and Edna H. Hong (Princeton, NJ: Princeton University Press, 1983), 123–231. Nietzsche's notion of the eternal return is, of course, articulated throughout his works, but see the exemplary statement in §341 of Friederich Nietzsche, *The Gay Science*, trans. Walter Kaufmann (New York: Vintage Books, 1974), 273–74. Repetition compulsion is the centerpiece of Freud's analysis in Sigmund Freud, *Beyond the Pleasure Principle*, trans. James Strachey (New York: W.W. Norton & Co., 1961). Repetition forms a subterranean and underexplored theme in Foucault's early work. For his most explicit treatments, see Michel Foucault, *The Archaeology of Knowledge* (New York: Pantheon Books, 1972), 100–5 and Michel Foucault, "Language to Infinity," in *Aesthetics, Method, and Epistemology*, vol. 2 of The Essential Works of Michel Foucault, 1954–1984, ed. James Faubion and Paul Rabinow, trans. Robert Hurley (New York: The New Press, 2000), 89–101. Derrida touches on the topic repeatedly, but generally either with reference to an epistemologized and aestheticized version of Freud's compulsion to repeat, as in Jacques Derrida, "To Speculate – On 'Freud'," in *The Postcard: From Socrates to Freud and Beyond*, trans. Alan Bass (Chicago, IL: University of Chicago Press, 1987), esp. 292–337, or through a concept of the iterability of signs developed in opposition to the centrality of intentionality in J.L. Austin's linguistic theory, as in Jacques Derrida, "Signature Event Context," in *Margins*, 307–30. Finally, for what amounts to an ontological treatise on repetition, see the whole of Gilles Deleuze, *Difference and Repetition*, trans. Paul Patterson (New York: Columbia University Press, 1994).
6. Insofar as this version of the problem turns around the metaphysical issue of unity in relation to multiplicity, see the excellent collection of essays in *Unità e molteplicità nel pensiero filosofico e scientifico di Leibniz*, ed. Antonio Lamarra and Roberto Palaia (Florence: L.S. Olschki, 2000).
7. On Leibniz's proposals for various schemes for the organization of the disciplines outside of a directly encyclopedic context, see Wilhelm Totok, "Die Einteilung der Wissenschaften bei Leibniz," in *Akten des II. Internationaler Leibniz Kongress, 1972, Band 4*, Studia Leibnitiana Supplementa 15 (Wiesbaden: Steiner, 1975), 87–96. On Leibniz's direct precursors in this area, see Joseph S. Freedman, "Sixteenth and

Seventeenth Century Classifications of Philosophical Disciplines: Leibniz and Some of His Predecessors," in *Akten des II. Internationaler Leibniz Kongress, 1972, Band 1*, Studia Leibnitiana Supplementa 12 (Wiesbaden: Steiner, 1975), 193–202. On the more general context of the problem of knowledge classification in the period, see Lorraine Daston, "Classifications of Knowledge in the Age of Louis XIV," in *Sun King: The Ascendancy of French Culture During the Reign of Louis XIV*, ed. David Rubin (Washington, DC: Folger Shakespeare Library, 1992), 207–20; Ann Blair, "Organizations of Knowledge," in *The Cambridge Companion to Renaissance Philosophy*, ed. James Hankins (Cambridge: Cambridge University Press, 2007), 287–303; and Ulrich G. Leinsle, "Wissenschaftstheorie oder Metaphysik als Grundlage der Enzyklopädie?" in *Enzyklopädien der Frühen Neuzeit: Beiträge zu ihrer Erforschung*, ed. Franz M. Eybl (Tübingen: Niemeyer, 1995), 98–119.

8. Literature dealing specifically with Leibniz's encyclopedia project includes Louis Couturat, *La logique de Leibniz*, 235–77; Herbert H. Knecht, *La Logique chez Leibniz: Essai sur le rationalisme baroque* (Lausanne: L'Âge d'homme, 1981), 257–91; and Gottfried Martin, "Thesaurus omnis humanae scientiae. Une requête de Leibniz," *Archives de Philosophie* 30, no. 3 (1967), 388–97.

9. Jorge Luis Borges, "John Wilkins' Analytical Language," *Non-Fictions*, 231.

10. Jorge Luis Borges, "Of Exactitude in Science," *Fictions*, 325. Jean Baudrillard, "The Precession of Simulacra," in *Simulations*, trans. Paul Foss, Paul Patton, and Philip Beitchman (New York: Semiotext[e], 1983), 1–2. Deleuze's fascination with Borges' "The Garden of Forking Paths" exercises less influence (*Fictions*, 119–28). Deleuze cites that story throughout his oeuvre, but a particularly relevant engagement for the discussion is *The Fold*, 62–63.

11. Josiah Royce, *The World and the Individual* (1899–1901), 2 vols. (New York: Macmillan, 1927), 1:502–7; Jorge Luis Borges, *Labyrinths: Selected Stories and Other Writings*, ed. Donald A. Yates and James E. Irby (New York: New Directions Books, 1962), 195–96; and Lewis Carroll, *Sylvie and Bruno Concluded* in *The Complete Works of Lewis Carroll* (New York: Random House, 1936), 616–17.

12. John Wilkins, *An Essay Towards a Real Character and a Philosophical Language* (1668; facsimile, Menston: Scolar Press, 1968).

13. At a 1999 lecture on Enlightenment classification systems and early-nineteenth-century libraries, I witnessed various audience members vehemently objecting to the speaker's mobilization of Foucault (on the rise of early modern epistemological classification procedures), offering nothing more than the indignant insistence that "Chinese encyclopedias are not really like that!" The lecturer himself, of course, was already quite aware that the Foucaultian reference was to a Borges fiction and not a historical account of Chinese encyclopedism. Jeffrey Garrett, "Books and Things: The Crisis of Representation in German Libraries after 1800" (presentation, Northwestern University, Evanston, IL,

March 8, 1999). See, however, George Huppert, "*Divinatio et Eruditio*: Thoughts on Foucault," *History and Theory* 13, no. 3 (1974), 191–207, which attacks Foucault's selection of sixteenth- and early-seventeenth-century texts used to build his account of the Renaissance *episteme*. For the development of a similar argument keyed particularly to the way aspects of Leibniz's thought defy Foucault's account of the conditions for discursive existence in the Baroque, see Robinet, "Leibniz: La Renaissance et l'Âge Classique," 32–36.

14. In particular, see Rule 8 of Descartes, *Rules for the Direction of Mind*, which will be treated extensively in Chapter 4 (*CSM*, 1:28–33).
15. Remnant and Bennett's claim can be found at Leibniz, *New Essays*, 532n1. On the history of the term "encyclopedia," see Ulrich von Dierse, *Enzyklopädie: zur Geschichte eines philosophischen und wissenschaftstheoretischen Begriffs* (Bonn: Bouvier, 1977), 7–8.
16. Antoine Furetière, *Dictionnaire universel contenant généralement tous les mots François* (Rotterdam: Leers, 1690), s.v. "Encyclopédie" reads "Science universelle, recueil ou enchaînement de toutes les sciences ensemble." *Dictionnaire de l'Académie française* (Paris: Coignard, 1694), s.v. "Encyclopédie" is "Enchaînement ou cercle où sont enfermées toutes les sciences."
17. On the changing notions of encyclopedism in the period leading up to Leibniz also see Jean Cérard, "Encyclopédie et encyclopédisme à la Renaissance," Walter Tega, "Encyclopédie et unité du savoir de Bacon à Leibniz," and J.-F. Maillard, "Fortunes de l'encyclopédie à la fin de la Renaissance," all in *L'Encyclopédisme: Actes du colloque de Caen, 12–16 janvier 1987*, ed. Annie Becq (Paris: Aux Amateurs de livres, 1991), 57–67, 69–96, and 319–25; and Arno Seifert, "Der enzyklopädische Gedanke von der Renaissance bis zu Leibniz," in *Leibniz et la Renaissance*, ed. Albert Heinekamp, Studia Leibnitiana Supplementa 23 (Wiesbaden: Steiner, 1983), 113–24.
18. Johann Heinrich Alsted, *Encyclopaedia septem tomis distincta*, 7 vols. (Herborn: Corvinus, 1630).
19. Leroy E. Loemker, "Leibniz and the Herborn Encyclopedists," *Journal of the History of Ideas* 22, no. 3 (1961), 324–26 and 332–33.
20. Howard Hotson, *Johann Heinrich Alsted, 1588–1638: Between Renaissance, Reformation, and Universal Reform* (Oxford: Clarendon Press, 2000), 163–72.
21. Gregor Reisch, *Margarita Philosophica, rationalis, moralis philosophiae principia, duodecim libris dialogice coplectens* (Basel: [Petreius], 1535). William West, *Theaters and Encyclopedias in Early Modern Europe* (Cambridge: Cambridge University Press, 2002), 22–28.
22. Leibniz's excerpts from and commentary on Alsted's work can be found at *A*, 6.2:394–97 and 6.4-b:1122–62. See also his notes on the encyclopedic work of Alsted's disciple Johann Amos Comenius' *Pansophiae prodromus* (London: Fawne & Gellibrand, 1639). Leibniz's references to Comenius are scattered, but see, for example, *A*, 6.4-a:683–85.
23. Portions of the book were already written in dialogue, but only after Locke's death does the whole work take this form. For Remnant and

Bennett's account of the composition of the text, see Leibniz, *New Essays*, xi–xii.
24. John Locke, *An Essay Concerning Human Understanding*, ed. Peter H. Nidditch (Oxford: Clarendon Press, 1975), 720–21.
25. On framing the issue of encyclopedic methodology see Robert McRae, *The Problem of the Unity of the Sciences: Bacon to Kant* (Toronto: University of Toronto Press, 1961), 69–88, esp. 83.
26. On Locke's division of the sciences, see John W. Yolton, *Locke and the Compass of Human Understanding: A Selective Commentary on the 'Essay'* (Cambridge: Cambridge University Press, 1970), 14-43.
27. For an excellent explanation of the relation of encyclopedic synthetic and analytic methodology in their wider philosophical signification for Leibniz, see François Duchesneau, *Leibniz et la méthode de la science* (Paris: Presses Universitaires de France, 1993), 41–55.
28. On the development of the index (and related textual tools) as a strategy for coping with the "multitude of books" in early modern print culture, see Ann Blair, "Annotating and Indexing Natural Philosophy," in *Books and the Sciences in History*, ed. Marina Frasca-Spada and Nick Jardine (Cambridge: Cambridge University Press, 2000), 69–89 and Ann Blair, "Reading Strategies for Coping with Information Overload, ca. 1550–1700," *Journal of the History of Ideas* 64, no. 1 (2003), 17–19.
29. Anthony Grafton, *The Footnote: A Curious History* (Cambridge, MA: Harvard University Press, 1997), 190–222. Pierre Bayle, *The Dictionary Historical and Critical of Mr. Peter Bayle*, trans. Pierre Desmaizeaux (London: Knapton et al., 1734–1738); translations frequently modified, via *Dictionnaire historique et critique*, 5th edn., 4 vols. (Amsterdam: Brunel et al., 1740). Hereafter cited as *Dict*.
30. On the implications of Bayle's use of notes, see H.H.M. (Leny) van Lieshout, *The Making of Pierre Bayle's "Dictionaire historique et critique,"* trans. Lynne Richards (Amsterdam: APA-Holland University Press, 2001), 68–79 and Pierre Rétat, "Le remarque baylienne," in *Critique, savoir et érudition à la veille des Lumières: le "Dictionnaire historique et critique" de Pierre Bayle*, ed. Hans Bots (Amsterdam: APA-Holland University Press, 1998), 27–39. On Bayle as encyclopedist, see Frank A. Kafker, *Notable Encyclopedias of the Seventeenth and Eighteenth Centuries: Nine Predecessors of the "Encyclopédie"* (Oxford: Voltaire Foundation, 1981), 83–104 and Sebastian Neumeister, "Unordnung als Methode: Pierre Bayles Platz in der Geschichte der Enzyklopädie," in *Enzyklopädien der Frühen Neuzeit: Beiträge zu ihrer Erforschung*, ed. Franz M. Eybl (Tübingen: Niemeyer, 1995), 188–99.
31. A foundational discussion of some of the central aspects of this graphic referential tradition (and especially the relation between the shifts it undergoes from the twelfth to the fourteenth centuries and the corresponding changes in the methodological demands of practices of philosophical reading) can be found in Malcolm Beckwith Parkes, "The Influence of the Concepts of *Ordinatio* and *Compilatio* on the Development of the Book," in *Medieval Learning and Literature: Essays Presented to Richard William Hunt*, ed. J.J.G. Alexander and

NOTES

M.T. Gibson (Oxford: Clarendon Press, 1976), 115–41. Also see Olga Weijers, "Funktionen des Alphabets im Mittelalter," in *Seine Welt wissen: Enzyklopädien in der Frühen Neuzeit*, ed. Ulrich Johannes Schneider (Darmstadt: Primus, 2006), 22–32.

32. For an account of the relationship between encyclopedic "text types" in the sixteenth century and their projects for the organization of knowledge, see Udo Friedrich, "Grenzen des Ordo im enzyklopädischen Schrifttum des 16. Jahrhunderts," in *Die Enzyklopädie im Wandel vom Hochmittelalter bis zur Frühen Neuzeit*, ed. Christel Meier, Stefan Schuler, and Marcus Heckenkamp (Munich: Fink, 2002), 391–408.
33. William W.E. Slights, "Back to the Future – Littorally: Annotating the Historical Page," in *The Future of the Page*, ed. Peter Stoicheff and Andrew Taylor (Toronto: University of Toronto Press, 2004), 71–72 and 87n1.
34. Henri-Jean Martin, *La Naissance du livre moderne (XIVe-XVIIe siècles): Mise en page et mise en texte du livre français* (Paris: Éditions du Cercle de la Libraire, 2000), 272–74.
35. For full translations of the textual exchange between Leibniz and Bayle, see *Leibniz's 'New System'*, 68–132.
36. On this exchange between Leibniz and Bayle, see Leny Van Lieshout, *Making*, 17–19 and Lief Nedergaard, "Le genèse du 'Dictionaire historique et critique' de Pierre Bayle," *Orbis Litterarum* 13, no. 2 (1958), 215–16.
37. Pierre Bayle, *Projet et fragmens d'un dictionnaire critique* (1692; reprint, Geneva: Slatkine, 1970), 383–400.
38. Denis Diderot, "The Encyclopedia" (1755) in *Rameau's Nephew and Other Works*, trans. Jacques Barzun and Ralph Bowen (Indianapolis, IN: Hackett, 2001), 295.
39. See Leibniz's fourth and fifth letters in G.W. Leibniz and Samuel Clarke, *Correspondence*, ed. and trans. Roger Ariew (Indianapolis, IN: Hackett, 2000), 22–28 and 36–66.
40. Murdoch gives a less traditional but equally valid "I am thinking, therefore I exist" for both the *Discourse* and the *Principles* claim about the cogito. (*CSM*, 1:127 and 195).

3 THE MATERIALIST ENCYCLOPEDIA

1. I owe both these references to Jean-Michel Gros, who magnificently describes the *Dictionary* as *un livre absolu*. Pierre Bayle, *Pour une histoire critique de la philosophie: Choix d'articles philosophiques du 'Dictionnaire historique et critique,'* ed. and intro. Jean-Michel Gros with the collaboration of Jacques Chomarat (Paris: Honoré Champion, 2001), 25–26. The labyrinth image comes from the preface to the third and fourth editions of *Pensées diverses sur la comète*. This and the stormy ocean image from Bayle's letter to Minutoli can be found in Pierre Bayle, *Oeuvres diverses*, 5 vols. (1731; reprint, Hildesheim: Olms, 1964-1968), 3:7 and 4:672.
2. Thomas M. Lennon, *Reading Bayle* (Toronto: University of Toronto Press, 1999), esp. 12–41. Hereafter cited as *RB*.

3. Lennon rejects what he sees as the excesses of the structuralist reading of Bayle offered by Weibel, while noting that its insistence on foregrounding the "discontinuous" nature of Bayle's texts is amenable to his own. Luc Weibel, *Le savoir et le corps: essai sur le Dictionnaire de Pierre Bayle* (Paris: L'Age d'Hommes, 1975).
4. Elisabeth Labrousse, "Reading Pierre Bayle in Paris," in *Anticipations of the Enlightenment in England, France and Germany*, ed. Alan Charles Kors and Paul J. Korshin (Philadelphia, PA: University of Pennsylvania Press, 1987), 7–16. Also see her *Pierre Bayle*, 2 vols. (The Hague: Nijhoff, 1964), 2:293–316 and 595–609. Labrousse argues that Bayle's thought must be radically recontextualized within the debates regarding grace and the problem of evil in late-seventeenth-century Calvinism. On the contradictions of the Dutch censorship regime (or comparative lack thereof), see S. Groenveld, "The Dutch Republic, an Island of Liberty of the Press in 17th Century Europe? The Authorities and the Book Trade," in *Commercium Litterarium: La communication dans la République des lettres, 1600–1750*, ed. Hans Bots and Françoise Waquet (Amsterdam: APA-Holland University Press, 1994), 281–300.
5. On the possibility of reading the philosophical force and power of Bayle's texts against their explicit endorsement or disavowal of particular positions, see *RB*, 14–20 and Anthony McKenna, "L'ironie de Bayle et son statut dans l'écriture philosophique," in *La Raison corrosive: Études sur la pensée critique de Pierre Bayle*, ed. Isabelle Delpla and Philippe de Robert (Paris: Honoré Champion, 2003), 245–66.
6. Thomas Holden, "Bayle and the Case for Actual Parts," *Journal of the History of Philosophy* 42, no. 2 (2004), 145–64. Hereafter cited as *HB*. For his insertion of this issue into the broader context of the history of early modern accounts of material parts see Thomas Holden, *The Architecture of Matter: Galileo to Kant* (Oxford: Clarendon Press, 2004).
7. Richard Popkin, *The High Road to Pyrrhonism* (Indianapolis, IN: Hackett, 1989) and Richard Popkin, Introduction, in Pierre Bayle, *Historical and Critical Dictionary: Selections*, ed. and trans. Richard Popkin (Indianapolis, IN: Hackett, 1991), xxiii–xvii.
8. Jonathan Israel, *Radical Enlightenment: Philosophy and the Making of Modernity, 1650–1750* (Oxford: Oxford University Press, 2001), 336. Hereafter cited as *RE*.
9. On the problem of superstition in relation to the issue of Bayle's fideism or skepticism see also Anthony McKenna, "Pierre Bayle et la superstition," in *La superstition à l'âge des Lumières*, ed. Bernard Dompnier (Paris: Honoré Champion, 1998), 64–5; Anthony McKenna "Rationalisme moral et fidéisme," in *Pierre Bayle: Citoyen du Monde*, ed. Hubert Bost and Phillippe de Robert (Paris: Honoré Champion, 1999), 257–74; Ruth Whelan, *The Anatomy of Superstition: A Study of the Historical Theory and Practice of Pierre Bayle* (Oxford: Voltaire Foundation, 1989); and Jean-Luc Solère, "Bayle et les apories de la raison humaine," in *La Raison corrosive: Études sur la pensée critique de Pierre Bayle*, ed. Isabelle Delpla and Philippe de Robert (Paris: Honoré Champion, 2003), 87–137.

NOTES

10. Gianluca Mori, *Bayle philosophe* (Paris: Honoré Champion, 1999), 15, 49–53, and 236–71. Mori argues that the true Baylean position is a "corrected" materialist Spinozism combined with an "overturned" Malebranchean occasionalism purged of its theology. Mori, *Bayle philosophe*, 149 and 189.
11. See Pliny the Elder, *Natural History: Books 8–11*, trans. H. Rackham, Loeb Classical Library 353 (Cambridge, MA: Harvard University Press, 1940), 8.1.
12. Foucault is discussing Ulisse Aldrovandi, *Serpentum, et draconum historia* (Bologna: Bernia, 1640), written prior to Aldrovandi's death in 1605 but not published until the mid-seventeenth century.
13. Foucault is referring to the discussion of Aldrovandi in the preface to Georges Buffon, *Histoire naturelle, générale et particuliére*, 44 vols. (Paris: Imprimerie royale, 1749–1804), vol. 1. Buffon is also discussed extensively in *OT*, 132–150.
14. Louis Moréri, *Le Grand dictionnaire historique, ou le Mélange curieux de l'histoire sacrée et profane* (Lyons: J. Girin and B. Rivière, 1694).
15. *Histoire des ouvrages des savants* (Sept.–Nov., 1690), 136. The announcement is published anonymously, as is the *Projet* itself.
16. For a comprehensive account of the composition, publication, and revision history of the *Dictionary*, see Leny Van Lieshout, *Making*, 1–54 and 259–75. On the history of its production and immediate reception, also see Elisabeth Labrousse, *Bayle*, 1:235–71. For the details of the collaboration and negotiation between Bayle and his printer Reinier Leers, see Otto S. Lankhorst, "Naissance typographique du *Dictionaire historique et critique* de Pierre Bayle," in *Critique, savoir et érudition à la veille des Lumières: le "Dictionnaire historique et critique" de Pierre Bayle*, ed. Hans Bots (Amsterdam: APA-Holland University Press, 1998), 3–16. Bayle gives his own perspective on the history of the *Dictionary* in its preface.
17. On the increasing speed of scholarly communication made possible by the diffusion of presses and bookstores in the early modern period (especially in the Dutch context), see the Eisenstein-indebted P.G. Hoftijzer, "Between Mercury and Minerva: Dutch Printing Offices and Bookshops as Intermediaries in Seventeenth-Century Scholarly Communication," in *Commercium Litterarium: La communication dans la République des lettres, 1600–1750*, ed. Hans Bots and Françoise Waquet (Amsterdam: APA-Holland University Press, 1994), 119–29. On the changing readership of the intellectual journals and the effects of their broad dispersion on the early modern intellectual milieu, see *RE*, 142–55; Hans Bots, "Le rôle des périodiques Néerlandais pour la diffusion du livre (1684–1747)," in *Le Magasin de l'univers: The Dutch Republic as the Centre of the European Book Trade*, ed. Christiane Berkvens-Stevelinck (New York: Brill, 1992), 47–70; Martha Ornstein, *The Rôle of Scientific Societies in the Seventeenth Century* (1938; reprint, Hamden, CT: Archon Books, 1963), 198–209; and Harcourt Brown, "History and the Learned Journal," *Journal of the History of Ideas* 33, no. 3 (1972), 365–78.

18. Michel Foucault, "What is an Author?" in *Aesthetics, Method, and Epistemology*, vol. 2 of *The Essential Works of Michel Foucault, 1954–1984*, ed. James Faubion and Paul Rabinow, trans. Robert Hurley (New York: The New Press, 2000), 205–22. For essential historical corrections to Foucault's thesis, see Roger Chartier, "Figures of the Author," in *The Order of Books: Readers, Authors, and Libraries in Europe between the Fourteenth and Eighteenth Centuries*, trans. Lydia G. Cochrane (Stanford, CA: Stanford University Press, 1994), 25–59; Roger Chartier, "Foucault's Chiasmus: Authorship between Science and Literature in the Seventeenth and Eighteenth Centuries, in *Scientific Authorship: Credit and Intellectual Property in Science*, ed. Mario Biagioli and Peter Galison (New York: Routledge, 2003), 13–31; and Adrian Johns, "The Ambivalence of Authorship in Early Modern Natural Philosophy," in *Scientific Authorship: Credit and Intellectual Property in Science*, ed. Mario Biagioli and Peter Galison (New York: Routledge, 2003), 67–89.
19. While many commentators cite brief passages from the "Ovid" article, sustained philosophical engagements are lacking. The only recent discussions I have been able to find are brief treatments in *RB*, 176–78 and Jean-Jacques Bouchardy, *Pierre Bayle: La nature et la 'nature des choses'* (Paris: Honoré Champion, 2001), 16–18.
20. Bayle explicitly presents Ovid's metaphysics as an "imitation" or "paraphrase" of what he finds in the writings of ancient Greek philosophers (*Dict.*, art. "Ovid," rem. G). The context makes it clear that Bayle is thinking specifically of Anaxagoras and Pythagoras who he eventually opposes to Leucippus, Democritus, and Epicurus by way of contrasting Ovid with Lucretius.
21. Publius Naso Ovid, *Metamorphoses*, trans. Frank Justis Miller and G.P. Goold, Loeb Classical Library 42 and 43, rev. edn. (Cambridge, MA: Harvard University Press, 1977), 1.1–2. Hereafter cited as *Met.*
22. Holden argues that this line of reasoning misidentifies substances with subjects (*HB*, 158–59).
23. Though arguing against the Cartesian inflections of Bayle's critique of Ovid's doctrine of chaos, six decades later Voltaire would take up the challenge to read Ovid as a natural philosopher and cosmologist, adapting Ovid's "doctrines" (against Bayle's quasi-Cartesian criticisms) to those of Newton. The key to this Newtonian response to Bayle is the assertion that a slightly corrected Ovid would never have separated weight from the essence of bodies, and would thereby have evaded Bayle's arguments altogether. How exactly this evasion would have been accomplished is not entirely clear in Voltaire's article. He also argues that Bayle has imported the notion—crucial to several of his arguments against Ovid—of the "homogeneity" of the universe via a mistranslation of the first lines of the *Metamorphoses*. Voltaire, *A Philosophical Dictionary*, in *The Works of Voltaire: A Contemporary Version*, trans. William Fleming, 42 vols. (Paris: E.R. DuMont, 1901), 12:131–38.
24. Indeed, as Holden has explicated, Bayle's *Systême Abrégé de Philosophie* (1675–1677) (*Oeuvres diverses*, 4:297 and 299)—a series of course notes

revised and published in textbook format—affirms that bodies extended in space must have distinct and actual parts.
25. Bayle cites book 3, ch. 39 of Guillaume Lamy, *De principiis rerum* (Paris: Petrum le Monnier, 1669), though it appears that he is referring to his commonplaced record of the text. While in one marginal note he gives the precise reference to Lamy's book, in another he refers to a 1682 abstract in the *Journal de Leipsic*, which notes that it was printed in 1680. Bayle insists that he read *De principiis rerum* in 1678 when it was already "old." This, too, is interesting, since it shows that for Bayle a mere decade after its printing a book was considered "old," whereas only two or three generations earlier such a book would have been considered to be freshly printed.
26. Lennon cites Bayle's engagement with Lamy, though he interprets Bayle's response as a "weak *ad hominem*" answer that displays the increased quality of arguments against finalism among late-seventeenth-century atomists as compared to those offered by Gassendi himself. Thomas M. Lennon, *The Battle of the Gods and Giants: The Legacies of Descartes and Gassendi, 1655–1715* (Princeton, NJ: Princeton University Press, 1993), 7n13. This engagement is also briefly referenced by Paolo Rossi, *The Dark Abyss of Time: The History of the Earth and the History of Nations from Hooke to Vico*, trans. Lydia G. Cochrane (Chicago, IL: University of Chicago Press, 1984), 47–49.
27. Aristotle, *On Coming-to-Be and Passing Away* in *On Sophistical Refutations; On Coming-to-Be and Passing Away; On the Cosmos*, trans. E.S. Foster and D.J. Furley, Loeb Classical Library 400 (Cambridge, MA: Harvard University Press, 1955), 1.3.318a25.

4 READING AND REPETITION

1. On the broad history and philosophical significance of the *sensus communis*, see Daniel Heller-Roazen, *The Inner Touch: Archaeology of a Sensation* (New York: Zone Books, 2007).
2. Those more familiar than Descartes with the engraving process will rightly object that producing an engraving involves a process and a set of technologies far more complicated than simply "a little ink placed here and there on a piece of paper."
3. On this moment in the Cartesian text, see Jean-Luc Nancy, "Dum Scribo," trans. Ian Macleod, *Oxford Literary Review* 3, no. 2 (1978), 6–21.
4. Also see Descartes' more straightforward recapitulation of this discussion in the 1648 *Conversation with Burman* (*CSM*, 3:344).
5. Cf. Descartes to Hogelande, February 8, 1639, where "the fewer items we fill our memory with, the sharper we will keep our native intelligence for increasing our knowledge" (*CSM*, 3:144).
6. For Descartes' early critical evaluation of the Lullist *ars memoria* and contemporary projects for the construction of encyclopedic universal languages, see Descartes to Mersenne, November 20, 1629 (*CSM*, 3:12–13). In the same letter, however, Descartes proposes the construction of his own universal language *qua* ordered symbolic system by

NOTES

which "all the thoughts which can come into the human mind must be arranged in an order like the natural order of numbers." The discovery of such a language, however, "depends upon the discovery of the true philosophy" for Descartes, whereas most seventeenth-century partisans of universal languages saw them as symbolic machines for the generation of "true philosophy" or at the very least, as systems useful for the art of discovery. For a general approach to early modern universal language projects, see Paolo Rossi, *Logic and the Art of Memory: The Quest for a Universal Language*, trans. Stephen Clucas (Chicago, IL: University of Chicago Press, 2000). For a general history of universal language projects, see Umberto Eco, *The Search for the Perfect Language,* trans. James Fentress (Oxford: Blackwell, 1995).

7. Instead of the print on the paper, Descartes may well be referring to the marginal notes he will recommend that his readers create while making their way through his own text.

8. For the earliest account of Descartes' reading practices, see Adrian Baillet's biography, *La vie de Monsieur Des-Cartes*, 2 vols. (1692; facsimile, New York: Garland Publishing, 1987), 2:467–71. I owe this reference to Ann Blair, "Focus: Scientific Readers, An Early Modernist's Perspective," *Isis* 95, no. 3 (2004), 427n18.

9. The distinction between science and history also occurs in the *Rules* (*CSM*, 1:13). In a February 8, 1639 letter to Hogeland, Descartes defines history as "everything which has been discovered already and is contained in books" and contrasts it to science, "the skill to solve every problem, and thus to discover by one's own efforts everything capable of being discovered . . . by means of our native human intelligence" (*CSM*, 3:144).

10. Descartes' notebook is now lost, and our only access to it depends on a fragmentary copy made by Leibniz and selected translations published by Baillet.

11. On the problem of "the multitude of books" and "early modern information overload," see Ann Blair, "Reading Strategies for Coping with Information Overload, ca. 1550–1700," *Journal of the History of Ideas* 63, no. 4 (2002), 11–28 and Brian W. Ogilvie, "The Many Books of Nature: Renaissance Naturalists and Information Overload," *Journal of the History of Ideas* 63, no. 4 (2002), 29–40. Specifically on the structure and use of commonplacing techniques, see Ann Moss, "Locating Knowledge," in *Cognition and the Book: Typologies of Formal Organisation of Knowledge in the Printed Book of the Early Modern Period*, ed. Karl A.E. Enenkel and Wolfgang Neuber (Leiden: Brill, 2005), 35–49.

12. Descartes' accusation that while Voetius may be erudite he lacks *doctrina* involves something of a polemical pun, since the main thrust of Voetius' attack on Cartesian philosophy was that it controverted accepted Church *doctrina*.

13. On the Scholastic structure of the *Principles,* see Jean-Luc Marion, *On Descartes' Metaphysical Prism: The Constitution and the Limits of Onto-theo-logy in Cartesian Thought*, trans. Jeffrey Kosky (Chicago, IL: University of Chicago Press, 1999), 22–25.

14. On Descartes' relationship to the Scholastic textbook tradition, see Roger Ariew, *Descartes and the Last Scholastics* (Ithaca, NY: Cornell University Press, 1999); Dennis Des Chene, *Physiologia: Natural Philosophy in Late Aristotelian and Cartesian Thought* (Ithaca, NY: Cornell University Press, 1996); Roger Ariew, "Descartes and the Tree of Knowledge," *Synthese* 92, no. 1 (1992), 101–16; and Jorge Secada, *Cartesian Metaphysics: The Scholastic Origins of Modern Philosophy* (Cambridge: Cambridge University Press, 2000).
15. Occasionally, the strategy Descartes proposed readers adopt for approaching the *Principles* radically backfired. Thomas Lennon quotes a February 26, 1693 letter from Huygens to Bayle: "Descartes had found the way to have his conjectures and fictions taken for truths, and what happened to those who read his *Principles of Philosophy* was something like what happens to those who read pleasant novels that make the same impression as true histories . . . It seemed to me that when I read this book of principles for the first time, everything went as well as could be, and when I found some difficulty, I believed it was my fault for not having properly understood his thought . . . But having since discovered from time to time things visibly false and others very improbable, I have thoroughly rejected my former opinion and I now find almost nothing I can certify as true in all his physics, metaphysics, or meteorology" (Thomas Lennon, *Gods and Giants*, 17).
16. The plan of the 36 rules is laid out in Rule 12 (*CSM*, 1:50–51).
17. Giovanni Crapulli, *Regulae ad directionem ingenii, Texte critique établi . . . avec la version hollandaise du XVIIème siècle* (The Hague: Martinus Nijhoff, 1966), hereafter cited as *CR*; Heinrich Springmeyer, Lüder Gäbe, and Hans Gunter Zekl, *Regulae ad directionem ingenii/Regeln zur Ausrichtung der Erkenntniskraft* (Hamburg: Felix Meiner, 1973); and George Heffernan, *Regulae ad directionem ingenii/Rules for the Direction of the Natural Intelligence* (Amsterdam: Rodopi, 1998). The critical translation (French translation facing another critical edition of the Latin text) is Jean-Luc Marion, *Règles utiles et claires pour la direction de l'esprit en la recherche de la vérité* (The Hague: Martinus Nijhoff, 1977). These are all in addition to the standard critical edition in *AT*, 10.
18. Étienne Gilson, *Index scolastico-cartésien* (Paris: F. Alcan, 1912); Étienne Gilson, *Études sur le rôle de la pensée médiévale dans la formation du système cartésien* (Paris: Vrin, 1951); Jean-Luc Marion, *Sur l'ontologie grise de Descartes* (Paris: Vrin, 1975); and André Robinet, *Aux Sources de l'esprit cartésien. L'Axe Ramée-Descartes, de la "Dialectique" de 1555 aux "Regulae"* (Paris: Vrin, 1996).
19. The "extant" texts of the inventory include two French manuscript copies (discovered in the papers of Huygens and Clerselier) and a Latin version published in 1656. While Adam and Tannery conjecture that the Latin version is a translation of Clerselier's text, they also allow that it may be based on a lost Latin original (*AT*, 10:1–12).
20. Prior to 1701, fragments and quotations appeared in publications by Baillet, Arnauld, and Nicholas Poisson, all of whom claim to have had

NOTES

access to the (lost) original manuscript while composing their texts (*AT*, 10:476–84).
21. While most editors accept that the genealogy of the Amsterdam text can be traced to de Raey, Herbert Breger and Jan-Erik Bos argue that it must be traced to the lost Tschirnhaus copy. They are able to demonstrate with relative certainty only that a copy by Tschirnhaus was the basis of the Hanover text, that it *might* have been the basis of the 1684 Dutch translation (both these texts are discussed in this chapter), but *not* that it is the basis of the Amsterdam text. Herbert Breger, "Über die Hannoversche Handschrift der Descartesschen *Regulae*," *Studia Leibnitiana* 15, no. 1 (1983), 108–14 and Jan-Erik Bos, "La Première publication de *La Recherche de la vérité* en 1684: *Onderzoek der Waarheid door 't Natuurlijk Licht*," *Nouvelles de la République de Lettres* 1 (1999), 13–26.
22. Breger, "Hannoversche Handschrift," 108–14 and Bos, "Première publication," 16–18. For even more on the battle over dating sparked by this note, see *AT*, 10:492–93; *CR*, xviii; and Heinrich Springmeyer, "Eine neue kritische Textausgabe der *Regulae ad directionem ingenii* von René Descartes," *Zeitschrift für philosophische Forschung* 24 (1970), 101–25.
23. Technically, this should be the "Dutch" text, but I have referred to it as the "Netherlands text" since it is referenced as "N" (for Niederländische manuskript).
24. Bos has argued that this translation is based on a copy of Tschirnhaus' copy of the autograph (possessed by Clerselier), rather than de Raey's copy. He is also the source of the claim about Glazemaker's death. Jan-Erik Bos, "Première publication," 15–22.
25. Jean-Paul Weber, *La Constitution du texte des "Regulae"* (Paris: Société d'édition d'enseignement supérieur, 1964).
26. *Uno aut altero exemplo* is perhaps more straightforwardly "one or two examples," but it also carries the meaning "one example or another." While *alter* is related to "two" (in the sense of "the other of two" or "another of two"), Descartes' translators have generally chosen to emphasize the word's distinction from the less restrictive *alius*. I am arguing that the initial injection of exemplarity into Rule 8 is explicitly figured in terms of the equivalence, interchangeability, and denotative identity of example: one example or another.
27. Beck notices the repetition of the entire methodological project in the *omnium nobilissimum exemplum,* writing, "In other words, we should be undertaking a study coextensive with that of the *Regulae.*" However, he sees no more significance in this relation than that of a convenient opportunity to explain Cartesian enumeration. Hamelin also identifies this methodological reflexivity, but misses its radical implications. Leslie John Beck, *The Method of Descartes: A Study of the "Regulae"* (Oxford: Clarendon Press, 1952), 28 and Octave Hamelin, *Le système de Descartes* (Paris: Alcan, 1911), 105–6.
28. The location of the three examples including the full text of their explanations: *AT,* 10:395.17–396.25; 396.26–397.26; 397.27–398.25.
29. Spinoza appropriates this metaphor in his *Treatise on the Emendation of the Intellect* when he attempts to avoid the infinite regress that threatens

the constitution of any philosophical method that denies its certification by an external subject. Baruch Spinoza, *Complete Works*, ed. Michael Morgan, trans. Samuel Shirley (Indianapolis, IN: Hackett, 2002), 9; *TdIE*, 29–30. Hereafter cited as *SW*.
30. Cf. Plato, *Statesman* in *Statesman, Philebus, Ion*, trans. Harold North Fowler and W.R.M. Lamb, Loeb Classical Library 164 (Cambridge, MA: Harvard University Press, 1995), 279a and Aristotle, *Art of Rhetoric*, trans. J.H. Freese, Loeb Classical Library 193 (Cambridge, MA: Harvard University Press, 1994), 1393a–1394a. An excellent discussion of early modern exemplarity is found in John Lyons, *Exemplum: the Rhetoric of Example in Early Modern France and Italy* (Princeton, NJ: Princeton University Press, 1989). One of the most useful structural analyses of the example is Sophie Fisher, "L'exemple des exemples: à propos d'objets linguistique," *Versus* 70–71 (1995), 31–47.
31. While commenting on the fragmentary nature of the work and rejecting the possibility that its variants require extraordinary explanation, Crapulli adds, "On the other hand, as much as its unfinished status, the 'syllogistic' nature of the treatise excludes the hypothesis of another revision." He recognizes, in other words, that the force brought into play by the content of the *Rules* reflexively exercises power over the text's own composition. *CR*, xxi.
32. The precise location of the mobile text block is *AT*, 10:393.22–396.26. The Amsterdam and Netherlands texts leave this passage intact, while the Hanover text moves it into an appendix.
33. Cf. the third iteration of Rule 8 and several other sections of Rule 12 (*AT*, 10:398; 410.18–19; 411.6–9; and 416.7–9).
34. Baillet points this out with regard to the *Studium*, and Adam and Tannery themselves conjecture that of all Baillet's marginal notes to that text, this is perhaps the only one directly borrowed from the manuscript itself (*AT*, 10:200). Adrian Baillet, *Vie de Descartes*, 2:66.
35. Rodis-Lewis points out this continuity. Geneviève Rodis-Lewis, ed., *L'Oeuvre de Descartes*, 2 vols. (Paris: Vrin, 1971), 1:78.
36. Robinet cites another repetition—the triple iteration of *semel in vita*—as evidence for the "defective" nature of the text. He claims, however, that "paleographically," it is the second iteration that is the definitive text, that the first should be eliminated as a draft, and that the third should be moved to Rule 12. He thus reverses the entire philological tradition, which has insisted on eliminating the first and second from the rule while claiming a definitive status for the third. André Robinet, *L'Axe*, 296–97.
37. Jean-Paul Weber, *Constitution*, 94. For Weber's full engagement with the passages from Rule 8, see *Constitution*, 91–96.
38. Springmeyer claims that the Hanover text has undergone less editorial revision, but as Heffernan comments, "In fact, this even leads to an ironic situation in which the unreliability of 'H[anover]' is adduced as evidence for its reliability." Heffernan, *Regulae*, 63.
39. Jean-Paul Weber, "La Méthode de Descartes, de après les Regulae" *Archives de Philosophie* 35 (1972), 54. The transposition in Rule 4 can be

found in *AT*, 10:374.16-379.13. In the Hanover text, this passage is removed from the rule completely and resituated in an appendix.

40. *Studeo* in the first iteration and *amo* in the third are conjugated in the third person plural: "qui serio student ad bonam mentem pervenire" and "qui tantillum amant veritatem" (*AT*, 10:395 and 398). In the second iteration, *accingo* takes the first person plural: "antequam ad res in particulari cognoscendas nos accingamus, oportet semel in vita" (*AT*, 10:396).
41. In the *Discourse*, "Good sense is the best distributed thing in the world," and is quickly identified with "reason" (*CSM*, 1:111). The earliest occurrences of *bona mens* are to be found, unsurprisingly, in *Studium bonae mentis*, whose title Baillet proposed translating as either *L'Étude du bon sens* or *L'Art de bien comprendre* (*AT*, 10:191–204). Adrian Baillet, *La vie de Descartes*, 2:406. Etienne de Courcelles' Latin translation of the *Discourse*, reviewed and corrected by Descartes, uses *bona mens* for *bon sens* in the first sentence of the text (*AT*, 6:540). For Descartes' tacit approval, see his note just after the index of *Specimina Philosophiae*, the volume including the Latin translations of the *Discourse, Optics*, and *Meteors* (*AT*, 6:539).
42. In the *Discourse*, by contrast, "It is not enough to have a good mind [*esprit bon*], but the principle thing is to use it well" (*CSM*, 1:113).
43. Étienne Gilson, *Discours de la méthode: Texte et commentaire* (Paris: Vrin, 1947), 81–82.

5 THE BODY AND THE BOOK

1. In Meditation Three Descartes never states this principle so succinctly. Spinoza takes it more or less directly from Axiom 4 of Descartes' geometrical restatement of the argument in the replies to the second set of objections (cf., *CSM*, 2:114). In Spinoza's *Principles of Cartesian Philosophy* this becomes Axiom 9.
2. To establish that my idea of the infinite is not "materially false" requires yet another argument, which I will not detail here as it is not relevant to Spinoza's book images in the *Principles of Cartesian Philosophy*.
3. In the replies to the second set of objections, Descartes frames the argument more succinctly: "The objective reality of our ideas requires a cause which contains the very same reality not merely objectively but formally or eminently. But we have an idea of God, and the objective reality of this idea is not contained in us either formally or eminently; moreover it cannot be contained in any other being except God himself. Therefore, this idea of God, which is in us, must have God for its cause; and hence God exists" (*CSM*, 2:118).
4. From the perspective of the work of Roger Chartier and Adrian Johns one might object that Spinoza is mistaken in assuming that any two books—even those written in the same hand or printed by the same early modern hand-press—are identical. Each still has its own particular provenance and history of readership, and it is unlikely if not impossible that even their material forms (the characters on the page or the paper on which they are printed) would be completely the same.

NOTES

5. An excellent explication of Spinoza's tripartite epistemology can be found in Spencer Carr, "Spinoza's Distinction between Rational and Intuitive Knowledge," *The Philosophical Review* 87, no. 2 (1978), 241–52.
6. While the interpretive issues associated with these two propositions are enormous, I have attempted to restrict myself to their minimal senses in order to allow my argument to progress. For some of the best attempts to explicate these propositions, see Martial Gueroult, *Spinoza II – L'âme ("Ethique," II)* (Paris: Aubier, 1974), 64–91; Pierre Macherey, *Introduction à l'Ethique de Spinoza*, 5 vols. (Paris: Presses Universitaires de France, 1995), 2:64–81 and 3:49–71; Jonathan Bennett, "Spinoza's Mind-Body Identity Thesis," *The Journal of Philosophy* 78, no. 10 (1981), 573–84; and Michael Della Rocca, "Spinoza's Argument for the Identity Theory," *The Philosophical Review* 102, no. 2 (1993), 183–213.
7. For work approaching Spinoza's critique of Descartes with respect to the issues treated in this chapter, see Frederick Ablondi and Steve Barbone, "Individual Identity in Descartes and Spinoza," *Studia Spinozana* 10 (1994), 69–91; John G. Cottingham, "The Intellect, the Will and the Passions: Spinoza's Critique of Descartes," *Journal of the History of Philosophy* 26, no. 2 (1988), 239–57; and R.S. Woolhouse, "Spinoza and Descartes and the Existence of Extended Substance," in *Central Themes in Early Modern Philosophy*, ed. J.A. Cover and Mark Kulstad (Indianapolis, IN: Hackett, 1990), 23–47.
8. Louis Althusser, "The Underground Current of the Materialism of the Encounter," in *Philosophy of the Encounter: Later Writings, 1978–87*, ed. François Matheron and Oliver Corpet, trans. G.M. Goshgarian (London: Verso, 2006), 169 and 193–94.
9. A view that heavily influenced Althusser's late interpretation of Spinoza but is ultimately quite different is offered by Deleuze. Interested in how the identity of freedom and necessity in Spinoza plays out at the level of existing singular things, Deleuze proposes a particular way of understanding Spinoza's ontological necessity. Absolute necessity rules the finite modal realm insofar as it is causally governed by structures of law-like determination (mechanistic principles under the attribute of extension, logical principles under the attribute of thinking; that is, the laws of motion and rest and the infinite intellect). But that same realm must be understood, at first, to be utterly fortuitous with regard to the particular encounters. Eventually—and this is the work of liberation from bondage—the aleatory can be left behind as an entity shifts from an inadequate mental life of perception and imagination to the formation of adequate ideas. We transform, in Deleuze's terms, from passive beings that merely undergo encounters to active beings that freely engage in the art of their organization. Gilles Deleuze, *Expressionism in Philosophy: Spinoza*, trans. Martin Joughin (New York: Zone Books, 1990). As far as it may be from typical accounts of Spinoza today, Deleuze's interpretation of the necessity involved in the causal determination of finite modes is quite close to that advanced by the dominant (and nearly only) English-language commentator on Spinoza in the late 1960s,

NOTES

Edwin Curley, *Spinoza's Metaphysics: An Essay in Interpretation* (Cambridge, MA: Harvard University Press, 1969). For more recent views on the necessitarianism issue, see Don Garrett, "Spinoza's Necessitarianism," in *God and Nature: Spinoza's Metaphysics (Ethica I)*, ed. Yirmiyahu Yovel (Leiden: Brill, 1991), 191–218. For a response to Garrett, see Edwin Curley and Gregory Walski, "Spinoza's Necessitarianism Reconsidered," in *New Essays on the Rationalists*, ed. Rocco Gennaro and Charles Huenemann (Oxford: Oxford University Press, 1999), 241–62.

10. On the status of matter in Spinoza, see Alexandre Matheron, *Individu et Communauté chez Spinoza* (Paris: Editions de Minuit, 1969); Warren Montag, *Bodies, Masses, Power: Spinoza and His Contemporaries* (London: Verso, 1999), hereafter cited as *MB*; Etienne Balibar, *Spinoza and Politics*, trans. Peter Snowdon (London: Verso, 1998), hereafter cited as *SP*; Antonio Negri, *The Savage Anomaly: The Power of Spinoza's Metaphysics and Politics*, trans. Michael Hardt (Minneapolis, MN: University of Minneapolis Press, 1991); J.A. Cover, "Spinoza's Extended Substance," in *New Essays on the Rationalists*, ed. Rocco Gennaro and Charles Huenemann (Oxford: Oxford University Press, 1999), 105–33; and Charles Huenemann, "Spinoza and Prime Matter," *Journal of the History of Philosophy* 42, no. 1 (2004), 21–32. Bennett gives an original interpretation of Spinoza in terms of a field metaphysics where the matter of bodies becomes a bundle of properties suspended in (or really, projected upon) the field of substance. While his reading bears an interesting relationship to the materialist readings of Spinoza, its relation to Spinoza's views themselves is less clear. Jonathan Bennett, *A Study of Spinoza's Ethics* (Indianapolis, IN: Hackett, 1984).

11. For a general critique of Althusser and Balibar's reading (including some pokes at Negri) that is nevertheless largely sympathetic to the attempt to read Spinoza as a materialist if not with attempts to connect this materialism to Marx, see Susan James, "Spinoza and Materialism," in *Current Continental Theory and Modern Philosophy*, ed. Stephen Daniels (Evanston, IL: Northwestern University Press, 2005), 100–13. Two of the strongest attacks on the materialist reading of Spinoza are R.S. Woolhouse, *Descartes, Spinoza, Leibniz: The Concept of Substance in Seventeenth-Century Metaphysics* (London: Routledge, 1993), 28–52 and Tad Schmaltz, "Spinoza on the Vacuum," *Archiv für Geschichte der Philosophie* 81 (1999), 174–205.

12. On Descartes' account of the body primarily in relation to his physics, see especially Daniel Garber, *Descartes' Metaphysical Physics* (Chicago, IL: University of Chicago Press, 1992); Stephen Gaukroger, *Descartes' System of Natural Philosophy* (Cambridge: Cambridge University Press, 2002); and Dennis Des Chene, *Physiologia*, 42–390.

13. On the "brief preface concerning the nature of bodies," see David Lachterman, "The Physics of Spinoza's *Ethics*," in *Spinoza: New Perspectives*, ed. Robert W. Shahan and John Biro (Norman, OK: University of Oklahoma Press, 1978), 71–111; Wim Klever, "Moles in Motu: Principles of Spinoza's Physics," *Studia Spinozana* 4 (1988): 165–94; and Frederick

Ablondi and Steve Barbone, "Individual Identity." Ablondi and Barbone argue (against Matheron and others) that "Spinoza's use of physics is adaptive rather than derivative," that is, that Spinoza's metaphysics cannot be understood to be a consequence of his physics (78n14).
14. For an excellent account of both motion as a mode of bodies and the "vicinity" or "neighborhood" concept in Descartes, see Daniel Garber, *Metaphysical Physics*, 156–75.
15. In this context, Althusser's reliance on Spinoza's dynamic materialism becomes most apparent. Also on this issue see Richard Mason, "Spinoza on the Causality of Individuals," *Journal of the History of Philosophy* 24, no. 2 (1986), 197–210 and Steve Barbone, "What Counts as an Individual for Spinoza?" in *Spinoza: Metaphysical Themes*, ed. Olli Koistinen and John Biro (Oxford: Oxford University Press, 2002), 89–112.
16. While Spinoza holds that to the extent that human beings live within a political community "the greater the number of men who unite in this one body [*in unum sic conveniunt*] the greater they will all collectively possess" (*SW*, 687; *TP*, 2.15), Barbone rightly insists that here, as in the other places where Spinoza uses the "uniting in one" language, he always qualifies it with caveats that show that the Spinozan body-politic never truly coheres in one body or one individual (such as his insertion of a *quasi* before a *corpore*). That position, rather, belongs to Hobbes, where the multitude becomes one when it congeals into the artificial body of the sovereign. Steve Barbone, "What Counts?" 101.
17. Thomas Hobbes, *Leviathan, with selected variants from the Latin edition of 1668*, ed. Edwin Curley (Indianapolis, IN: Hackett, 1994), 4. Hereafter cited as *Lev*. An engagement with figures of inscription in Hobbes could constitute an entirely separate chapter. On this, see especially Gary Shapiro, "Reading and Writing in the Text of Hobbes's *Leviathan*," *Journal of the History of Philosophy* 18, no. 2 (1980), 147–57 and James R. Martel, *Subverting the Leviathan: Reading Thomas Hobbes as a Radical Democrat* (Ithaca, NY: Cornell University Press, 2007).
18. The theory of "personation" is developed in chapter 26 (*Lev.*, 101–5). On the rhetoric and theory of personation and the distinction between the natural and artificial persons, see Quentin Skinner, "Hobbes and the Purely Artificial Person of the State," *The Journal of Political Philosophy* 7, no. 1 (1999), 1–29 and Philip Pettit, *Made with Words: Hobbes on Language, Mind, and Politics* (Princeton, NJ: Princeton University Press, 2008), 55–69.
19. This passage parallels Spinoza's description of his project in the *Ethics*, where he writes, "I shall, then, treat of the nature and strength of the affects, and the mind's power over them, by the same method I have used in treating of God and the mind, and I shall consider human actions and appetites just as if it were an investigation into lines, planes, and bodies" (*CSW*, 278; *E*, 3Pref).
20. See, for example, Antonio Negri, *Insurgencies: Constituent Power and the Modern State*, trans. Maurizia Boscagli (Minneapolis, MN: University of Minnesota Press, 1999).

21. The *potential/potestas* distinction has been discussed by many commentators. See especially Balibar's *SP*; Antonio Negri, *The Savage Anomaly*; Steve Barbone, "Power in the *Tractatus theologico-politicus*," in *Piety, Peace, and the Freedom to Philosophize*, ed. Paul Bagley (Dordrecht: Kluwer, 2000), 91–110; and Steve Barbone and Lee Rice, introduction to Baruch Spinoza, *Political Treatise*, trans. Samuel Shirley (Indianapolis, IN: Hackett, 2000), 15–19. Curley denies that the terminological distinction is consistent in Spinoza's work, and while he is right with respect to the broad oeuvre, I think it is clear that the distinction is operative in the *Political Treatise* and in the *Theological-Political Treatise* (though not *completely* consistently). Edwin Curley, "Kissinger, Spinoza, and Genghis Khan," in *The Cambridge Companion to Spinoza*, ed. Don Garrett (Cambridge: Cambridge University Press, 1995), 315–42. Curley, Barbone, and Rice all offer interpretations of the right and power equation that take Spinoza to essentially hold that "might makes right," a perspective with which I obviously disagree.
22. Cf., Etienne Balibar, "Jus-Pactum-Lex: On the Constitution of the Subject in the *Theologico-Political Treatise*," in *The New Spinoza*, ed. Warren Montag and Ted Stolze (Minneapolis, MN: University of Minnesota Press, 1997), 171–205.
23. This reading of the *Theological-Political Treatise* is heavily indebted to Montag's "Scripture and Nature: The Materiality of the Letter" (*MB*, 1–25).
24. See Leo Strauss, *Persecution and the Art of Writing* (Chicago, IL: University of Chicago Press, 1988), 142–201 and André Tosel, "Superstition and Reading," in *The New Spinoza*, ed. Warren Montag and Ted Stolze (Minneapolis, MN: University of Minnesota Press, 1997), 147–67.
25. As Montag puts it, "We see an abandonment of the theme, essential to any hermeneutic, of the interior and exterior of scripture. There is no reserve of meaning, no residue beyond its surface. Meaning and form coincide exactly in the graphic materiality apart from which Scripture has no existence" (*MB*, 20).
26. This claim is repeated in chapter 12 where Spinoza insists that the word of God "is not confined within the compass of a set number of books" (*SW*, 504–5; *TTP*, 12) and that "It can thus readily be seen in what sense God can be understood as the author of the Bible: it is not because God willed to confer upon men a set number of books, but because of the true religion that is taught therein" (*SW*, 507; *TTP*, 12).
27. It should be noted that on Spinoza's account, the affective power of devotion does not result in an assembly-line production of obedient subjects. Given the differences among people's characters and the subsequent variation in the way they are "influenced by their beliefs," "what moves one man to devotion will move another to ridicule and contempt" (*SW*, 517; *TTP*, 14).

NOTES

CONCLUSION

1. Roger Chartier, "Languages, Books, and Reading from the Printed Word to the Digital Text," *Critical Inquiry* 31 (Autumn, 2004), 133–54. Also see his "The Printing Revolution: A Reappraisal," in *Agent of Change: Print Culture Studies after Elizabeth L. Eisenstein*, ed. Sabrina Alcorn Baron, Eric N. Lindquist, and Eleanor F. Shevlin (Amherst, MA: University of Massachusetts Press, 2007), 397–408.
2. For example, many of the most nuanced discussions of the effects of the wide availability to the academic community of scanned files of pre-nineteenth-century books (through databases such as Early English Books Online or Gallica) are shockingly similar—down to the details of their arguments—to discussions in the 1920s of the "complete revolution in bibliographical and research work" wrought by the photostat machine. Compare, for example, the exemplary theoretical discussion in Joseph A. Dane, *Abstractions of Evidence in the Study of Manuscripts and Early Printed Books* (Burlington, VT: Ashgate, 2009), 92–94 with the articles collected in a special issue on the photostat, George Winship, Carl B. Roden, and Andrew Keogh, eds., *The Papers of the Bibliographical Society of America* 15, no. 1 (1921). On the other hand, Dane cites this material directly, so some of the connections are no doubt intentional. Many such examples, however, can be readily adduced.
3. See the articles by Ann Blair, Brian Ogilvie, Jonathan Sheehan, and Richard Yeo collected in the symposium on "Early Modern Information Overload," ed. and intro. Daniel Rosenberg, *Journal of the History of Ideas* 64, no. 1 (January 2003), 1–72.
4. Gilles Deleuze and Félix Guattari, *A Thousand Plateaus: Capitalism and Schizophrenia*, trans. Brian Massumi (Minneapolis, MN: University of Minnesota Press, 1987), 3–25. Hereafter cited as *ATP*.
5. Ironically, this introduction is the only section of *A Thousand Plateaus* that Deleuze and Guattari provide with a definite structural location (the beginning) in their assemblage of "plateaus" through which the reader is meant to freely wander.
6. Umberto Eco, *Semiotics and the Philosophy of Language* (Bloomington, IN: Indiana University Press, 1986), 46–68.
7. Mobilizing another aspect of their neologistic terminology, Deleuze and Guattari add, "The book assures the deterritorialization of the world, but the world effects a reterritorialization of the book, which in turn deterritorializes itself in the world (if it is capable, if it can)" (*ATP*, 11).

BIBLIOGRAPHY

Aarsleff, Hans. *From Locke to Saussure: Essays on the Study of Language and Intellectual History*. Minneapolis, MN: University of Minnesota Press, 1982.
Ablondi, Frederick and Steve Barbone. "Individual Identity in Descartes and Spinoza." *Studia Spinozana* 10 (1994), 69–91.
Agamben, Giorgio. *Potentialities: Collected Essays in Philosophy*. Ed. and trans. Daniel Heller-Roazen. Stanford, CA: Stanford University Press, 1999.
Aldrovandi, Ulisse. *Serpentum, et draconum historia*. Bologna: Bernia, 1640.
Alsted, Johann Heinrich. *Encyclopaedia septem tomis distincta*. 7 vols. Herborn: Corvinus, 1630.
Althusser, Louis. *Philosophy of the Encounter: Later Writings, 1978–87*. Ed. François Matheron and Oliver Corpet. Trans. G.M. Goshgarian. London: Verso, 2006.
Aquinas, Thomas. *Knowledge in God (1a. 14-18)*. Vol. 4 of *Summa Theologicae*. Trans. Thomas Gornall. New York: McGraw-Hill, 1964.
Ariew, Roger. *Descartes and the Last Scholastics*. Ithaca, NY: Cornell University Press, 1999.
—. "Descartes and the Tree of Knowledge." *Synthese* 92, no. 1 (1992), 101–16.
Aristotle. *Art of Rhetoric*. Trans. J.H. Freese. Loeb Classical Library 193. Cambridge, MA: Harvard University Press, 1994.
—. *Metaphysics*. Trans. Hugh Tredennick. Loeb Classical Library 270 and 271. Cambridge, MA: Harvard University Press, 1975.
—. *On Sophistical Refutations; On Coming-to-Be and Passing Away; On the Cosmos*. Trans. E.S. Foster and D.J. Furley. Loeb Classical Library 400. Cambridge, MA: Harvard University Press, 1955.
Bacon, Francis. *Collected Works of Francis Bacon*. Ed. James Spedding, Robert Leslie Ellis, and Douglas Denon Heath. 12 vols. 1876. Reprint, London: Routledge, 1996.
Baillet, Adrian. *La vie de Monsieur Des-Cartes*. 2 vols. 1691. Facsimile, New York: Garland Publishing, 1987.
Balibar, Etienne. "Jus-Pactum-Lex: On the Constitution of the Subject in the *Theologico-Political Treatise*." In *The New Spinoza*. Ed. Warren Montag and Ted Stolze. Minneapolis, MN: University of Minnesota Press, 1997, 171–205.
—. *Spinoza and Politics*. Trans. Peter Snowdon. London: Verso, 1998.

BIBLIOGRAPHY

Barbone, Steve. "Power in the *Tractatus theologico-politicus.*" In *Piety, Peace, and the Freedom to Philosophize.* Ed. Paul Bagley. Dordrecht: Kluwer, 2000, 91–110.
—. "What Counts as an Individual for Spinoza?" In *Spinoza: Metaphysical Themes.* Ed. Olli Koistinen and John Biro. Oxford: Oxford University Press, 2002, 89–112.
Baudrillard, Jean. *Simulations.* Trans. Paul Foss, Paul Patton, and Philip Beitchman. New York: Semiotext(e), 1983.
Bayle, Pierre. *The Dictionary Historical and Critical of Mr. Peter Bayle.* Trans. Pierre Desmaizeaux. 5 vols. London: Knapton et al., 1734–1738.
—. *Dictionnaire historique et critique.* 2 vols. Rotterdam: Leers, 1697.
—. *Dictionnaire historique et critique.* 2nd edn. 3 vols. Rotterdam: Leers, 1702.
—. *Dictionnaire historique et critique.* 5th edn. 4 vols. Amsterdam: Brunel et al., 1740.
—. *Historical and Critical Dictionary: Selections.* Ed. and trans. Richard Popkin. Indianapolis, IN: Hackett, 1991.
—. *Oeuvres diverses.* 5 vols. 1731. Reprint. Hildesheim: Olms, 1964–1968.
—. *Pour une histoire critique de la philosophie: Choix d'articles philosophiques du 'Dictionnaire historique et critique'.* Ed. and intro. Jean-Michel Gros. Coll. Jacques Chomarat. Paris: Honoré Champion, 2001.
—. *Projet et fragmens d'un dictionnaire critique.* 1692. Reprint, Geneva: Slatkine, 1970.
—. [Untitled announcement]. *Histoire des ouvrages des savants* (Sept.–Nov. 1690), 136.
Beck, Leslie John. *The Method of Descartes: A Study of the "Regulae."* Oxford: Clarendon Press, 1952.
Benjamin, Walter. *The Arcades Project.* Trans. Howard Eiland and Kevin McLaughlin. Cambridge, MA: Harvard University Press, 1999.
—. *The Origin of German Tragic Drama.* Trans. John Osborne. London: Verso, 1998.
Bennett, Jonathan. "Spinoza's Mind-Body Identity Thesis." *The Journal of Philosophy* 78, no. 10 (1981), 573–84.
—. *A Study of Spinoza's Ethics.* Indianapolis, IN: Hackett, 1984.
Black, Robert and Gabriella Pomaro. *Boethius' Consolation of Philosophy in Italian Medieval and Renaissance Education.* Florence: Galluzzo, 2000.
Blair, Ann. "Annotating and Indexing Natural Philosophy." In *Books and the Sciences in History.* Ed. Marina Frasca-Spada and Nick Jardine. Cambridge: Cambridge University Press, 2000, 69–89.
—. "Focus: Scientific Readers, An Early Modernist's Perspective." *Isis* 95, no. 3 (2004), 420–30.
—. "Organizations of Knowledge." In *The Cambridge Companion to Renaissance Philosophy.* Ed. James Hankins. Cambridge: Cambridge University Press, 2007, 287–303.
—. "Reading Strategies for Coping with Information Overload, ca. 1550–1700." *Journal of the History of Ideas* 64, no. 1 (2003), 11–28.
Blondel, Maurice. *Une énigme historique: Le 'Vinculum substantiale' d'après Leibniz et l'ébauche d'un réalisme supérieur.* Paris: Gabriel Beauchesne, 1930.

BIBLIOGRAPHY

Blumenberg, Hans. *Die Lesbarkeit der Welt*. Frankfurt am Main: Suhrkamp, 1981.
Boehm, Alfred. *Le 'Vinculum substantiale' chez Leibniz: Ses origines historiques*. Paris: Vrin, 1938.
Boethius, Anicius Manlius Severinus. *The Theological Tractates and the Consolation of Philosophy*. Ed. and trans. H.F. Stewart, E.K. Rand, and S.J. Tester. Loeb Classical Library 74. Cambridge, MA: Harvard University Press, 1973.
Borges, Jorge Luis. *Collected Fictions*. Trans. Andrew Hurley. New York: Penguin Books, 1998.
—. *Labyrinths: Selected Stories and Other Writing*. Ed. Donald A. Yates and James E. Irby. New York: New Directions Books, 1962.
—. *Selected Non-Fictions*. Ed. Eliot Weinberger. Trans. Esther Allen, Suzanne Jill Levine, and Eliot Weinberger. New York: Penguin Books, 1999.
Borges, Jorge Luis and Adolfo Bioy Casares. *Extraordinary Tales*. Trans. Anthony Kerrigan. New York: Herder and Herder, 1971.
Bos, Jan-Erik. "La Première publication de *La Recherche de la vérité* en 1684: *Onderzoek der Waarheid door 't Natuurlijk Licht*." *Nouvelles de la République de Lettres* 1 (1999), 13–26.
Bots, Hans. "Le rôle des périodiques Néerlandais pour la diffusion du livre (1684–1747)." In *Le Magasin de l'univers: The Dutch Republic as the Centre of the European Book Trade*. Ed. Christiane Berkvens-Stevelinck. New York: Brill, 1992, 47–70.
Bouchardy, Jean-Jacques. *Pierre Bayle: La nature et la 'nature des choses'*. Paris: Honoré Champion, 2001.
Bowker, John, ed. *The Oxford Dictionary of World Religions*. Oxford: Oxford University Press, 1997.
Boyle, Robert. *The Works of Robert Boyle*. Ed. Michael Hunter and Edward B. Davis. 14 vols. London: Pickering & Chatto, 1999–2000.
Braun, Lucien. *Iconographie et philosophie: Essai de définition d'un champ de recherche*. Strasbourg: Presses Universitaires de Strasbourg, 1994.
Breger, Herbert. "Über die Hannoversche Handschrift der Descartesschen Regulae." *Studia Leibnitiana* 15, no. 1 (1983), 108–14.
Brown, Harcourt. "History and the Learned Journal." *Journal of the History of Ideas* 33, no. 3 (1972), 365–78.
Buffon, Georges-Louis Leclerc, Comte de. *Histoire naturelle, générale et particuliére*. 44 vols. Paris: Imprimerie royale, 1749–1804.
Camporeale, Salvatore. "Lorenzo Valla: The Transcending of Philosophy through Rhetoric." *Romance Notes* 30, no. 3 (1990), 269–84.
Capella, Martianus. *The Marriage of Philology and Mercury*. Vol. 2 of *Martianus Capella and the Seven Liberal Arts*. Ed. William Stahl, Richard Johnson, and E.L. Burge. New York: Columbia University Press, 1977.
Carr, Spencer. "Spinoza's Distinction between Rational and Intuitive Knowledge." *The Philosophical Review* 87, no. 2 (1978), 241–52.
Carroll, Lewis. *The Complete Works of Lewis Carroll*. New York: Random House, 1936.
Celenza, Christopher S. "Lorenzo Valla, 'Paganism,' and Orthodoxy." *MLN* 119, Supplement (2004), s66–87.

Cérard, Jean. "Encyclopédie et encyclopédisme à la Renaissance." In *L'Encyclopédisme: Actes du colloque de Caen, 12-16 janvier 1987.* Ed. Annie Becq. Paris: Aux Amateurs de Livres, 1991, 57–67.
Chadwick, Henry. *Boethius: The Consolations of Music, Logic, Theology, and Philosophy.* Oxford: Clarendon, 1981.
Chartier, Roger. *The Cultural Uses of Print in Early Modern France.* Trans. Lydia G. Cochrane. Princeton, NJ: Princeton University Press, 1987.
—. "Foucault's Chiasmus: Authorship between Science and Literature in the Seventeenth and Eighteenth Centuries." In *Scientific Authorship: Credit and Intellectual Property in Science.* Ed. Mario Biagioli and Peter Galison. New York: Routledge, 2003, 13–31.
—. "Languages, Books, and Reading from the Printed Word to the Digital Text." *Critical Inquiry* 31 (Autumn, 2004), 133–54.
—. *The Order of Books: Readers, Authors, and Libraries in Europe between the Fourteenth and Eighteenth Centuries.* Trans. Lydia G. Cochrane. Stanford, CA: Stanford University Press, 1994.
—. "The Printing Revolution: A Reappraisal." In *Agent of Change: Print Culture Studies after Elizabeth L. Eisenstein.* Ed. Sabrina Alcorn Baron, Eric N. Lindquist, and Eleanor F. Shevlin. Amherst, MA: University of Massachusetts Press, 2007, 397–408.
Cicero, Marcus Tullius. *Tusculan Disputations.* Trans. J.E. King. Loeb Classical Library 141. Cambridge, MA: Harvard University Press, 1927.
Comenius, Johann Amos. *Pansophiae prodromus.* London: Fawne & Gellibrand, 1639.
Cottingham, John G. "The Intellect, the Will and the Passions: Spinoza's Critique of Descartes." *Journal of the History of Philosophy* 26, no. 2 (1988), 239–57.
Courcelle, Pierre. *La 'Consolation de Philosophie' dans la tradition littéraire: Antécédents et postérité de Boèce.* Paris: Études Augustiniennes, 1969.
—. *Histoire littéraire des grandes invasions germaniques.* Paris: Études Augustiniennes, 1964.
Couturat, Louis. *La logique de Leibniz d'après des documents inédits.* 1901. Reprint, Hildesheim: Olms, 1961.
Cover, J.A. "Spinoza's Extended Substance." In *New Essays on the Rationalists.* Ed. Rocco Gennaro and Charles Huenemann. Oxford: Oxford University Press, 1999, 105–33.
Curley, Edwin. "Kissinger, Spinoza, and Genghis Khan." In *The Cambridge Companion to Spinoza.* Ed. Don Garrett. Cambridge: Cambridge University Press, 1995, 315–42.
—. *Spinoza's Metaphysics: An Essay in Interpretation.* Cambridge, MA: Harvard University Press, 1969.
Curley, Edwin and Gregory Walski. "Spinoza's Necessitarianism Reconsidered." In *New Essays on the Rationalists.* Ed. Rocco Gennaro and Charles Huenemann. Oxford: Oxford University Press, 1999, 241–62.
Curtius, Ernst Robert. *European Literature and the Latin Middle Ages.* Trans. Willard R. Trask. Princeton, NJ: Princeton University Press, 1991.
Dane, Joseph A. *Abstractions of Evidence in the Study of Manuscripts and Early Printed Books.* Burlington, VT: Ashgate, 2009.

Dascal, Marcelo. *Leibniz: Language, Signs, and Thought*. Amsterdam: Benjamins, 1987.
Daston, Lorraine. "Classifications of Knowledge in the Age of Louis XIV." In *Sun King: The Ascendancy of French Culture During the Reign of Louis XIV*. Ed. David Rubin. Washington, DC: Folger Shakespeare Library, 1992, 207–20.
De Man, Paul. *Allegories of Reading: Figural Language in Rousseau, Nietzsche, Rilke, and Proust*. New Haven, CT: Yale University Press, 1979.
—. *Blindness and Insight: Essays in the Rhetoric of Contemporary Criticism*. 2nd rev. edn. Minneapolis, MN: University of Minnesota Press, 1983.
Deleuze, Gilles. *Difference and Repetition*. Trans. Paul Patterson. New York: Columbia University Press, 1994.
—. *Expressionism in Philosophy: Spinoza*. Trans. Martin Joughin. New York: Zone Books, 1990.
—. *The Fold: Leibniz and the Baroque*. Trans. Tom Conley. Minneapolis, MN: University of Minnesota Press, 1993.
Deleuze, Gilles and Félix Guattari. *A Thousand Plateaus: Capitalism and Schizophrenia*. Trans. Brian Massumi. Minneapolis, MN: University of Minnesota Press, 1987.
Della Rocca, Michael. *Representation and the Mind-Body Problem in Spinoza*. Oxford: Oxford University Press, 1996.
—. "Spinoza's Argument for the Identity Theory." *The Philosophical Review*, 102, no. 2 (1993), 183–213.
Derrida, Jacques. *Margins of Philosophy*. Trans. Alan Bass. Chicago, IL: University of Chicago Press, 1982.
—. *Of Grammatology*. Trans. Gayatri Chakravorty Spivak. Baltimore, MD: The Johns Hopkins University Press, 1974.
—. *Paper Machine*. Trans. Rachel Bowlby. Stanford, CA: Stanford University Press, 2005.
—. *The Postcard: From Socrates to Freud and Beyond*. Trans. Alan Bass. Chicago, IL: University of Chicago Press, 1987.
—. *Writing and Difference*. Trans. Alan Bass. Chicago, IL: University of Chicago Press, 1978.
Des Chene, Dennis. *Physiologia: Natural Philosophy in Late Aristotelian and Cartesian Thought*. Ithaca, NY: Cornell University Press, 1996.
Descartes, René. *Discours de la méthode: Texte et commentaire*. Ed. Étienne Gilson. Paris: Vrin, 1947.
—. *Oeuvres de Descartes*. Ed. Charles Adam and Paul Tannery. Rev. edn. 11 vols. Paris: Vrin, 1996.
—. *The Philosophical Writings of Descartes*. Ed. and trans. John Cottingham, Robert Stoothoff, and Dugald Murdoch. 3 vols. Cambridge: Cambridge University Press, 1984–1991.
—. *Règles utiles et claires pour la direction de l'esprit en la recherche de la vérité*. Ed. and trans. Jean-Luc Marion. The Hague: Martinus Nijhoff, 1977.
—. *Regulae ad directionem ingenii/Regeln zur Ausrichtung der Erkenntniskraft*. Ed. Heinrich Springmeyer, Lüder Gäbe, and Hans Gunter Zekl. Hamburg: Felix Meiner, 1973.

BIBLIOGRAPHY

—. *Regulae ad directionem ingenii/Rules for the Direction of the Natural Intelligence.* Ed. and trans. George Heffernan. Amsterdam: Rodopi, 1998.
—. *Regulae ad directionem ingenii. Texte critique établi . . . avec la version hollandaise du XVIIème siècle.* Ed., trans., and commentary Giovanni Crapulli. The Hague: Martinus Nijhoff, 1966.
Dictionnaire de l'Académie Française. 2 vols. Paris: Coignard, 1694.
Diderot, Denis. *Rameau's Nephew and Other Works.* Trans. Jacques Barzun and Ralph Bowen. Indianapolis, IN: Hackett, 2001.
Diderot, Denis, Jean Le Rond d'Alembert, and Pierre Mouchon. *Encyclopédie ou Dictionnaire raisonné des sciences, des arts et des métiers, par une Société de Gens de lettres.* 17 vols. Paris: Breton et al., 1751–1765.
Doob, Penelope Reed. *The Idea of the Labyrinth from Classical Antiquity through the Middle Ages.* Ithaca, NY: Cornell University Press, 1990.
Drake, Stillman. "Early Science and the Printed Book: The Spread of Science beyond the Universities." *Renaissance and Reformation* 6 (1970), 43–52.
Duchesneau, François. *Leibniz et la méthode de la science.* Paris: Presses Universitaires de France, 1993.
Eco, Umberto. *The Search for the Perfect Language.* Trans. James Fentress. Oxford: Blackwell, 1995.
—. *Semiotics and the Philosophy of Language.* Bloomington, IN: Indiana University Press, 1986.
Eisenstein, Elizabeth L. *The Printing Press as an Agent of Change: Communications and Cultural Transformations in Early-Modern Europe*, 1 vol. edn. Cambridge: Cambridge University Press, 1979.
—. "Reply." *The American Historical Review* 107, no. 1 (2002), 126–28.
—. "An Unacknowledged Revolution Revisited." *The American Historical Review* 107, no. 1 (2002), 87–105.
Febvre, Lucien Paul Victor and Henri-Jean Martin, *The Coming of the Book: The Impact of Printing 1450-1800.* Trans. David Gerard. London: Verso, 1976.
Feldman, Karen S. "*Per canales Troporum*: On Tropes and Performativity in Leibniz's Preface to Nizolius." *Journal of the History of Ideas* 65, no. 1 (2004), 39–51.
Fenves, Peter. *Arresting Language: From Leibniz to Benjamin.* Stanford, CA: Stanford University Press, 2001.
—. "Continuing the Fiction: From Leibniz's 'petit fable' to Kafka's *In der Strafkolonie.*" *MLN* 116, no. 3 (2001), 502–20.
Fichant, Michel. "Ewige Wiederkehr oder unendlicher Fortschritt: Die Apokatastasisfrage bei Leibniz." *Studia Leibnitiana* 23, no. 2 (1991), 133–50.
Fisher, Saul. *Pierre Gassendi's Philosophy and Science: Atomism for Empiricists.* Leiden: Brill, 2005.
Fisher, Sophie. "L'exemple des exemples: À propos d'objets linguistique." *Versus* 70–71 (1995), 31–47.
Ford, Philip. "Lucretius in Early Modern France." In *The Cambridge Companion to Lucretius.* Ed. Stuart Gillespie and Philip Hardie. Cambridge: Cambridge University Press, 227–41.

BIBLIOGRAPHY

Foucault, Michel. *The Archaeology of Knowledge*. New York: Pantheon Books, 1972.
—. *The Essential Works of Michel Foucault, 1954-1984*. Ed. James Faubion and Paul Rabinow. Trans. Robert Hurley et al. 3 vols. New York: The New Press, 1997–2001.
—. *The Order of Things: An Archaeology of the Human Sciences*. Trans. Alan Sheridan. New York: Vintage, 1970.
Freedman, Joseph S. "Sixteenth and Seventeenth Century Classifications of Philosophical Disciplines: Leibniz and Some of His Predecessors." In *Akten des II. Internationaler Leibniz Kongress, 1972, Band 1*. Studia Leibnitiana Supplementa 12. Wiesbaden: Steiner, 1975, 193–202.
Frémont, Christiane. *L'Être et la relation*. Paris: Vrin, 1981.
—. *Singularités: Individus et relations dans le système de Leibniz*. Paris: Vrin, 2003.
Freud, Sigmund. *Beyond the Pleasure Principle*. Trans. James Strachey. New York: W.W. Norton & Co., 1961.
Friedrich, Udo. "Grenzen des Ordo im enzyklopädischen Schrifttum des 16. Jahrhunderts." In *Die Enzyklopädie im Wandel vom Hochmittelalter bis zur Frühen Neuzeit*. Ed. Christel Meier, Stefan Schuler, and Marcus Heckenkamp. Munich: Fink, 2002, 391–408.
Froidmont, Libert. *Labyrinthus, sive, De compositione continui liber unus: philosophis, mathematicis, theologis utilis ac iucundus*. Antwerp: Ex officina Plantiniana Balthasaris Moreti, 1631.
Furetière, Antoine. *Dictionnaire universel, contenant generalement tous les mots françois*. 3 vols. Rotterdam: Leers, 1690.
Galilei, Galileo. *The Assayer* in *The Controversy of the Comets of 1618*. Ed. and trans. Stillman Drake and C.D. O'Malley. Philadelphia, PA: Pennsylvania University Press, 1960.
Garber, Daniel. *Descartes' Metaphysical Physics*. Chicago, IL: University of Chicago Press, 1992.
Garrett, Don. "Spinoza's Necessitarianism." In *God and Nature: Spinoza's Metaphysics (Ethica I)*. Ed. Yirmiyahu Yovel. Leiden: Brill, 1991, 191–218.
Garrett, Jeffrey. "Books and Things: The Crisis of Representation in German Libraries after 1800." Presentation at Northwestern University, Evanston, IL, March 8, 1999.
Gassendi, Pierre. *The Selected Works of Pierre Gassendi*. Ed. and trans. Craig B. Brush. New York: Johnson Reprint Corporation, 1972.
Gaukroger, Stephen. *Descartes' System of Natural Philosophy*. Cambridge: Cambridge University Press, 2002.
Gerl-Falkovitz, Hanna. *Rhetorik als Philosophie: Lorenzo Valla*. Munich: Fink, 1974.
Gilson, Étienne. *Études sur le rôle de la pensée médiévale dans la formation du système cartésien*. Paris: Vrin, 1951.
—. *Index scolastico-cartésien*. Paris: Alcan, 1912.
Grafton, Anthony. "Epilogue: Boethius in the Renaissance." In *Boethius: His Life, Thought, and Influence*. Ed. Margaret Gibson. Oxford: Blackwell, 1981, 410–13.

BIBLIOGRAPHY

—. *The Footnote: A Curious History*. Cambridge, MA: Harvard University Press, 1997.

—. "The Humanist as Reader." In *A History of Reading in the West*. Ed. Guglielmo Cavallo and Roger Chartier. Trans. Lydia G. Cochrane. Amherst: University of Massachusetts Press, 1999, 179–212.

—. "The Importance of Being Printed." Review of Elizabeth L. Eisenstein, 'The Printing Press as an Agent of Change.' *Journal of Interdisciplinary History* 11, no. 2 (Autumn, 1980), 265–86.

—. "Introduction" *The American Historical Review* 107, no. 1 (2002), 84–6.

Grassi, Ernesto. *Einführung in philosophische Probleme des Humanismus*. Darmstadt: Wissenschaftliche Buchgesellschaft, 1986.

Groenveld, S. "The Dutch Republic, an Island of Liberty of the Press in 17th-Century Europe? The Authorities and the Book Trade." In *Commercium Litterarium: La communication dans la République des lettres, 1600–1750*. Ed. Hans Bots and Françoise Waquet. Amsterdam: APA-Holland University Press, 1994, 281–300.

Gruber, Joachim. "Die Erscheinung der Philosophie in der *Consolatio Philosophiae* des Boethius." *Rheinisches Museum für Philologie* 121 (1969), 166–86.

—. *Kommentar zu Boethius De Consolatione philosophiae*. Berlin: de Gruyter, 1978.

Gueroult, Martial. *Spinoza II – L'âme ("Ethique," II)*. Paris: Aubier, 1974.

Hamelin, Octave. *Le système, De consolatione*. Paris: Alcan, 1911.

Hegel, G.W.F. *Phenomenology of Spirit*. Trans. A.V. Miller. Oxford: Oxford University Press, 1977.

—. *Science of Logic*. Trans. A.V. Miller. Atlantic Highlands, NJ: Humanities Press International, 1989.

Heinekamp, Albert. "Sprache und Wirklichkeit nach Leibniz." In *History of Linguistic Thought and Contemporary Linguistics*. Ed. Herman Parret. Berlin: de Gruyter, 1976, 518-70.

Heller-Roazen, Daniel. *The Inner Touch: Archaeology of a Sensation*. New York: Zone Books, 2007.

Hobbes, Thomas. *Leviathan, with selected variants from the Latin edition of 1668*. Ed. Edwin Curley. Indianapolis, IN: Hackett, 1994.

Hoftijzer, Paul Gerardus. "Between Mercury and Minerva: Dutch Printing Offices and Bookshops as Intermediaries in Seventeenth-Century Scholarly Communication." In *Commercium Litterarium: La communication dans la République des lettres, 1600-1750*. Ed. Hans Bots and Françoise Waquet. Amsterdam: APA-Holland University Press, 1994, 119–29.

Holden, Thomas. *The Architecture of Matter: Galileo to Kant*. Oxford: Clarendon Press, 2004.

—. "Bayle and the Case for Actual Parts." *Journal of the History of Philosophy* 42, no. 2 (2004), 145–64.

Homer. *Iliad*. Trans. A.T. Murray. Rev. William F. Wyatt. Loeb Classical Library 170 and 171. Cambridge, MA: Harvard University Press, 1999.

Hotson, Howard. *Johann Heinrich Alsted, 1588-1638: Between Renaissance, Reformation, and Universal Reform*. Oxford: Clarendon Press, 2000.

BIBLIOGRAPHY

Hübener, Wolfgang. "Die notwendige Grenze des Erkenntnisfortschritts als Konsequenz der Aussagenkombinatorik nach Leibniz' unveröffentlichten Traktat 'De l'Horizon de la doctrine humaine'." In *Akten des II. Internationaler Leibniz Kongress, 1972, Band 4*. Studia Leibnitiana Supplementa 15. Wiesbaden: Steiner, 1975, 55–71.

Huenemann, Charles. "Spinoza and Prime Matter." *Journal of the History of Philosophy* 42, no. 1 (2004), 21–32.

Hume, David. *An Enquiry Concerning Human Understanding*. Ed. Eric Steinberg. 2nd edn. Indianapolis, IN: Hackett, 1993.

Huppert, George. "*Divinatio et Eruditio*: Thoughts on Foucault." *History and Theory* 13, no. 3 (1974), 191–207.

Ishiguro, Hidé. *Leibniz's Philosophy of Logic and Language*. Cambridge: Cambridge University Press, 1990.

Israel, Jonathan. *Radical Enlightenment: Philosophy and the Making of Modernity, 1650-1750*. Oxford: Oxford University Press, 2001.

James, Susan. "Spinoza and Materialism." In *Current Continental Theory and Modern Philosophy*. Ed. Stephen Daniels. Evanston, IL: Northwestern University Press, 2005, 100–13.

Jardine, Lisa. "Lorenzo Valla: Academic Skepticism and the New Humanist Dialectic." In *The Skeptical Tradition*. Ed. Myles Burnyeat. Berkeley, CA: University of California Press, 1983, 253–86.

—. "Lorenzo Valla and the Intellectual Origins of Humanist Dialectic." *Journal of the History of Philosophy* 15, no. 2 (1977), 143–64.

Johns, Adrian. "The Ambivalence of Authorship in Early Modern Natural Philosophy." In *Scientific Authorship: Credit and Intellectual Property in Science*. Ed. Mario Biagioli and Peter Galison. New York: Routledge, 2003, 67–89.

—. "How to Acknowledge a Revolution." *The American Historical Review* 107, no. 1 (2002), 106–25.

—. *The Nature of the Book: Print and Knowledge in the Making*. Chicago, IL: University of Chicago Press, 1998.

Johnson, George. "Vatican's Celestial Eye, Seeking Not Angels but Data." *New York Times*. June 23, 2009, D2.

Jones, Howard. *The Epicurean Tradition*. London: Routledge, 1989.

Joy, Lynn Sumida. *Gassendi the Atomist: Advocate of History in an Age of Science*. Cambridge: Cambridge University Press, 1987.

Kafker, Frank A. *Notable Encyclopedias of the Seventeenth and Eighteenth Centuries: Nine Predecessors of the "Encyclopédie."* Oxford: Voltaire Foundation, 1981.

Kahn, Victoria. "The Rhetoric of Faith and the Use of Usage in Lorenzo Valla's *De libero arbitrio*." *Journal of Medieval and Renaissance Studies* 13 (1983), 91–109.

Kelley, Donald R., ed. "Special Issue: Salvatore Camporeale, Lorenzo Valla, Humanism, and Theology." *Journal of the History of Ideas* 66, no. 4 (2005).

Kern, Hermann. *Labyrinthe: Erscheinungsformen und Deutungen 5000 Jahre Gegenwart eines Urbilds*. Munich: Prestel Verlag, 1982.

Kern, Thomas and Janet Backhouse, ed. *Renaissance Painting in Manuscripts: Treasures from the British Library*. New York: Hudson Hills Press, 1983.

Kierkegaard, Søren. *Fear and Trembling. Repetition*. Ed. and trans. Howard V. Hong and Edna H. Hong. Princeton, NJ: Princeton University Press, 1983.

Klever, Wim. "Moles in Motu: Principles of Spinoza's Physics." *Studia Spinozana* 4 (1988): 165–94.

Knecht, Herbert H. *La Logique chez Leibniz: Essai sur le rationalisme baroque*. Lausanne: L'Age d'Homme, 1981.

Knoppik, Jürgen. "Leibniz' Fortschrittskriterium: Das Übergehen zu Neuem." *Studia Leibnitiana* 14, no. 1 (1997), 45–62.

Kristeller, Paul Oskar. *Eight Philosophers of the Italian Renaissance*. Stanford, CA: Stanford University Press, 1964.

Labrousse, Elisabeth. *Pierre Bayle*. 2 vols. The Hague: Nijhoff, 1964.

—. "Reading Pierre Bayle in Paris." In *Anticipations of the Enlightenment in England, France, and Germany*. Ed. Alan Charles Kors and Paul J. Korshin. Philadelphia, PA: University of Pennsylvania Press, 1987, 7–16.

Lachterman, David. "The Physics of Spinoza's *Ethics*." In *Spinoza: New Perspectives*. Ed. Robert W. Shahan and John Biro. Norman, OK: University of Oklahoma Press, 1978, 71–111.

Laertius, Diogenes. *Lives of Eminent Philosophers*. Trans. R.D. Hicks. Loeb Classical Library 184 and 185. Cambridge: Harvard University Press, 1925.

Lamarra, Antonio and Roberto Palaia. Ed. *Unità e molteplicità nel pensiero filosofico e scientifico di Leibniz*. Florence: Olschki, 2000.

Lamy, Guillaume. *De principiis rerum*. Paris: Petrum le Monnier, 1669.

Lankhorst, Otto S. "Naissance typographique du *Dictionaire historique et critique* de Pierre Bayle." In *Critique, savoir et érudition à la veille des Lumières: Le "Dictionnaire historique et critique" de Pierre Bayle*. Ed. Hans Bots. Amsterdam: APA-Holland University Press, 1998, 3–16.

Lasswitz, Kurd. "The Universal Library." Trans. Willy Ley. In *Fantasia Mathematica*. Ed. Clifton Fadiman. New York: Simon and Schuster, 1958, 237–43.

Latour, Bruno, *We Have Never Been Modern*. Trans. Catherine Porter. Cambridge, MA: Harvard University Press, 1993.

Le Doeuff, Michèle. *The Philosophical Imaginary*. Trans. Colin Gordon. London: Continuum, 2002.

Lebel, Robert and Isabelle Waldberg, ed. *Encyclopaedia Da Costa* (1947). In *Encyclopaedia Acephalica*. Ed. Alastair Brotchie. Trans. Iain White. London: Atlas Press, 1995, 107–56.

Leibniz, Gottfried Wilhelm. *De l'horizon de la doctrine humaine (1693); Apocatastase panton (La Restitution universelle, 1715)*. Ed. and trans. Michel Fichant. Paris: Vrin, 1991.

—. *Leibniz's 'New System' and Associated Contemporary Texts*. Ed. and trans. R.S. Woolhouse and Richard Francks. Oxford: Clarendon Press, 1997.

—. *Mathematische Schriften*. Ed. C.I. Gerhardt. 7 vols. 1849–1863. Reprint, Hildesheim: Olms, 1971.

BIBLIOGRAPHY

—. *New Essays on Human Understanding*. Ed. and trans. Peter Remnant and Jonathan Bennett. Cambridge: Cambridge University Press, 1993.
—. *Opuscules et fragments inédits de Leibniz*. Ed. Louis Couturat. Paris: Alcan, 1903.
—. *Philosophical Essays*. Ed. and trans. Roger Ariew and Daniel Garber. Indianapolis, IN: Hackett, 1989.
—. *Philosophical Papers and Letters*. 2nd edn. Ed. and trans. Leroy E. Loemker. Dordrecht: Kluwer, 1989.
—. *Die Philosophischen Schriften*. Ed. Carl I. Gerhardt. 7 vols. 1875–1890. Reprint, Hildesheim: Olms, 1996.
—. *Sämtliche Schriften und Briefe*. Ed. Berlin-Brandenburgerischen [form. Preussische] Akademie der Wissenschaften and Akademie der Wissenschaften in Göttingen. 48 vols. in 8 series. Berlin: Akademie Verlag, 1923–present.
—. *Theodicy: Essays on the Goodness of God, the Freedom of Man, and the Origin of Evil*. Ed. Austin Marsden Farrer. Trans. E.M. Huggard. La Salle, IL: Open Court, 1985.
Leibniz, G.W. and Samuel Clarke. *Correspondence*. Ed. and trans. Roger Ariew. Indianapolis, IN: Hackett, 2000.
Leinsle, Ulrich G. "Wissenschaftstheorie oder Metaphysik als Grundlage der Enzyklopädie?" In *Enzyklopädien der Frühen Neuzeit: Beiträge zu ihrer Erforschung*. Ed. Franz M. Eybl. Tübingen: Niemeyer, 1995, 98–119.
Lennon, Thomas M. *The Battle of the Gods and Giants: The Legacies of Descartes and Gassendi, 1655–1715*. Princeton, NJ: Princeton University Press, 1993.
—. *Reading Bayle*. Toronto: University of Toronto Press, 1999.
Lerer, Seth. *Boethius and Dialogue: Literary Method in the Consolation of Philosophy*. Princeton, NJ: Princeton University Press, 1985.
Levy, Samuel. "Leibniz on Mathematics and the Actually Infinite Division of Matter." *The Philosophical Review* 107, no. 1 (1998), 49–96.
—. "Matter and Two Concepts of Continuity in Leibniz." *Philosophical Studies* 94, no. 1–2 (1999), 81–118.
Locke, John. *An Essay Concerning Human Understanding*. Ed. Peter H. Nidditch. Oxford: Clarendon Press, 1975.
Loemker, Leroy E. "Leibniz and the Herborn Encyclopedists." *Journal of the History of Ideas* 22, no. 3 (1961), 323–38.
Lolordo, Antonia. *Pierre Gassendi and the Birth of Early Modern Philosophy*. Cambridge: Cambridge University Press, 2007.
Look, Brandon. *Leibniz and the 'Vinculum Substantiale.'* Studia Leibnitiana Sonderheft 30. Stuttgart: Franz Steiner, 1999.
Lucretius, Titus Carus. *De rerum natura*. Trans. W.H.D. Rouse and Martin Ferguson Smith. Rev. edn. Loeb Classical Library 181. Cambridge, MA: Harvard University Press, 1975.
Lyons, John. *Exemplum: The Rhetoric of Example in Early Modern France and Italy*. Princeton, NJ: Princeton University Press, 1989.
Macherey, Pierre. *Introduction à l'Ethique de Spinoza*. 5 vols. Paris: Presses Universitaires de France, 1994–1998.

Maillard, Jean-François. "Fortunes de l'encyclopédie à la fin de la Renaissance." In *L'Encyclopédisme: Actes du colloque de Caen, 12–16 janvier 1987*. Ed. Annie Becq. Paris: Aux Amateurs de Livres, 1991, 319–25.
Marion, Jean-Luc. *On Descartes' Metaphysical Prism: The Constitution and the Limits of Onto-theo-logy in Cartesian Thought*. Trans. Jeffrey Kosky. Chicago, IL: University of Chicago Press, 1999.
——. *Sur l'ontologie grise de Descartes*. Paris: Vrin, 1975.
Martel, James R. *Subverting the Leviathan: Reading Thomas Hobbes as a Radical Democrat*. Ithaca, NY: Cornell University Press, 2007.
Martin, Gottfried. "Thesaurus omnis humanae scientiae. Une requête de Leibniz." *Archives de Philosophie* 30, no. 3 (1967), 388–97.
Martin, Henri-Jean. *The History and Power of Writing*. Trans. Lydia G. Cochrane. Chicago, IL: University of Chicago Press, 1994.
——. *La Naissance du livre moderne (XIVe-XVIIe siècles): Mise en page et mise en texte du livre français*. Paris: Éditions du Cercle de la Libraire, 2000.
Mason, Richard. "Spinoza on the Causality of Individuals." *Journal of the History of Philosophy* 24, no. 2 (1986), 197–210.
Matheron, Alexandre. *Individu et Communauté chez Spinoza*. Paris: Editions de Minuit, 1969.
McKenna, Anthony. "L'ironie de Bayle et son statut dans l'écriture philosophique." In *La Raison corrosive: Études sur la pensée critique de Pierre Bayle*. Ed. Isabelle Delpla and Philippe de Robert. Paris: Honoré Champion, 2003, 245–66.
——. "Pierre Bayle et la superstition." In *La superstition à l'âge des Lumières*. Ed. Bernard Dompnier, Paris: Honoré Champion, 1998, 49–65.
——. "Rationalisme moral et fidéisme." In *Pierre Bayle: Citoyen du Monde*. Ed. Hubert Bost and Phillippe de Robert. Paris: Honoré Champion, 1999, 257–74.
McKenzie, Douglas. "Printers of the Mind: Some Notes on Bibliographical Theories and Printing-House Practices." *Studies in Bibliography* 22 (1969), 1–75.
McKitterick, David. *Print, Manuscript, and the Search for Order 1450–1830*. Cambridge: Cambridge University Press, 2003.
McRae, Robert. *The Problem of the Unity of the Sciences: Bacon to Kant*. Toronto: University of Toronto Press, 1961.
Monfasani, John. "Humanism and Rhetoric." In *Renaissance Humanism: Foundations, Forms, and Legacy*. Ed. Albert Rabil, Jr. 3 vols. Philadelphia, PA: University of Pennsylvania Press, 1988, 171–235.
——. "Was Lorenzo Valla an Ordinary Language Philosopher?" *Journal of the History of Ideas* 50, no. 2 (1989), 309–23.
Montag, Warren. *Bodies, Masses, Power: Spinoza and His Contemporaries*. London: Verso, 1999.
Moréri, Louis. *Le Grand dictionnaire historique, ou le Mélange curieux de l'histoire sacrée et profane*. Lyons: J. Girin and B. Rivière, 1674.
Mori, Gianluca. *Bayle philosophe*. Paris: Honoré Champion. 1999.
Moss, Ann. "Locating Knowledge." In *Cognition and the Book: Typologies of Formal Organisation of Knowledge in the Printed Book of the Early*

Modern Period. Ed. Karl A.E. Enenkel and Wolfgang Neuber. Leiden: Brill, 2005, 35–49.
Nancy, Jean-Luc. "Dum Scribo." Trans. Ian Macleod. *Oxford Literary Review* 3, no. 2 (1978), 6–21.
Nauta, Lodi. "Lorenzo Valla and the Rise of Humanist Dialectic." In *The Cambridge Companion to Renaissance Philosophy*. Ed. James Hankins. Cambridge: Cambridge University Press, 2007, 193–210.
——. "'Magis sit Platonicus quam Aristotelicus': Interpretations of Boethius's Platonism in the *Consolatio philosophiae* from the Twelfth to the Seventeenth Century." In *The Platonic Tradition in the Middle Ages: A Doxographic Approach*. Ed. Stephen Gersh and Maarten J.F.M. Hoenen. Berlin: de Gruyter, 2002, 165–204.
——. "Some Aspects of Boethius' *Consolatio Philosophiae* in the Renaissance." In *Boèce, ou la chaîne des savoirs*. Ed. Alain Galonnier. Louvain: Peeters, 2003, 767–78.
Nedergaard, Lief. "Le genèse du 'Dictionnaire historique et critique' de Pierre Bayle." *Orbis Litterarum* 13, no. 2 (1958), 210–27.
Negri, Antonio. *Insurgencies: Constituent Power and the Modern State*. Trans. Maurizia Boscagli. Minneapolis, MN: University of Minnesota Press, 1999.
——. *The Savage Anomaly: The Power of Spinoza's Metaphysics and Politics*. Trans. Michael Hardt. Minneapolis, MN: University of Minnesota Press, 1991.
Neumeister, Sebastian. "Unordnung als Methode: Pierre Bayles Platz in der Geschichte der Enzyklopädie." In *Enzyklopädien der Frühen Neuzeit: Beiträge zu ihrer Erforschung*. Ed. Franz M. Eybl. Tübingen: Niemeyer, 1995, 188–99.
Nietzsche, Friedrich. *The Gay Science*. Trans. Walter Kaufmann. New York: Vintage Books, 1974.
——. *Twilight of the Idols/The Anti-Christ*. Trans. R.J. Hollingdale. New York: Penguin, 1990.
Ockham, William of. *Predestination, God's Foreknowledge, and Future Contingents*. Trans. Marilyn McCord Adams and Norman Kretzmann. Indianapolis, IN: Hackett, 1983.
Ogilvie, Brian W. "The Many Books of Nature: Renaissance Naturalists and Information Overload." *Journal of the History of Ideas* 63, no. 4 (2002), 29–40.
Origen of Alexandria. *The Writings of Origen*. Trans. Frederick Crombie. Vol. 10 of the Ante-Nicene Christian Library: Translations of the Writings of the Fathers Down to A.D. 325. Ed. Alexander Roberts and James Donaldson. Edinburgh: T. & T. Clark, 1869.
Ornstein, Martha. *The Rôle of Scientific Societies in the Seventeenth Century*. 1938. Reprint. Hamden, CT: Archon Books, 1963.
Ovid, Publius Naso. *Metamorphoses*. Trans. Frank Justis Miller and G.P. Goold. Loeb Classical Library 42 and 43. Rev. edn. Cambridge, MA: Harvard University Press, 1977.
Palumbo, Margherita. *Leibniz e la 'res bibliothecaria': Bibliografie, 'historiae literariae' e cataloghi nella biblioteca privata leibniziana*. Rome: Bulzoni, 1993.

BIBLIOGRAPHY

Parkes, Malcolm Beckwith. "The Influence of the Concepts of *Ordinatio* and *Compilatio* on the Development of the Book." In *Medieval Learning and Literature: Essays Presented to Richard William Hunt*. Ed. J.J.G. Alexander and M.T. Gibson. Oxford: Clarendon Press, 1976, 115–41.

Petrarch, Francesco. *Letters on Familiar Matters*: *Rerum familiarium libri XVII-XXIV*. Trans. Aldo S. Bernardo. Baltimore, MD: The Johns Hopkins University Press, 1985.

Pettit, Philip. *Made with Words: Hobbes on Language, Mind, and Politics*. Princeton, NJ: Princeton University Press, 2008.

Phemister, Pauline. *Leibniz and the Natural World: Activity, Passivity and Corporeal Substances in Leibniz's Philosophy*. Dordrecht: Springer, 2005.

Piro, Francesco. "Are the 'Canals of Tropes' Navigable? Rhetorical Concepts in Leibniz' Philosophy of Language." In *Im Spiegel des Verstandes: Studien zu Leibniz*. Ed. Klaus D. Dutz and Stefano Gensini. Munster: Nodus, 1996, 137–60.

Plato. *Lysis, Symposium, Gorgias*. Trans. W.R.M. Lamb. Loeb Classical Library 166. Cambridge, MA: Harvard University Press, 1925.

—. *Statesman, Philebus, Ion*. Trans. Harold North Fowler and W.R.M. Lamb. Loeb Classical Library 164. Cambridge, MA: Harvard University Press, 1995.

—. *Timaeus, Critias, Cleitophon, Menexenus, Epistles*. Trans. R.G. Bury. Loeb Classical Library 234. Cambridge, MA: Harvard University Press, 1929.

Pliny the Elder. *Natural History, Books 8-11*. Trans. H. Rackham. Loeb Classical Library 353. Cambridge, MA: Harvard University Press, 1940.

Popkin, Richard H. *The High Road to Pyrrhonism*. Indianapolis, IN: Hackett, 1989.

Reisch, Gregor. *Margarita Philosophica, rationalis, moralis philosophiae principia, duodecim libris dialogice coplectens*. Basel: [Petreius], 1535.

Rétat, Pierre. "Le remarque baylienne." In *Critique, savoir et érudition à la veille des Lumières: Le "Dictionnaire historique et critique" de Pierre Bayle*. Ed. Hans Bots. Amsterdam: APA-Holland University Press, 1998, 27–39.

Robinet, André. *Aux Sources de l'esprit cartésien. L'Axe Ramée-Descartes, de la 'Dialectique' de 1555 aux 'Regulae.'* Paris: Vrin, 1996.

—. "Leibniz: La Renaissance et l'Âge Classique." In *Leibniz et la Renaissance*. Studia Leibnitiana Supplementa 23. Ed. Albert Heinekamp. Wiesbaden: Steiner, 1983, 12–36.

Rodis-Lewis, Geneviève. *L'Oeuvre de Descartes*. 2 vols. Paris: Vrin, 1971.

Roncaglia, Gino. "*Cum Deus calculat:* God's Evaluation of Possible Worlds and Logical Calculus." *Topoi* 9, no. 1 (1990), 83–90.

Rossi, Paolo. *The Dark Abyss of Time: The History of the Earth and the History of Nations from Hooke to Vico*. Trans. Lydia G. Cochrane. Chicago, IL: University of Chicago Press, 1984.

—. *Logic and the Art of Memory: The Quest for a Universal Language*. Trans. Stephen Clucas. Chicago, IL: University of Chicago Press, 2000.

—. "The Twisted Roots of Leibniz's Characteristic." In *The Leibniz Renaissance*. Ed. Centro Fiorentino di Storia e Filosofia della Scienza. Florence: Olschki, 1989, 271–89.

BIBLIOGRAPHY

Royce, Josiah. *The World and the Individual.* 2 vols. New York: Macmillan, 1927.
Rutherford, Donald. *Leibniz and the Rational Order of Nature.* Cambridge: Cambridge University Press, 1995.
—. "Philosophy and Language in Leibniz." In *The Cambridge Companion to Leibniz.* Ed. Nicholas Jolley. Cambridge: Cambridge University Press, 1995, 224–69.
Saxl, Fritz and Hans Meier. *Catalogue of Astrological and Mythological Illuminated Manuscripts of the Latin Middle Ages.* Vol. 3. Manuscripts in English Libraries. London: The Warburg Institute, 1953.
Schaefer, Claude, "Les débuts de l'altier de Jean Colombe. Jean Colombe et André Rousseau, prêtre, librarire et escrivain." *Gazette des Beaux-Arts* 40 (1977), 137–50.
Schelling, F.W.J. *System of Transcendental Idealism (1800).* Trans. Peter Heath. Charlottesville, VA: University of Virginia Press, 1993.
Schenk, Richard. "Daedalus medii aevi? Die Labyrinthe der Theodizee im Mittelalter." *Jahrbuch für Philosophie des Forschungsinstituts für Philosophie, Hannover,* 9 (1998), 15–35.
Schmaltz, Tad. "Spinoza on the Vacuum." *Archiv für Geschichte der Philosophie* 81 (1999), 174–205.
Scotus, John Duns. *Contingency and Freedom.* Trans. A. Vos. Dordrecht: Kluwer, 1994.
Secada, Jorge. *Cartesian Metaphysics: The Scholastic Origins of Modern Philosophy.* Cambridge: Cambridge University Press, 2000.
Seifert, Arno. "Der enzyklopädische Gedanke von der Renaissance bis zu Leibniz." In *Leibniz et la Renaissance.* Ed. Albert Heinekamp. Studia Leibnitiana Supplementa 23. Wiesbaden: Steiner, 1983, 113–24.
Shapin, Steven. *A Social History of Truth: Civility and Science in Seventeenth-Century England.* Chicago, IL: University of Chicago Press, 1994.
Shapin, Steven and Simon Schaffer. *Leviathan and the Air-Pump: Hobbes, Boyle, and the Experimental Life.* Princeton, NJ: Princeton University Press, 1986.
Shapiro, Gary. "Reading and Writing in the Text of Hobbes's *Leviathan.*" *Journal of the History of Philosophy* 18, no. 2 (1980), 147–57.
Skinner, Quentin. "Hobbes and the Purely Artificial Person of the State." *The Journal of Political Philosophy* 7, no. 1 (1999), 1–29.
Slights, William W.E. "Back to the Future – Littorally: Annotating the Historical Page." In *The Future of the Page.* Ed. Peter Stoicheff and Andrew Taylor. Toronto: University of Toronto Press, 2004, 71–89.
Solère, Jean-Luc. "Bayle et les apories de la raison humaine." In *La Raison corrosive: Études sur la pensée critique de Pierre Bayle.* Ed. Isabelle Delpla and Philippe de Robert. Paris: Honoré Champion, 2003, 87–137.
Spinoza, Baruch. *Complete Works.* Ed. Michael L. Morgan. Trans. Samuel Shirley. Indianapolis, IN: Hackett, 2002.
—. *Political Treatise.* Trans. Samuel Shirley. Intro. Steve Barbone and Lee Rice. Indianapolis, IN: Hackett, 2000.

Springmeyer, Heinrich. "Eine neue kritische Textausgabe der *Regulae ad directionem ingenii* von René Descartes." *Zeitschrift für philosophische Forschung* 24 (1970), 101–25.
Steierwald, Ulrike. *Wissen und System: Zu Gottfried Wilhelm Leibniz' Theorie einer Universalbibliothek*. Köln: Greven Verlag, 1995.
Stoddard, Roger. "Morphology and the Book from an American Perspective." *Printing History* 17 (1987), 2–14.
Strauss, Leo. *Persecution and the Art of Writing*. Chicago, IL: University of Chicago Press, 1988.
Struever, Nancy S. *Theory as Practice: Ethical Inquiry in the Renaissance*. Chicago, IL: University of Chicago Press, 1992.
Tega, Walter. "Encyclopédie et unité du savoir de Bacon à Leibniz." In *L'Encyclopédisme: Actes du colloque de Caen, 12-16 janvier 1987*. Ed. Annie Becq. Paris: Aux Amateurs de livres, 1991, 69–96.
Tosel, André. "Superstition and Reading." In *The New Spinoza*. Ed. Warren Montag and Ted Stolze. Minneapolis, MN: University of Minnesota Press, 1997, 147–67.
Totok, Wilhelm. "Die Einteilung der Wissenschaften bei Leibniz." In *Akten des II. Internationaler Leibniz Kongress, 1972, Band 4*. Studia Leibnitiana Supplementa 15. Wiesbaden: Steiner, 1975, 87–96.
Uhlfelder, Myra L. "The Role of the Liberal Arts in Boethius' *Consolatio*." In *Boethius and the Liberal Arts*. Ed. Michael Masi. Berne: Peter Lang, 1981, 17–34.
Valla, Lorenzo. "Dialogue on Free Will." Trans. Charles Trinkhaus. In *The Renaissance Philosophy of Man*. Ed. Ernst Cassirer, Paul Oskar Kristeller, and John Herman Randall, Jr. Chicago, IL: University of Chicago Press, 1948, 155–82.
Van Berkel, Klaas and Arjo Vanderjagt, eds. *The Book of Nature in Early Modern and Modern History*. Leuven: Peeters, 2006.
Van Lieshout, H.H.M. (Leny). *The Making of Pierre Bayle's "Dictionaire historique et critique."* Trans. Lynne Richards. Amsterdam: APA-Holland University Press, 2001.
Vanderjagt, Arjo and Klaas van Berkel, eds. *The Book of Nature in Antiquity and the Middle Ages*. Leuven: Peeters, 2005.
Voltaire. *The Works of Voltaire: A Contemporary Version*. Trans. William Fleming. 42 vols. Paris: DuMont, 1901.
Von Dierse, Ulrich. *Enzyklopädie: Zur Geschichte eines philosophischen und wissenschaftstheoretischen Begriffs*. Bonn: Bouvier, 1977.
Weber, Jean-Paul. *La Constitution du texte des 'Regulae.'* Paris: Société d'édition d'enseignement supérieur, 1964.
—. "La Méthode de Descartes de après les *Regulae*." *Archives de Philosophie* 35 (1972), 51–60.
Weibel, Luc. *Le savoir et le corps: Essai sur le Dictionnaire de Pierre Bayle*. Paris: L'Age d'Hommes, 1975.
Weijers, Olga. "Funktionen des Alphabets im Mittelalter." In *Seine Welt wissen: Enzyklopädien in der Frühen Neuzeit*. Ed. Ulrich Johannes Schneider. Darmstadt: Primus, 2006, 22–32.

West, William. *Theaters and Encyclopedias in Early Modern Europe*. Cambridge: Cambridge University Press, 2002.

Whelan, Ruth. *The Anatomy of Superstition: A Study of the Historical Theory and Practice of Pierre Bayle*. Oxford: Voltaire Foundation, 1989.

Whitman, Jon. *Allegory: The Dynamics of an Ancient and Medieval Technique*. Cambridge, MA: Harvard University Press, 1987.

Wilkins, John. *An Essay Towards a Real Character and a Philosophical Language*. 1668. Facsimile, Menston: Scolar Press, 1968.

Wilson, Catherine. *Leibniz's Metaphysics: A Historical and Comparative Study*. Manchester: Manchester University Press, 1989.

Winship, George, Carl B. Roden, and Andrew Keogh, eds. Special Issue on the Photostat. *The Papers of the Bibliographical Society of America* 15, no. 1 (1921).

Wittkower, Rudolf. *Allegory and the Migration of Symbols*. Boulder, CO: Westview Press, 1977.

Woolhouse, R.S. *Descartes, Spinoza, Leibniz: The Concept of Substance in Seventeenth-Century Metaphysics*. London: Routledge, 1993.

—. "Spinoza and Descartes and the Existence of Extended Substance." In *Central Themes in Early Modern Philosophy*. Ed. J.A. Cover and Mark Kulstad. Indianapolis, IN: Hackett, 1990, 23–47.

Yolton, John W. *Locke and the Compass of Human Understanding: A Selective Commentary on the 'Essay'*. Cambridge: Cambridge University Press, 1970.

INDEX

actual
  Leibnizian difference between ideal and 23, 25–9, 48
Adam, Charles 152–3, 154, 155–6
affect
  definition 190
  of devotion 190–1, 232n.27
Agamben, Giorgio 46, 55
Aldrovandi, Ulisse 97–8
allegory
  doubled 32, 40, 42–3, 49–50
  Leibniz's use of 30–1, 43–9, 52–3
  multiplication 37–43, 165
  philosophy and 30–2
  Valla's use of 35–7
Alsted, Johann Heinrich 64–6
Althusser, Louis 174–5
apokatastasis 30
  bibliographical 53–7
  theological 55
Apollo (deity) 35–6, 44
arche-writing 7, 9–10, 214n.3
artificial machines 25
The Assayer (Galileo) 11–12
atomism
  Bayle's stance 113, 115
  Epicurean 1–2, 23, 115
  Lucretian 116–17, 119
  material 26–7
  spiritual 23
  substantial 27–8, 55–7
authorship 101–2

Bacon, Francis 10, 11
  on method 25
Balibar, Etienne 179
Baudrillard, Jean 62–3
Bayle, Pierre 18, 19–20, 26, 72–7, 89–94, 98–103, 104, 106–10, 112–21, 165
  Voltaire's critique of 222n.23
  see also *Historical and Critical Dictionary* (Bayle)
being
  arborescent images of 198–9
  infinite 169
  metaphysical continuum of 117–18, 119
Blumenberg, Hans 7
Boethius, Anicius Manlius Severinus 30, 31
  distinction between divine and human knowledge 41–2
  Leibniz's critique of Valla's readings of 43–4
  on nature of eternal 42
  philosophical allegory 32, 37–40, 42, 49–50
  on subordination of fate to providence 40–1
book(s)
  Cartesian critique of 5, 123, 129–34, 164–5
  materialist historiography of 12–16
  Valla's rejection of 34–6

INDEX

book, figures of 7–8, 194–5
  book of nature 10–12
  book of the world 5, 7, 10–11, 129, 134
  dematerialization 6–10
  radicle-book 198–9, 200
  rhizome-book 197, 199–201
  root-book 198–9, 200
  sacralization 10–12
  Spinozan 166–7, 170–4, 175, 183
Borges, Jorge Luis 57, 60, 61–3
Boyle, Robert 10–11, 176
Buffon, Georges 97–8

Casares, Adolfo Bioy 62
chance
  atomism and 90, 114–17
Chartier, Roger 195–6
  critique of Eisenstein 14–15
Clarke, Samuel 79–80
Colombe, Jean 50–2
Comenius, Johann Amos 132–3
Conatuum Comeniorum Praeludia (Comenius) 132–3
Consolation of Philosophy (Boethius) 30, 31, 37–43, 49–50
  illuminated manuscript of 50–2
continuum
  of being 117–18, 119
  composition of 18–19, 23, 24, 26–30, 48, 54, 57
corporeality 3–4
  Althusser's 175
  scriptive 122–3, 135, 138
cosmogony
  Bayle's reading of Ovid's 105–7, 119
  Leibniz's 166
Crapulli, Giovanni 143–4, 154
cross-referencing 19
  analogous techniques 77–8
  Bayle's *Dictionary* and 72–5, 76
  early modern practice 75, 97–8

  as evidence 94–8, 101–2
  Leibniz's proposals 61, 72, 76–8, 79, 82–3, 85–8
Curtius, Ernst Robert 7

Deleuze, Gilles 197–201, 229n.9
De Man, Paul 31
De rerum natura (Lucretius) 1, 2–3, 105
Derrida, Jacques
  on books 6–10, 190
Descartes, René 18, 20
  on corporeality of writing and reading 122–4
  definition of history and science 224n.9
  "I am, I exist" (*ego sum, ego existo*) 83–5
  on mechanism 95–6
  on methodological thinking 24–5, 63, 83–4, 130, 139–40, 145–6, 148–52, 158–60
  on motion 111–12, 177
  on objective reality 21, 164, 168–9, 228n.3
  on orderliness of world 111–12
  on representative signs and sensory objects 124–7
  Spinoza's reading of 21, 163–4, 167
  on writing and affection of sense organs 127
  on writing and memory 128–9, 152–3
  see also Rules for the Direction of Mind (Descartes)
devotion as affect 179, 189–93, 232n.27
  definition 191
Dialogue on Free Will (Valla) 30, 33–7, 49
Diderot, Denis 78

INDEX

Discourse on Metaphysics (Leibniz) 70, 82, 86
Discourse on Method (Descartes) 83–4, 129–30, 134
  Descartes' instructions for reading 134–5
  Geometry (Descartes) 135, 138
Dissertation on the Art of Combinations (Leibniz) 59
divine foreknowledge
  human freedom and 33–4, 35–6, 37, 41–2, 44, 45
dynamic materialism 175–7, 178–9, 201
  political ramifications 179–83

Eisenstein, Elizabeth 13–15
Encyclopaedia septem tomis distincta (Alsted) 64–6
  typographical variations 75
encyclopedia/encyclopedism
  Alstedian 64–7
  analytical and practical method 71–2, 79
  anti-encyclopedia 76
  Cartesian critique of Comenuis' 132–3
  "civil" method 71
  conceptual structure 68–70, 85
  critique of Locke's proposal 61, 67–8
  formal structure 79–80, 81–2, 85
  holistic approach 68
  imaginary Newtonian model 80–1
  Leibnizian model 19, 60–1, 63–4, 66–70
  linguistic and numerical system 58–60
  as a method for production of truths 66
  nominalist method 68

readings of Leibniz's use of the term 64, 66
  referentiality 19, 77–9, 82–3, 85–6
  synthetic and theoretical method 71, 72, 79
An Essay Concerning Human Understanding (Locke) 67
An Essay Toward a Real Character and a Philosophical Language (Wilkins) 63
eternity 42, 49
  eternal library 54–5
Ethics (Spinoza) 171, 172, 177–9, 190–1
Eustache de Saint-Paul 137
"Of Exactitude in Science" (Borges) 62
exemplarity
  Cartesian 123, 140, 147–52, 155–7

fate 40–1, 47, 48, 49
finite machines 24–30
footnotes 72
formalism
  Cartesian 83–5
  Leibnizian 61, 79–80, 81, 83, 85–6
formal reality 170
  Cartesian 21, 168
  Spinozan 173, 187–8, 192
Foucault, Michel 63
  on origin of his taxonomy project 61–2
  on resemblance and similitude 97–8
Foucher, Simon 25, 28
freedom 19, 23, 32
  divine foreknowledge and 33–6, 37, 41–2, 44, 45
Frémont, Christiane 48
Froidmont, Libert 24, 25

253

INDEX

Galileo 176
  secularization of book of nature 11–12
Gassendi, Pierre 1, 2, 176
Gilson, Étienne 141, 159
Glazemaker, Jan Hendriksz 142–3
God, existence of
  objective perfection proof 164, 168–9
  Spinoza on 172
  textual reproduction and 166–7
Grafton, Anthony 72
Of Grammatology (Derrida) 7–10, 198
Grand Dictionnaire historique (Moréri) 99
Grassi, Oratio 12
Great Instauration (Bacon) 25
Guattari, Félix 197–201

Historical and Critical Dictionary (Bayle) 19–20, 87, 121
  citational structure 72–6, 90, 94–8
  critique of error 72, 76, 90, 92, 98–100, 102–3
  history 99
  Labrousse's reading of 91
  on Lucretian materialism 116–17
  materialism within 90, 104, 106–14
  mise en page 72, 73, 76–7, 89, 107, 165
  textual function 94, 100–1
historical criticism 100–3
Hobbes, Thomas 18
  political theory 180
Holden, Thomas 92, 113
Hotson, Howard 65, 75

ideality
  Leibnizian difference between actuality and 23, 25–9, 48
Illiad (Homer) 115

infinite library, figures of 18, 22–3, 29–32, 46–50, 51–3, 165
  allegorical reason and 29–32
infinite machines 24–9, 48
ink, figures of
  Cartesian 20, 124–9
  Spinozan 186–9, 192–3
Israel, Jonathan
  reading of Bayle's theoretical position 92–3

Jelles, Jarig 172
Johns, Adrian
  critique of Eisenstein's early modern textual stability and fixity 14–16
"John Wilkins' Analytical Language" (Borges) 61–2
Jupiter (deity) 35–6, 44–6
  as librarian 47

knowledge
  capacities for 41–2
  division of *see* encyclopedia/encyclopedism
  encyclopedia as knowledge 64
  Lockean divisions of 67, 68, 87

Labrousse, Elisabeth
  reading of Bayle's *Dictionary* 91
labyrinth 23, 24–5, 26–9, 57
The Labyrinth, or On the Composition of the Continuum (Froidmont) 24
Lamy, Guillaume 18, 26, 115
Leibniz, Gottfried Wilhelm 6, 18, 165
  on *apokatastasis* 53–7
  in Bayle's *Dictionary* 77
  critique of *Projet et fragmens* 99
  on cross-referencing 77–8, 85–6
  differences between mechanism, finite and infinite 24–9

INDEX

encyclopedic project 60–1, 63–4,
   66–7, 79–80, 81, 82–3, 85–6,
   87–8
 on existence of God 166–7
 Hanover text of Descartes'
   Rules and 142, 144, 152,
   154, 225n.21, 227n.38
 on individual substances 70–1,
   82–3, 86
 on knowledge organization
   structures 58–61, 165–6
 on methodological
   reflexivity 63–4
 on repetition 60
 theory of preestablished
   harmony 95, 96
 use of allegory 30–1, 43–9,
   52–3
 use of figure of infinite
   library 22–3, 32, 46–8
Lennon, Thomas 119
 reading of Bayle's theoretical
   position 90–1
Leucippus
 Bayle's *Dictionary* article on 113
Locke, John
 Leibniz's critique of encyclopedic
   scheme of 61, 67–8, 87
Loemker, Leroy E. 64–5
Lucretius 1–2, 105, 114–19
 Bayle's *Dictionary* article
   on 115–17

Margarita Philosophica (Reisch) 66
marginal notes 73–5
Marion, Jean-Luc 141
Martin, Henri-Jean 75
material atomism
 Leibnizian rejection 26–7
material inscription, figures of 11,
   16–21, 194–5, 201–2
 Cartesian corporeality and 123–4
 notion 4–6

philosophical discourse
   and 197–201
 technological shifts 195–7
materialism
 Althusser's 174–5
 Bayle's 90, 106–14
 Cartesian 176
 classical 174
 Lucretian 116–17
 mechanical 176
 neo-Epicureans 176
 ontological status 103–4
 Spinozan 21, 167–8, 175–88,
   201–2
 of textual organization 76–7, 89–90
materialist historiography of
   book 12–16
 secularization 12
mechanism
 Cartesian 95–6
 Leibnizian finite and infinite
   machines 24–9
Meditations of First Philosophy
   (Descartes) 83–4, 122–3, 169
 Descartes' instructions for
   reading 135–7
memory
 Cartesian 128–9, 152–3
Metamorphoses (Ovid) 105–11,
   117–19, 121
method
 Bacon on 25
 Cartesian 24, 123–4
 *see also Rules for the Direction of
   Mind* (Descartes)
methodological reflexivity
 Cartesian 63, 140, 147
 Leibnizian 63–4
methodological thinking
 Baconian 25
 Cartesian 24–5, 63, 83–5, 130,
   139–40, 145–6, 148–52,
   158–60

255

INDEX

Meyer, Lodewijk 163–4
Molière 119
monad 23, 29, 48, 53, 54
Moréri, Louis 99
motion
  matter and 20, 103–4, 110–14, 177
  Zeno's position 92
multitude
  Hobbesian 180
  Spinozan 182–3

natural/divine machines 25–6, 28, 48
  infinite division of 56–7
natural history
  Aldrovandi's 97–8
  Buffon's 97–8
natural philosophy 70
  Cartesian 111–12, 114, 177
  Spinozan 186
natural power 181–3
natural right 181–3
New Essays on Human Understanding (Leibniz) 29, 60–1, 67–70, 71–2, 78–9, 81–3, 85–8
New System of Nature (Leibniz) 23, 25–30, 77, 95
Newtonianism
  Clarke's 80
Nietzsche, Friedrich 34–5
  of eternal return 55, 60
Nouvelles des république des lettres (journal) 100–1

objective reality
  Cartesian 21, 164, 168–9, 228n.3
  Spinozan 173
Optics (Descartes) 125–6, 147
optimum
  Leibnizian 30, 45, 48–9, 53, 212n.42
order
  Cartesian 140, 144–7

The Order of Things (Foucault) 61
organic substances 23, 25
Origen of Alexandria 55, 60, 213n.47
Ovid
  Bayle on doctrine of chaos of 19–20, 104–5, 107–11, 112, 114, 117–19
  Voltaire's critique of Bayle's reading of 222n.23

page
  dematerialization 8–9, 10
  ontology of 18, 20
paper, figures of
  Cartesian 20, 124–9
  Spinozan treatment 186–9, 192–3
pen, figures of
  Cartesian 20, 124–9
phenomenalism 80
philosophy
  allegorization of 30–2
  Bayle's critical and historical approach 90–4
  Boethius personification of 38–40, 49–50, 51–2
  Colombe's miniature of 51–2
  as corrosive powder 93–4, 102
  Leibnizian personification of 44–5
  Valla's rejection of 34–7
political theory
  Hobbesian 180
  Spinozan 179–83
Political Treatise (Spinoza) 180–3
Popkin, Richard
  reading of Bayle as skeptic 92
possible worlds 30, 43–50, 54, 165
"Preface to a Universal Characteristic" (Leibniz) 58–9
principle of the identity of indiscernibles 24, 26, 82

INDEX

Principles of Cartesian Philosophy
  (Spinoza) 163–4, 167, 173–4, 175
Principles of Philosophy
  (Descartes) 21, 83–4, 110, 111, 112, 125, 173
  Descartes' instructions for reading 137–9, 225n.15
print artifacts
  Chartier and Jones on 14–15
  stability and fixity of 13–15
print culture 13–14, 15
The Printing Press as an Agent of Change (Eisenstein) 13–14
Projet et fragmens d'un dictionnaire critique (Bayle) 77, 99
  contemporary reception 99
providence 40–1, 44

Raey, Jean de 142, 225n.21
Ramus, Peter 64
reading
  Cartesian corporeality of 20, 122–3
  Cartesian instructions for 123–4, 134–9
  Cartesian materialized critique 130–2
reality
  formal 21, 168, 170, 173, 187–8, 192
  objective 21, 164, 168–9, 173, 228n.3
Renaissance
  encyclopedism 64–6, 67
  system of resemblance and similitude 97–8
  typographical conventions 73–5
repetition
  Cartesian 20, 123, 140, 146, 148–50, 152, 155–8, 161, 227n.36
  forms in philosophical and theoretical discourses 60

Hegelian 214n.5
Leibnizian 54–7, 64, 68–9, 79, 81–2, 165–6
metaphysical notion 60
propositional repetition 68–71, 72
Spinozan 21, 173–4
Rorarius, Jerome
  Bayle's *Dictionary* article on 73–5, 77, 95–6, 99–100
Rules for the Direction of Mind
  (Descartes) 20, 24, 128, 130, 135, 139–41, 160–2
  Amsterdam text 142, 143, 144, 152, 154, 225n.21
  definition and notion of method 144–5
  Hanover text 142, 144, 152, 154, 225n.21, 227n.38
  Netherlands text 142–3, 144
  Rule 1 159
  Rule 4 145, 154
  Rule 5 144–5, 153
  Rule 8 140, 145–7, 154, 161
  Rule 8, examples in 147–52, 154–7
  Rule 10 153
  sources 141–3, 225n.19

Schuller, Georg 142
The Search for Truth by Means of Natural Light
  (Descartes) 133, 153
similitude and resemblance
  Cartesian critique of iconic systems of 124–7
  Gassendi on 2
  Lucretius on 1–2
  Renaissance 97–8
singularity 26–8, 29, 53, 54, 86
  metaphysical identity of 60–1
skepticism
  question of Bayle's stance 92–4
sovereignty 181–3

INDEX

space and spatiality
 Leibnizian conception 28, 80
Spinoza, Baruch 5–6, 18, 21, 163
 break from Cartesianism 21, 174
 conception of materialism 167–8, 175–83, 201–2
 figures of book and 163, 166–7, 170–4, 175
 interpretation and 184–8
 ontological necessity 229n.9
 political theory 179–83
 typology of bodies 177–8
Studium bonae mentis (Descartes) 153
Suarez, Francisco 168
subjectivity
 Cartesian 157–60
sufficient reason
 existence of God 166–7
Summa Philosophica Quadripartia (Eustache) 137

textual authority 101–2
 Cartesian critique 20
textual multiplication 13–14, 21, 68–9
 existence of God and 166–7
textual organization
 Bayle's *Dictionary* 72–7
 Leibniz's suggestions to Bayle 77
Theodicy (Leibniz) 23–4, 30–1, 43–8, 53, 165
Theological-Political Treatise (Spinoza) 175, 179, 181–2, 184–8, 189, 191
theology
 Bayle's on 91–2

A Thousand Plateaus (Deleuze and Guattari) 197–201
time 42, 49
 Clarke's conception 80
 Leibnizian conception 80
truth
 Cartesian search 24, 133–4
 encyclopedia as method for production of 66
Tschirnhaus, Ehrenfried Walter von 142, 143
typography 5
 Bayle's *Dictionary* 73–5, 104
 Renaissance conventions 75
 typographical fixity 13, 15, 16

"On the Ultimate Origination of Things" (Leibniz) 46, 162, 166

Valla, Lorenzo 19, 30, 31, 32–3, 165
 critique of Boethius 43
 Leibniz's critique of 43–4
 use of dialogue and allegory 31, 34–7
Voét, Gilbert 133
Voltaire 222n.23

Weber, Jean-Paul 144, 154–6
Wilkins, John 63
The World (Descartes) 110, 111, 124
writing
 Cartesian corporeality of 20, 122–3, 128–9, 152–3
 Derrida on 9–10

Zeno of Elea 37, 92, 209n.28